Igniting STEM Learning

A Guide to Designing an Authentic Primary School STEM Program

Dr Adrian Bertolini

© 2023 Adrian Bertolini

All rights reserved. No part of this book may be reproduced or transmitted in any form or by any means, electronic or mechanical, including photocopying, recording or by any information storage and retrieval system, without prior permission in writing from the publisher.

Access the resources, templates and reproducibles from the book at
https://intuyuconsulting.com.au/igniting-stem-learning/ or
https://ambapress.com.au/products/igniting-stem-learning

Published in 2023 by Amba Press, Melbourne, Australia.
www.ambapress.com.au

Previously published in 2022 by Hawker Brownlow Education.
This edition replaces all previous editions.

ISBN: 9781923116238 (pbk)
ISBN: 9781923116245 (ebk)

A catalogue record for this book is available from the National Library of Australia.

ACKNOWLEDGEMENTS

While this book may have been written over the past three years it has actually been forming and expressing itself in my conversations, discussions and workshops for decades. If your name is not specifically mentioned, please don't hold it against me. Just know that I am deeply grateful for your contribution!

I would first like to thank the hundreds of teachers and schools I've worked with over the past twenty years testing ideas, approaches and structures. Every activity and structure within the book began in a workshop I led or as part of a coaching conversation with a teacher. Specifically I want to thank the extraordinary STEM teachers and school leaders from around Australia who shared their experiences, allowed me to interview them, generously gave me the opportunity to run workshops in their schools, or discussed elements of the book: Ann Adams, Lucy Angelico, Chris Bracken, Jacqui Butler, Anna Danson, Jodi-Ann Gulley, Serena Hinds, Reid Moule, Julia Murrie, Lauren Newton, Stephanie Pollard, Tim Rowberry, Josh Velez and Shelley Waldon. Your contributions, thoughts and feedback made a difference to my thinking in many ways.

I would also like to thank the team at Hawker Brownlow Education for their patience, trust and empowerment. It all began with Elaine Brownlow, who gave me the opportunity to present at one of the Hawker Brownlow conferences. This was the sliding doors moment that led to this book. Thank you especially to my editors Olivia Tolich and Lauren Mitchell. Your insightful questions, feedback and encouragement helped me through those times I felt stuck, overwhelmed and needing a break.

Finally I want to offer a huge thank you to my family for giving me the time and the space over two years of Melbourne lockdowns to invest in bringing this to life. My enormous gratitude goes to the amazing Rachel Manneke-Jones, who makes sure I keep connected to what matters, and to my children Ty and Chiara who I learn from every day. Many thanks go to my parents, Sergio and Mary Bertolini, for cultivating the seeds of my curiosity and willingness to give things a try – especially when I failed.

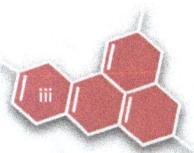

TABLE OF CONTENTS

Acknowledgements	iii
About the author	vii
Introduction	1
Chapter 1: Understanding the purpose of STEM	7
Chapter 2: Developing a whole-school skill and mindset map	37
Chapter 3: Developing curriculum and learning ladder maps	51
Chapter 4: First steps in planning transdisciplinary STEM units	73
Chapter 5: Beginning small with bounded STEM projects	97
Chapter 6: Getting real-world with open-ended STEM projects	123
Chapter 7: Assessing STEM learning	143
Chapter 8: Growing teacher capacity to lead STEM learning	179
Chapter 9: Leading the STEM curriculum and pedagogical change	195
Epilogue	213
References	217
Index	225

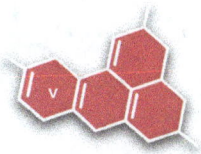

ABOUT THE AUTHOR

Dr Adrian Bertolini has spent over thirty years working with and learning from students, educators and adults about what makes a difference to learning. He has taught physics, numerical analysis and engineering design at university. He rewrote the ruMAD (aRe yoU Making A Difference) program, which then won the 2009 Garth Boomer Award for curriculum development. Through the ruMAD program he led workshops and coached students in developing projects that made a huge difference in their communities.

Adrian has also led transformational leadership programs and coached adults to develop projects that made a difference in their communities. Some of the people he has coached or taught have gone on to start ventures that now make a difference in the world. These include Marita Cheng (founder of Robogals), the founders of Engineers Without Borders Australia, Jacqueline Savage (founder of MedCorp) and Guido Pozzebon (founder of One Umbrella, which led to FareShare) to name a few.

For the past fifteen years Adrian has been the founder and director of learning for Intuyu Consulting Pty Ltd, where he coaches teachers and school leaders from government, Catholic and independent schools in curriculum planning and assessment, growing leadership and excellence in practice in schools, and supporting the development of STEM thinking and learning in schools. He coaches schools around Australia as they enact projects funded by Schools Plus. He has also coached a group of teacher coaches as they enacted curriculum and pedagogical change in their schools as part of a Victorian Department of Education initiative.

In recent years Adrian also founded the It Takes a Spark STEM conference, which currently runs in four states around Australia. The intent of the conferences is to ignite leadership and passion in students and their teachers for STEM, not because it is required by governments or the economy but because it nurtures the problem-solving, creative and entrepreneurial mindset that makes a difference. The conferences are crowd-sourced affairs, with sessions run by students and teachers from schools local to the conference as well as local industry, organisations, charities, TAFEs and universities.

Introduction

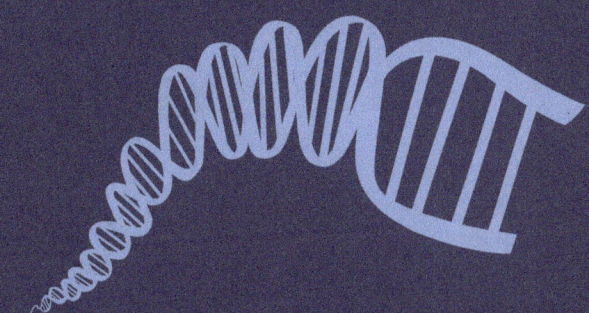

He who would learn to fly one day must first learn to stand and walk and run and dance; one cannot fly into flying.

Friedrich Nietzsche, *Thus Spoke Zarathustra*

GROWING UP A LEARNER AND PROBLEM-SOLVER

I grew up in the south-eastern suburbs of Melbourne in a low socio-economic area filled with working-class families. Dad was an Italian immigrant who worked as a solid plasterer and Mum worked from home running a household products small business while bringing up three adventurous boys. We had a huge vegetable garden, fruit trees in the backyard, chickens for eggs and rabbits to play with (and for other purposes later on), but we never seemed to have new clothes or go on the trips that my friends did. We also had second-hand bikes.

Our bikes were our access to adventures and income. Since Mum and Dad were always busy, I would often go riding around the neighbourhood to catch up with my friends. We'd head out to the local creeks to go tadpoling, to the football ground to kick a ball, to the shops to get groceries, or through the streets on a paper run to earn some money. Along the way my brothers and I would occasionally find stuff tossed out in hard rubbish and bring it home to see if we could repair or use it in some other way. Toasters, watches, clocks, kettles, old bikes and more used to be collected and pulled apart. Dad had a great workshop in the back shed, so we could usually find the right tools. More often than not we couldn't repair what we brought home, but sometimes we could use the parts in other things – like a cool billycart. I grew up curious and wondering what made things work the way they did.

Given the scarcity we grew up in we learned to be quite entrepreneurial. Not only did we ride our bikes to deliver papers, but we also collected aluminium cans to recycle, glass soft drink bottles to return to the local milk bar for a refund, and even vast amounts of beer bottles from the neighbours in the area to make a small fortune (to us) from the bottle recycling guy!

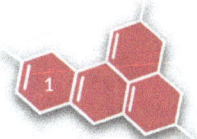

Igniting STEM *Learning*

Figure 1.1: That's me on the far right on the tricycle when I was six

When I think about my schooling, I don't really remember much of the curriculum we covered or what I learned at different times. What I remember most are certain moments and relationships that made a difference to me. I remember being overjoyed when the wonderful Mrs Barnfield, my Year 4 teacher, announced that she would be teaching us again in Year 5. I remember the friends that I made at school, lying on my back in the grass with them at lunchtime imagining fantastic shapes out of the clouds, or inventing new games using the only equipment we had (a worn tennis ball). I remember, embarrassingly, my voice breaking in Year 7 during a performance of *The Sound of Music* and how that affected my confidence to communicate in front of groups for many years. I remember Mrs James in Year 11 and her commitment to all of us, but especially how she challenged and extended my thinking and passion for learning. I remember helping other students with their study and finding that I learned a lot by explaining my thinking to others.

The combination of my curiosity, wanting to know how things worked and learning through teaching others led me to be quite good at school. I loved my maths and science, and I did well enough in Year 12 to be accepted into a double degree in science and engineering. University was a huge growing-up and learning experience for me. I struggled academically for a few years and learned that some people are way brighter and work way harder than me to achieve their results. I learned to learn collaboratively, to trust myself and my abilities, and I worked out how I learned best. At the end of five years I had a Bachelor of Science with a major in computer science and a minor in maths, plus a first class honours in mechanical engineering. Six years later I had a PhD in engineering that brought together my maths, computer science and engineering knowledge and had presented at conferences around the world. I eventually jumped at the chance to teach aerospace engineering (yes, rocket science) at RMIT.

It was while I was teaching aerospace engineering that I realised my passion was not specifically the maths, science, engineering or computing, but developing learners and problem-solvers. As the selection officer and first-year coordinator for the aerospace degrees, I saw how many of these extraordinarily capable students weren't developed as independent thinkers, problem-solvers and learners. In any year, up to half of the cohort failed a subject for the first time and over 25 per cent dropped out. I had to do something about it. Thus began my journey into education. I worked with my students to improve my teaching and began developing online asynchronous support materials for the subjects I taught. I then left the university and spent three years with a not-for-profit running a program called ruMAD (aRe yoU Making A Difference) which empowered primary and secondary students to create and deliver projects that made a difference in their communities. This led me to found an educational consultancy because I realised that if I wanted to make a difference to more young people I needed to work with teachers and school leaders. There is no doubt that the years I spent studying, teaching and then applying the concepts and approaches from engineering, computer science and maths disciplines has made a huge difference to my ability to coach teachers and schools in STEM learning. However, when I reflect on my life's journey, I grew up in a culture of curiosity, creativity, problem-solving, self-agency and entrepreneurialism. Not everyone has had that opportunity. I have written this book to support teachers and schools in the thinking, structures and practices that will allow both students and teachers to thrive as learners, thinkers and problem-solvers.

GETTING THE MOST OUT OF THIS BOOK

This STEM book is not designed, like many STEM books, to be a series of projects that can be picked up and run in your school. Those books are great resources and are useful if you need examples of what you could do immediately. But that is not what this book is about. Equally, this book is unlikely to be something you consume quickly. It distils decades of thinking and practice across many disciplines – not just STEM. The blend of theory and practice has been designed to challenge teachers and leaders to stop, think and explore the largely unexamined structures and approaches that exist within most schools. It is likely you will discover something new each time you read this book.

Getting the most out of this STEM book will require a passionate commitment to creating a learning environment that empowers students and teachers as learners, problem-solvers and thinkers. The embedding of an authentic and sustainable STEM program will be transformational for a school and the lives of its students, teachers and leaders. This can't be done by simply reading what is written. It will require grasping the purpose of STEM and the Australian Curriculum: Technologies, and investing the time and effort to authentically embed it – rather than simply treating it as another thing to do. It will require teachers and school leaders to grow their understanding of systems thinking, design thinking and computational thinking and how they can be applied to structuring learning within schools. It will require practice, trial and error, failing and making mistakes, reflection and refinement. It will require developing a mindset of 'having a go' and 'we can figure it out together' – both critical to the process of design and learning. It will require putting in the intellectual effort to think your way through the process of creating a school environment that actually develops young people to be the problem-solvers, critical and creative thinkers, and collaborative, adaptable learners they need to be in their futures. The outcome will not only be a sustainable STEM program, but also a school culture and approach that empowers everyone involved.

SOME HIDDEN INFLUENCES TO OVERCOME

There are a number of hidden and often unexamined influences that will constrain the process of developing a sustainable and authentic STEM program within a school. While not exhaustive, it is

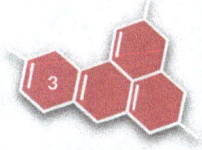

important for schools to be aware of the following influences and to think about how they can be addressed when implementing the strategies discussed in this book.

Firstly, the vast majority of teachers and school leaders have not been trained to think, plan and operate from the thinking frameworks at the core of the Australian Curriculum: Technologies (and all STEM learning): systems thinking, design thinking and computational thinking. This lack of understanding influences how schools are organised, what is valued, what is focused on and habitual practices and processes. Some examples of the constraining influences include a grading system focused on achievement rather than progress, the siloing of disciplines and a focus on ensuring that the curriculum knowledge is 'covered' – often to the detriment of consolidating skills, thinking and mindsets. Even more challenging is that the lack of understanding of STEM and these thinking frameworks influences the ability of schools to create a systemic approach to developing independent, self-regulated learners and thinkers. Curiosity, engagement, empowerment, joy of learning, self-regulation, choice, reflective learning, feedback, adaptiveness, problem-solving and much more are all outcomes of a school centred on STEM learning. If a school is going to begin to embed an authentic STEM program, it must confront the fact that many of their systems, processes, practices and structures are unlikely to support that endeavour.

What happens within schools is only one piece of the STEM-learning puzzle. Most parents have also not been trained to think, plan and operate from the thinking, mindset and practices underlying STEM learning. As all teachers and schools recognise, how parents support their children's learning at home makes a profound difference to the capacity of a child to learn and problem-solve. Research has shown that parental engagement has a positive effect on a child's academic attainment, regardless of age or socio-economic status (Axford et al., 2019). So how could your school support parents to encourage and empower their children to be problem-solvers and to think and adapt as learners? What could homework look like? What could the Foundation-year induction program for parents look like? What could parent–teacher meetings look like? What could reports look like? What could the school encourage parents to be doing at home? These questions and more will need to be considered and explored as a school progresses along its STEM journey.

Finally, most adults do not yet relate to students as able to drive their own learning. Sir Ken Robinson (2006) in his famous TED talk went so far as to say that we educate this drive out of them. Just like learner drivers need to actually drive a car to learn how to drive, young people cannot learn to be problem-solvers, think critically or drive their own learning if they do not have sufficient opportunities to develop those capabilities. Unfortunately, many primary schools take in children who are highly curious, independent learners and enculturate them to be passive learners waiting to be taught. Young people are extraordinary – if we relate to them in that way. Of course they will make mistakes. Of course they will fail. Of course they won't have all the necessary knowledge, skills, thinking and mindsets to tackle the world – yet. It begins with teachers, school leaders and all adults seeing themselves as activators and coaches as well as teachers. Those young people who we laud publicly as exceptional and remarkable tend to be supported by at least one adult who relates to them as extraordinary.

HOW THIS BOOK IS ORGANISED

This book is organised to take you through a design process so you can create and build an authentic STEM program in your primary school that not only addresses the Australian Curriculum but also grows independent learners, problem-solvers and thinkers. Each chapter is a mix of research, practical structures, examples and activities. My recommendation is that teachers and

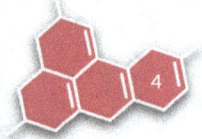

Introduction

school teams use the chapters to provoke discussion, thinking and planning. The whole process will take a significant investment of time and effort over a number of years.

Chapter 1 begins with the 'Empathise' and 'Define' aspects of the design thinking process. The chapter leads readers through the process of examining existing beliefs and perceptions of STEM; unpacks how developing learning based on the computational, design and systems thinking frameworks provides the real value in STEM learning; and lays the foundational thinking for discussions throughout the book by exploring what creates powerful learning. The chapter ends with two exercises that will support schools to define a clear design brief for STEM learning.

The process of taking a school from the design brief to a viable and sustainable STEM learning program begins in Chapter 2. The chapter goes through a process to create a progressive year-level map of desired mindsets and key STEM skills for students. This is an important early step that is often overlooked by schools and teachers. This approach supports teachers and schools to think from a systems perspective: looking at how their school will develop STEM learners from the moment they arrive to the day they graduate. Teachers will identify the mindset they will nurture across a year, the key skills for each year level, the habitual practices that they want students to develop, the associated learning norms and agreements, and the structures, routines and strategies that can be used to support the students to internalise particular habits and norms.

Chapter 3 builds on this work by examining how teachers and school leaders can use a whole-school curriculum mapping process to logically develop a progression of knowledge, skills and thinking while addressing all the required elements of the Australian Curriculum. Surprisingly, many schools don't do this work. This systems-thinking process will provide clarity and certainty for both teachers and school leaders. The whole-school and year-level documents produced will lay a rigorous foundation for being able to develop authentic STEM units, nurture STEM learners and thinkers, and support easy integration of new initiatives and approaches. The chapter ends by discussing the process of developing a 'learning ladder' to support the resourcing and digital literacy-building required to address the technological elements of a STEM program.

Chapter 4 demonstrates a simplified process of backward planning STEM and transdisciplinary units based on the curriculum mapping for each term. The process will show how to extract learning intentions and success criteria directly from the Australian Curriculum and define a logical sequence of understandings for a transdisciplinary STEM unit. The development of the logical sequence of understandings addresses one of the questions students ask of teachers: 'Why are we doing this?' The sequence will be also used to frame teaching throughout the unit as the design of appropriate real-life and authentic culminating tasks.

Chapter 5 introduces Hattie and Donoghue's (2016) conceptual model of learning to guide the thinking required to design STEM learning that progressively builds knowledge, skills and thinking through a school year. This chapter specifically outlines how teachers can create small, bounded STEM projects. Bounded activities and projects, which a multitude of STEM books promote, are great ways for learners to practise computational, design and systems thinking in projects that have a clear beginning, middle and end. Beginning small is critical for students to quickly acquire and consolidate knowledge, skills and thinking before tackling larger and more complex STEM learning. Chapter 6 then outlines how to create authentic open-ended projects that will support students to apply the knowledge, skills and thinking they have developed to real-life projects.

Chapter 7 explores assessing STEM learning. The chapter begins by examining and discussing the strengths and potential challenges of a range of STEM assessment approaches and then defines what aspects are worth assessing to achieve the most desirable outcomes from designing and leading STEM learning. In essence there are three aspects to consider: assessing the knowledge,

skills and thinking specific to the curriculum areas being covered (science, technologies, maths and so on); assessing learning progression in the underlying thinking frameworks (computational, design and system); and assessing learning progression in the general capabilities, especially self-regulation. A range of structures and templates will be provided to assist teachers to embed assessment within the everyday practice of STEM learning.

Chapter 8 shares stories and experiences from a range of Australian teachers to highlight some of the pathways and lessons in the journey towards leading STEM learning more effectively. Their stories are used to identify six broad areas teachers will need to develop their skill and capacity in to be effective at creating, planning and running STEM learning. Teachers will also be encouraged to create a mini action-research project to bring rigour to the process of developing themselves as teachers and learners.

Chapter 9 returns to the big picture and discusses the concept of socially constructed and led organisational change, and how that applies to embedding an authentic and sustainable STEM program. John Kotter's (1995) eight-step change management model is used to identify key steps that school leaders can take to lead the organisational change required. Each of the eight steps is unpacked in detail alongside examples from a range of Australian schools that have already started their STEM journey.

The book concludes with the encouragement to take the first step of what can be a challenging journey but one that is ultimately rewarding – for teachers, students and school leaders.

KEY POINTS

- Most teachers and school leaders (and parents) do not think from the systems thinking, design thinking and computational thinking frameworks. This is a huge lack in schools.
- Schools need to support parents to encourage and empower their children to be problem-solvers and to think and adapt as learners.
- Learners – students and teachers alike – cannot learn to be problem-solvers, entrepreneurs and critical thinkers or begin to drive their own learning if they do not have sufficient opportunities to practise the skills. The embedding of an authentic and sustainable STEM program will be transformational for a school and the lives of the students, teachers and school leaders.
- This book was written to support teachers and schools in the thinking, structures and practices that will allow students and teachers to thrive as learners, thinkers and problem-solvers. The blend of theory and practice has been designed to challenge teachers and schools leaders to stop, think and explore the largely unexamined structures and approaches that exist within most schools.
- This book will take readers through the process of creating and building an authentic STEM program in a primary school. The whole process will take a significant investment of time and effort over a number of years.

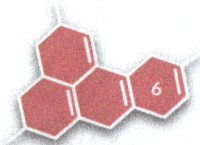

CHAPTER 1

Understanding the purpose of STEM

Tomorrow belongs to those who can hear it coming.

David Bowie, Heroes

EXAMINING THE UNEXAMINED

As every teacher and school leader understands, when a student walks into a school to learn they arrive with a world of pre-existing knowledge, skills and thinking, as well as a raft of subconscious habits and beliefs. All of these have been formed and internalised over a period of time based on the interactions and experiences they have had (and continue to have) with the people and situations in their lives. Teachers realise that some of the knowledge, skills, thinking, habits and beliefs are consistent with being self-directed learners and thinkers, while some of them are not. Therefore, as part of the teaching and learning process, effective teachers and schools invest the time to find out what students know, what they are able to do, how they think and what beliefs they have about themselves and learning. They then design targeted and differentiated learning experiences and teaching to meet the requirements of the curriculum while nurturing the growth of the human beings in front of them.

Equally, every teacher comes to teach with a range of pre-existing knowledge, skills, thinking and unconscious habits and beliefs. As Judith Lloyd Yero (2010) points out in her research, a teacher's beliefs and thinking about the nature of teaching and learning, about knowledge and about the purpose of education shapes that teacher's practices and can determine which approaches and practices thrive and which cannot be sustained. These beliefs and thinking are made visible through the language teachers use with their students; the way that they plan, deliver and assess the curriculum; the way they set up and structure learning in their classroom; the teaching and learning strategies that they use or don't use; the way they interact and communicate with others; and even the way they organise (or don't organise) themselves (Yero, 2010).

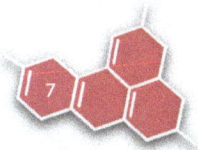

None of this should be a surprise. Of course students and teachers come to the task of learning with pre-existing knowledge, skills, thinking, habits and beliefs! So why do so many schools attempt to design and embed STEM activities and programs without beginning with an examination of the existing knowledge, thinking and beliefs?

Just like a house or a building cannot be built on a shoddy foundation, a sustainable and authentic STEM program cannot be created if schools have not grappled with or explored the pre-existing understandings, thinking and learning structures within the school. What do teachers and school leaders believe STEM learning is? What do students and teachers believe is important to know and understand about science, maths, technology and engineering? What teaching practices and habits do teachers currently have? How do these practices and habits create effective learners and learning? How do these practices and habits relate to effective STEM learning? How do the beliefs and perceptions of students, teachers and school leaders influence the embedding of effective STEM learning structures and approaches? Which teachers, school practices and structures are consistent with a STEM-learning approach, and which are not? Unfortunately, very few teachers or school leaders have the rich collaborative discussions that arise from exploring such questions. This is predominantly why STEM programs fall apart when key people leave. Sustainable STEM programs are built on a shared common understanding of learning and how STEM fits into the school vision and strategic goals.

This chapter supports schools to become clear about their starting point. It begins with two empathising activities that can be used to gain a deeper understanding of what is understood about STEM, the perceived needs that a school is attempting to address, the barriers to enacting STEM in the school and the desired outcomes for STEM and learning at the school. This lays the groundwork for a discussion about one of the major misconceptions about STEM and how the three thinking frameworks within the technologies curriculum can become an empowering context to think from when enacting aspects of STEM and the technologies curriculum. Three key learning concepts are also examined to lay the foundation for the thinking throughout this book. The chapter ends with the invitation for a design team to create a shared vision and define a meaningful purpose for an authentic STEM program.

UNDERSTANDING THE EXISTING PERCEPTIONS

It is a fundamental tenet of good design that you cannot design a solution to a challenge or problem without first coming to a deep understanding of the challenge or problem. The creation of an authentic and sustainable STEM program must begin with the process of empathising.

> ... gain an empathic understanding of the people you're designing for and the problem you are trying to solve. This process involves observing, engaging, and empathising with the people you are designing for in order to understand their experiences and motivations, as well as immersing yourself in their physical environment in order to have a deeper personal understanding of the issues, needs and challenges involved. (Interaction Design Foundation, 2021, 'Empathise' section)

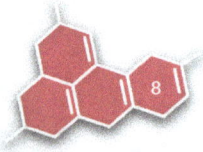

Understanding the purpose of STEM

Teachers and school leaders can begin to break down existing barriers and walls by examining the current beliefs, practices and assumptions about learning and STEM (as well as their impact). This process will support gaining a deeper understanding of the issues, needs and challenges that will have to be addressed by any STEM program that is proposed. Without having done this work, it is unlikely that any proposed solution will be sustainable. Even worse, the proposed program may perpetuate misconceptions and undermine the transformational possibilities made available by embedding STEM in a school.

The following two exercises are designed to spark a lively discussion within a design team exploring the implementation of STEM learning within a school. The activities encourage participants to voice their concerns, fears and existing understandings so that a shared understanding about the purpose of STEM can be created.

Exercise: Empathise 1

Form a design team made up of representatives from classroom teachers, middle leaders and senior leadership. If your school culture is particularly transformational, it is worthwhile to also include student and parent representatives. As members of the design team respond to the following questions they should think not only about their own perspectives, but also about those of all students, parents and other teachers of the school.

Reflect on and answer the following questions:
- What are our perceptions of STEM and its purpose?
- What do we understand? What do we not understand?
- Whose needs are we particularly trying to address by enacting a STEM program?
- What are the needs for each of the stakeholders?
- What barriers or challenges are there to enacting STEM in this school?
- What are the current experiences of students and teachers of STEM within this school?
- Are there any other perceptions or concerns in the community we have not yet captured?

This first exercise begins the process of uncovering the existing perceptions and knowledge around STEM learning. As can be seen from a selection of common responses shown in table 1.1, the responses will begin to capture the experiences, understandings and motivations present in the design team. Some responses demonstrate an incomplete understanding or skewed perception of what STEM is and how it can support school goals. Some indicate a perception that STEM is only about science, technology, engineering and mathematics, or that STEM is an add-on. Other responses highlight that the purpose of STEM is to develop a set of transferable skills (curiosity, problem-solving, critical thinking, collaboration and so on) or about preparing students for the future. Some show an understanding that STEM is transdisciplinary, student-led and can involve learning from mistakes. Across the board, the responses indicate a wondering about how to authentically implement STEM into the current curriculum, teaching and assessment practices.

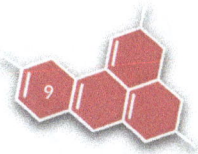

Table 1.1: Sample responses to some of the questions from 'Exercise: Empathise 1'

Perception of STEM and its purpose	Understandings about STEM	What is not understood about STEM	The needs to be addressed	The barriers or challenges
STEM only involves science and maths Problem-based learning (PBL) Acronym can vary Is an add-on to the current curriculum Coding is important 'It's got nothing to do with me' Students will get a positive association with maths and technology Purpose = to prepare kids for the world beyond traditional education To prepare students to work collaboratively To support students in problem-solving To make students globally aware Filling skill shortage in the industry Problem-solving Critical thinking Real-world problems	Teachers and students need to be open to make mistakes and willing to try new things It's problem based Teacher is the facilitator It is transdisciplinary and student-led STEM leads to entrepreneurial skills, leadership opportunities, new initiatives Rich differentiation possibility It will create a positive memory for students of their experience Will give students a real-world application for maths and science	Application – how to do it How do I implement STEM into literacy? How does it relate to other curriculum areas? Where intervention can sit How subjects that aren't in the acronym fit into STEM How do we manage timetabling and staffing? How is this going to impact the current curriculum? How are we going to promote this to parents? Best model? How to teach the teachers to be facilitators? How do we assess some of these skills? How do we know our kids are better in the future because of this?	Student social-emotional capabilities Students who need to be challenged Addressing the changing world and trying to change our approach based on how the world is going Connecting the learnings across learning areas and one topic to another Engaging and meaningful learning Helping students and teachers think conceptually rather than about content Curiosity Thinking Critical- and creative-thinking skills Real-world issues Community problems	Resistance to change Shifting staff perception and thinking Time to plan together Structure of current curriculum planning and teaching practices Timetable Getting all staff on board Teachers' confidence to let go of the control and become facilitators People will be out of their comfort zones, will be a break in routine Finance, resources, leadership Behavioural issues in students Assessment – How? Process?

The first exercise has the design team thinking and talking about their existing understandings of STEM and paints the broad picture of the issues, needs and challenges. The second exercise digs a little deeper and provides an opportunity for the design team to explore, discuss and think about why things are the way they are and how they would like them to be. This exercise often allows the participants to voice issues, concerns and barriers that were not picked up in the first exercise. It also requires the participants to begin the process of articulating a desirable future that addresses the potential causes of the current reality.

Understanding the purpose of STEM

Exercise: Empathise 2

Given the responses in 'Exercise: Empathise 1' (page 9), reflect on and answer the following questions:
- What is the school's current reality around STEM and learning?
- What are the possible causes of it being this way?
- What would be the desired future for STEM and learning?

Table 1.2: Sample responses to the questions from 'Exercise: Empathise 2'

Current reality	Possible causes	Desired future
School is starting to build an integrated approach across curriculum areas	Lack of transparency across learning areas	Distinguish the underlying perceptions and biases that people have, and create a richer point of view
Teachers have been discussing and working on differentiation	Lack of time for collaborative team planning? Always done it that way (tradition works)	Shift the way that teachers and parents think about learning – perhaps re-imagination of schooling
Teachers are hooked on delivering content and the school is hooked on curriculum and systems	Inconsistent communication because of misinterpretations or biases	Having breaker spaces (break down technology, deconstruction processes in learning areas) and then maker spaces
There is confusion and limited dialogue outside specific curriculum focus areas	Traditional assessment and reporting structures	Leadership supporting and trusting teachers through $$, time and structures
The STEM acronym is a problem because people can say it has nothing to do with them – it is polarising	Not giving students the permission to make mistakes and learn from attempts	Collaborative planning embedded in school practice
Some teachers do not know how to start. Do we use PBL? IBL?	Teachers and students not having the freedom to experiment within bounds (lack of trust?)	Assessment appropriately aligned to process of learning
Perception that only high-performing academic students can do it		School identifies themes or concepts that they value at the start and embed in the whole curriculum
Fixed perception of the roles of teachers and students		Teachers collaborating
There is limited physical as well as timetable space		Students collaborating
Concern about another tokenistic idea		Developing socio-emotional learning and emotional intelligence
		Drafting and conferencing processes embedded in the way learning occurs in the classroom

The responses shown in table 1.2 demonstrate the range of challenges and barriers schools face when they explore implementing STEM learning. The discussion is important to have because it means the design team considers the necessity of looking at the whole system of teaching and learning, rather than taking a piecemeal approach. How do teachers collaborate to plan learning? Is there a shared common understanding or are teachers accidentally adding to the variance in student understanding? Do the reporting structure and timetable constrain effective learning? Are there misunderstandings, biases or silos of learning occurring? Is there a culture of risk-taking in learning – for teachers and students?

As highlighted throughout this book, a well-designed STEM program empowers the agency and leadership of students and teachers. It models and grows thinking, skills and knowledge in a planned manner across the years of schooling. It is consistent with highly effective, evidence-based teaching and learning practices. It challenges the existing systems and processes of learning and demands that schools do the thinking, planning and acting to build a systemic approach to high-quality learning.

THE HIDDEN POWER OF STEM AND THE AUSTRALIAN CURRICULUM: TECHNOLOGIES

A common challenge that is highlighted by the two exercises is the shallow understanding of the purpose of STEM and Australian Curriculum: Technologies. Some teachers and school leaders think it is just yet another thing that they need to put in to an already crowded curriculum. Some people get hooked on the STEM acronym and think that it is only about the disciplines of science, technology, engineering and mathematics. Others argue that we should include *A* for *arts* (STEAM) to address creativity and the arts, or *H* for *humanities* (SHTEAM) to include the social sciences. Some teachers use the acronym to exclude themselves from thinking about even the possibility of STEM because they believe it doesn't apply to them. As one STEM teacher-leader pointed out to me, one of the biggest barriers she finds when she works with teachers is the mindset that they can't teach new technology or programs because they don't know enough about technology and don't have all the answers they need to teach.

In the Australian Curriculum: Technologies, the two elements (design and technologies, and digital technologies) both have the aim of using thinking frameworks to generate and produce designed solutions for authentic needs and opportunities. Along the way, students will use 'systems and data; design thinking, systems thinking and computational thinking; and technologies processes and production skills, project management skills, and enterprise skills and innovation; taking into account interactions and impact' (Australian Curriculum, Assessment and Reporting Authority [ACARA], n.d.-s, 'Structure: Core concepts' section).

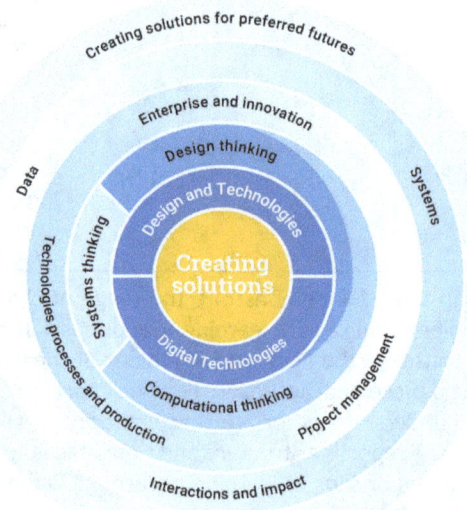

Figure 1.1: Overview of the Australian Curriculum: Technologies core concepts
Source: ACARA (n.d.-s)

The Australian Curriculum: Technologies documentation and videos are quite clear when they describe the intent of the curriculum: the focus is on the thinking first and foremost, and the content is the vehicle for this thinking. This is also true when you examine the curriculum for science, humanities and maths. The true value of the Australian Curriculum: Technologies and STEM are the thinking frameworks and the mindsets that are developed by attempting to create solutions to meet particular needs. If teachers and schools miss this point, they can become trapped by STEM being yet another thing to jam into an already full curriculum. Conversely, if you really grapple with and understand the thinking frameworks underscoring STEM and the Australian Curriculum: Technologies, you may realise that it will transform how learning in schools occurs.

THINKING FRAMEWORKS

Having a framework for thinking provides you with a systematic way of approaching problems and situations that allows you to be effective in creating a solution. This is particularly important when one is learning something new. For example, many English teachers use TEEL (topic sentence, explanation, evidence, link) as a framework to teach students how to write structured paragraphs that link to form an argument. Edward de Bono's (2019) six thinking hats provide a systematic framework of thinking so that by mentally wearing and switching 'hats' you can easily focus or redirect thoughts or the conversation. DIE (diagnose, intervene, evaluate) is a process promoted by John Hattie (2015) when developing teachers to be data informed in their practice. When learning something new, thinking frameworks support the learner to develop clarity of understanding, connect what they are learning to prior knowledge and bring rigour to their thinking.

There are many thinking frameworks present in the Australian Curriculum, though they aren't necessarily described as such. The inquiry skills that are core to science, geography and history can be considered to be thinking frameworks for approaching situations in those disciplines. In maths the 'framework of thinking' is described as mathematical reasoning and represents 'an increasingly sophisticated capacity for logical thought and actions, such as analysing, proving, evaluating, explaining, inferring, justifying and generalising' (ACARA, n.d.-l, 'Reasoning' section).

The three thinking frameworks at the heart of the Australian Curriculum: Technologies are extraordinarily powerful in that they are useful in all learning. By shifting the focus from the acronym of STEM to the underlying thinking frameworks, a whole new vista opens wherein specific thinking skills and processes can be transferred across multiple disciplines. If teachers and schools start to focus on the skills and processes inherent within each of the three thinking frameworks, every teacher can become a STEM teacher and schools can deliver on their curriculum requirements while developing highly capable learners.

COMPUTATIONAL THINKING

Computational thinking describes the problem-solving processes and approaches to create solutions that can be implemented using digital technologies. When thinking computationally we often draw on approaches such as breaking down problems into parts (decomposition), recognising and interpreting patterns, abstraction, logical reasoning, designing and using algorithms, and creating models to represent processes.

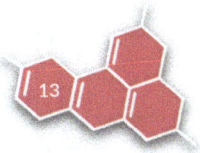

Igniting STEM *Learning*

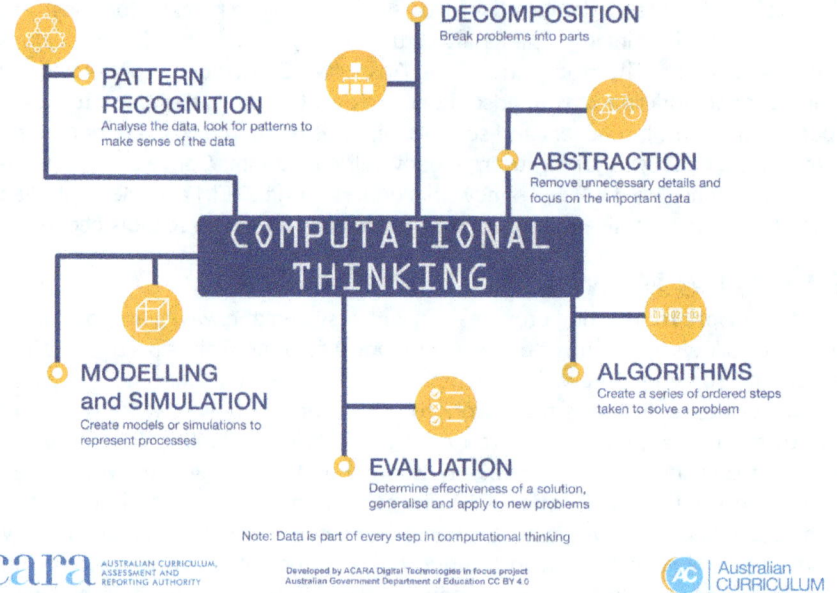

Figure 1.2: Overview of computational thinking skills and concepts
Source: ACARA (n.d.-a)

Figure 1.2 is ACARA's brief overview of the skills and concepts related to computational thinking. While the computational thinking framework is an articulation of the skills and concepts that are applicable to digital technology and digital systems, it is not hard to see how they are transferable across other curriculum areas. Building on this, table 1.3 unpacks each of the computational thinking skills into a description of the process, example success criteria, examples of where the skill is used in different disciplines and examples of how it can be used.

Understanding the purpose of STEM

Table 1.3: Examples of computational thinking skills across disciplines

Computational thinking skills		
Skill	**Examples of where to use it**	**Examples of how to use it**
Decomposition Decomposition is the process of solving a problem by breaking it down into parts that are easier to solve, understand or manage. **Example can-do statements:** - I can identify why I need to break down a problem/question. - I can identify the parts, essential elements, features of the problem/question. - I can identify parts of a problem that has been broken down into smaller components or stages. - I can break down a problem into smaller parts. - I can use a decision tree to break down a problem and identify requirements and constraints. - I can identify key elements by decomposing the problem.	**Digital technologies:** - We can break down a complex problem or system into smaller parts that are more manageable and easier to understand. The smaller parts can then be examined and solved or designed individually as they are simpler to work with. **English and the arts:** - Deconstruction is an approach to breaking down something (sentence/paragraph/text) into its separate parts to understand its meaning. - Identifying the key words and ideas in a text is the first step to being able to infer and attribute meaning. - Analysis is built on the skill of deconstruction. - To create an interactive story, one can decompose the problem to a list of characters and their characteristics, the actions of the characters, the backdrops and the sequence of scenes with reference to which characters, actions and backdrops are involved in each scene. - Genres in English can be distinguished between based on the way students decompose them. For example, the structure of poetry is different from the structure of a report; metre and rhyme are not relevant in the report genre, just as logical structure is not necessarily relevant in a poem. **Mathematics:** - Teaching learners how to deconstruct a worded problem using strategies, such as identifying the key words and creating a diagrammatic representation of the problem, is the first step in being able to apply the appropriate strategy to solve the problem. - Decomposition may be represented in diagrams. **Science:** - The process of identifying the independent and dependent variables so one can pose a hypothesis and design a valid test is a process of decomposition.	When something seems complex, the first step is to see if you can break it down into smaller parts. Let's decompose the problem into smaller parts. Let's deconstruct that sentence/paragraph to understand its meaning. Let's deconstruct that, identifying the key words and ideas. Let's deconstruct that by drawing what the question is asking. Let's decompose the question by identifying the independent and dependent variables. We will now use the skill of decomposition to break down the problem into more manageable/understandable parts. Problem-solving is puzzle solving. Each smaller problem is a smaller piece of the puzzle to find and solve. To solve the question/text/problem we need to decompose it into smaller parts. What are the pieces of your puzzle? How are you going to find them? Are these easier to solve?

Continued ...

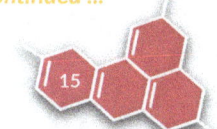

Igniting STEM Learning

Skill	Examples of where to use it	Examples of how to use it
Pattern recognition Pattern recognition is the process of finding patterns and order in information, and looking for similarities among and within problems so you can analyse, interpret and communicate it. **Example can-do statements**<ul><li>I can identify …</li><li>I can compare …</li><li>I can contrast …</li><li>I can sort and classify …</li><li>I can sort data into groups and describe each group type.</li><li>I can organise the data so I can make sense of the data.</li><li>I can describe patterns in the data.</li><li>I can represent data in different ways using symbols and images.</li><li>I can identify features and characteristics of books that allow for them to be sorted.</li><li>I can sort and organise data and identify patterns in data.</li><li>I can accurately organise data in spreadsheet software and can use that data to generate a graph.</li></ul>	**Science and geography:**<ul><li>Looking for patterns in data and observations helps to make predictions and identify cause and effect.</li></ul>**History:**<ul><li>Recognising patterns in societies and cultures allows the analysis and interpretation of societal trends. We make sense of our world by looking for patterns.</li></ul>**Mathematics:**<ul><li>Pattern recognition is core to maths and the fields of probability, statistics and number. There are patterns in the times tables and patterns in recognising shapes.</li></ul>**English:**<ul><li>There are patterns in the similarities and differences to the sounds of letters and words.</li><li>Pattern recognition is used when students are connecting read words to pictures.</li><li>Compare and contrast is a pattern finding approach.</li></ul>**The arts:**<ul><li>Patterns are absolutely everywhere – colour, drawing, concepts etc.</li></ul>**Science:**<ul><li>Observation is all about pattern recognition.</li><li>Dichotomous keys are based on pattern recognition.</li></ul>	What are the patterns here? How can we use the patterns or organise the information? How is this problem similar to that problem? What are the similarities and differences here? How can we use the patterns to sort the …? If that is the pattern how can we use it to interpret the …? How can we use the patterns to sort the …? How can we use the pattern to communicate the idea better? What are the patterns in the data? When you can recognise the patterns in the information/data, it helps you to analyse and interpret what is going on.

Understanding the purpose of STEM

Abstraction	Design and technologies:	
Abstraction is the process of filtering out or ignoring details that are not relevant or that we don't need to concentrate on information that is important or needed so that a solution can be developed. **Example can-do statements:**<ul><li>I can point out the details of …</li><li>I can identify what is important and what is not.</li><li>I can identify what is relevant to a topic and what is not.</li><li>I can use the patterns in the data/information to classify it.</li><li>I can simplify the information into categories.</li><li>I can identify the main ideas.</li><li>I can explain why something is important or not.</li><li>I can justify why something is important or not.</li></ul>	<ul><li>The define phase of the design thinking process involves not only looking for patterns in all the information gathered but getting clear about what is important and what is not so that the designer can narrow the focus for designing a solution.</li></ul>**Science:**<ul><li>The careful and creative use of abstraction is core to forming theories. Einstein's theory of relativity, for example, was built on filtering out what he felt was not important and concentrating on certain characteristics of the patterns he saw.</li><li>Occam's razor is a principle that suggests that if two explanations exist for an occurrence the one that requires the smallest number of assumptions is usually correct.</li></ul>**The arts:**<ul><li>Abstract art does not attempt to represent an accurate depiction of a visual reality but instead use shapes, colours, forms and gestural marks to represent and communicate specific ideas and characteristics to a viewer.</li></ul>**English:**<ul><li>The art of persuasion, argument and debate is built on the skill of abstraction.</li></ul>**Mathematics:**<ul><li>Abstraction helps us understand the idea that a cricket ball is a sphere in the same way that a soccer ball is.</li><li>Data can be organised in records made up of fields irrespective of whether the data are numbers, text, images or something else.</li></ul>	When we read the text, what are the key words? What is the important information in the question? Can you draw what the question is asking? What information is relevant/important here? What information is not relevant/important here? What should we concentrate on? Now that we have identified the patterns, what should we focus on? How can we simplify the information so we can decide what to focus on? Can you explain why that is relevant/important? Can you justify why that is relevant/important?

Continued …

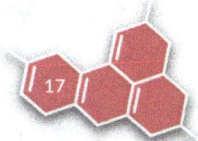

Skill	Examples of where to use it	Examples of how to use it
Algorithms Algorithms use a series of ordered steps to solve a problem or complete a task. **Example can-do statements:** - I can identify and follow a series of steps to complete a task. - I can follow a sequence of steps to solve a problem. - I can describe the steps of an algorithm for a task. - I can define an algorithm as a series of steps. - I can create a flow chart for an algorithm. - I can follow an algorithm. - I can describe an algorithm and what each part means. - I can describe an algorithm for a familiar task. - I can explain how to create an algorithm for a simple task. - I can create an algorithm and identify where user input results in possible different actions. - I can explain how to improve an algorithm. - I can seek feedback to improve an algorithm. - I can order steps in the right sequence if I'm given the steps of the task. - I can identify parts of the algorithm where choices are made (branching) and different events or actions result from user input.	**Health and PE:** - Health and PE are replete with tasks that have steps that need to be done in a particular order (algorithms). - Most recipes follow a series of steps to make a particular dish, dance steps follow choreography timed to music, even sport activities such as kicking a ball or throwing a ball can be broken down into a sequence of steps. This enables learners to understand how to complete a particular task and can be used to coach them to be more effective. **General capabilities:** - Unconscious algorithms exist in the automatic things that we all do in the mornings such as the steps to get ready for school, steps to brush our teeth, steps to be ready to learn in class, even planning to achieve a goal. These can be highlighted as forms of algorithms and be used to coach students on developing themselves in the capabilities. **English:** - Routines such as TEEL to write persuasive essays are algorithms. - Teachers can examine similar routines and begin to language them as algorithms. **Mathematics:** - Procedures in maths are algorithms (e.g. the method one uses to solve long or short division). One could even flowchart a mathematical procedure to make it visible to the students. **Digital technologies:** - Apart from programming, the steps a computer goes through to boot up can be considered an algorithm. - Having students create flow charts showing the flow of the steps, any branching and any iteration is a great visualisation tool for algorithms.	What is the sequence of steps of …? What are the steps you take to get ready for school? Describe the steps you took to solve that. Can we make an algorithm for doing that task? Can you follow that algorithm? Please follow the algorithm we put up for writing the essay. What are the decision points in the IF-THEN algorithm?

Understanding the purpose of STEM

Modelling/simulation

Modelling/simulation is creating a model that represents the operation of a process or a system to gain insight on the workings, structure and relationships within an object, system or idea so that predictions can be made.

Example can-do statements:
- I can create a model of a process.
- I can create a model of a digital system and explain the parts and software it uses.
- I can use data to model an object or event.
- I can design a prototype model of a real-life solution.
- I can create a paper prototype of my design to show how it will work.
- I can create a storyboard to predict the flow of a story.
- I can annotate a sequence to explain how a prototype meets user needs.
- I can discuss the relationship between a model and the real-world system it represents.

English:
- Prior to students writing a story, they can create a storyboard which models the flow of the story with the relationships between different incidents and characters. This will enable them to have a more coherent picture of the story as they write it.

Mathematics:
- Mathematical models are used constantly to represent real-life data and systems. This includes fitting trendlines to data and using mathematical models to represent collated real-life data.

Science:
- Models are used to represent particular real-world phenomena that aren't necessarily visible (e.g. cells, atoms). This allows scientists to create hypotheses and design theories.
- Scientists also use data from a simulation or a simplified model to make a prediction (e.g. climate change).

Design and technologies:
- During the design process it is normal to create a drawing of the product or system during the ideation process. The drawings then become more detailed and can even be annotated to explain particular features. This allows a more accurate prototype or model to be built before creating a full-sized version. They are low-cost simulations designed that allow fast problem-solving and evaluation of the concepts.

How can we simulate that so we can understand how it could work?

How can we model that?

What is a simplified version of that?

Before we write the story, we can create a storyboard (or model) of the flow of the story.

Models are used to give us insight into how things work.

Can we use the model to make a prediction?

Can we use the model to explain how it works?

Designers make prototypes to test a process or concept. They can then evaluate a new design quickly and cheaply.

Continued ...

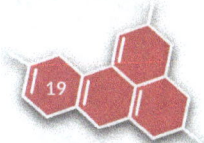

Skill	Examples of where to use it	Examples of how to use it
Evaluation Evaluation is the process of examining and judging the merit, significance or value of something to determine its effectiveness in meeting criteria. **Example can-do statements:** - I can use criteria to evaluate my ideas. - I can evaluate the effectiveness of … - I can determine the purpose and criteria for this evaluation. - I can examine the ideas, works, solutions and/or methods. - I can determine the merit, value or significance of the ideas, works, solutions or methods. - I can appraise the strengths, limitations, implications in relation to the selected criteria. - I can review the evaluation to ensure the criteria have been applied and the reason for this evaluation has been met. - I can evaluate the usefulness of the published information or product against agreed criteria. - I can evaluate a game and describe its usefulness.	**Design and technologies:** - The process of evaluating ideas and design concepts against set criteria is part of the improvement cycle in design and is fundamental to creating products that meet articulated needs. **General capabilities:** - The process of evaluation is core to developing self-regulated learners. For example, they could evaluate their behaviour against a norm or agreement to ensure they are operating as a team. Equally, they could compare their work against a rubric or existing piece of work to improve the quality of what they are expected to deliver. **English and languages:** - Persuasive writing involves evaluating information to draw conclusions and justify opinions. It is a key skill required to be a critical thinker and writer. **HASS and science:** - Evaluating evidence is critical to forming and assessing hypotheses. Evaluation is part of the inquiry skills in these disciplines. **Mathematics:** - Once a student has arrived at a solution it is important for them to evaluate the reasonableness of the solution. They need to ask questions such as: Does it make sense? Is it approximately what they thought it should be? This ensures they have not made a mistake in their calculations.	*Evaluate* is a key cognitive verb used throughout the curriculum in many contexts. We can begin the process of evaluating by coming up with a set of criteria. How could we judge the merit of that idea? How will we know if we are effective? We can evaluate … What can we do to assist in evaluating the impact of recent changes? How would we evaluate the results of the experiment? What is the significance of …? How do you know it is valuable? We first have to have some criteria to judge the value of X and then evaluate against that criteria.

Teachers can begin to develop student understanding and use of the skills and concepts inherent in computational thinking by using the language and strategies in all learning areas. As will be pointed out later in this chapter and in Chapter 5, deep learning and the ability to transfer learning to new situations is enhanced when students internalise the language and usage of learning strategies across multiple learning areas.

DESIGN THINKING

Design thinking is embedded in both the digital technologies, and design and technologies curriculums. It is an iterative and non-linear process used to solve complex problems and find useful solutions. As the Australian Curriculum articulates, design thinking 'helps people to empathise and understand needs, opportunities and problems; generate, iterate and represent innovative, user-centred ideas; and analyse and evaluate those ideas' (ACARA, n.d.-s, 'Structure: Design thinking' section).

When introducing the design thinking process to schools I prefer to use the Stanford d.school model (see a variation on this model in figure 1.3) as it is easier to explain to teachers and students in comparison to the descriptors used in the Australian Curriculum. Table 1.4 shows the relationships between the d.school model and the Australian Curriculum processes and production skills.

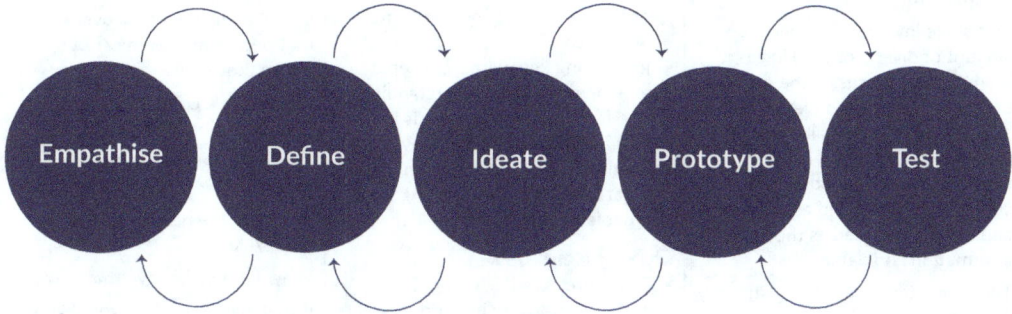

Figure 1.3: Variation on the design thinking model
Source: Adapted from Hasso-Plattner Institute of Design (2020)

Table 1.4: Relationships between the Stanford d.school model of design thinking and the Australian Curriculum processes and production skills

Stanford d.school model of design thinking	Australian Curriculum processes and production skills	Across the design process
Empathy	Investigating	Collaborating and managing
Define	Defining	
Ideate	Generating and designing	
Prototype	Producing and implementing	
Test	Evaluating	

Source: Adapted from Hasso-Plattner Institute of Design (2020) and ACARA (n.d.-s)

The skills inherent in the design thinking process, much like in computational thinking, are transferable and applicable in many disciplines. Table 1.5 unpacks each of the design thinking skills into a description of the process, example success criteria, examples of where the skill is used in different disciplines and examples of how it can be used.

Table 1.5: Use of design thinking skills across disciplines

Design thinking skills		
Skill	**Examples of where to use it**	**Examples of how to use it**
Empathising Empathising is the process of identifying goals and sub-goals, giving up assumptions, gathering information and data, and putting yourself in the shoes of the user to come to a deep understanding of a challenge and who you are designing for. This stage involves a significant amount of divergent thinking as it is an analysis process – the process of breaking down complex concepts and problems into smaller, easier-to-understand parts. It requires the learner to give up their pre-conceived notions and assumptions and be open-minded as they gather information and data. The computational thinking strategy of decomposition is particularly useful for empathising as it allows students to identify the elements of a task so they can seek information to understand. **Example can-do statements:** - I can identify … - I can describe … - I can use clues to … - I can locate … - I can identify and describe the parts of … - I can define a problem and break it into smaller parts. - I can gather information. - I can collect/record data. - I can identify the key words, ideas or concepts. - I can identify the needs of the user. - I can describe the pros and cons of … - I can describe different points of views.	**English:** - Empathising is a key skill of the literacy strand. - When you read a text you are looking for clues and information, within the text and outside the text, so you can gain an insight into the possible context for the actions and behaviours of the characters or the ideas and concepts being discussed. - Identifying key words, concepts and ideas leads to understanding. - The more skilled a learner is in empathising, the better they are at coming to a deep understanding of what is written and inferring from what is written. **Other disciplines:** - The more skilled a learner is in empathising, the deeper they will understand the situation and how to communicate it. - Experimentation in science and art is about empathising and looking for data/information so that patterns can be recognised. - Watching/reading about other people's perspectives is an empathising process. - Identifying key words and drawing the situation leads to clarity in maths – particularly worded problems.	If we are to empathise with users, we should always try to adopt the mindset of a beginner. What are we observing? What are the assumptions here? What is the key information we are looking for? Photographing or recording target users can help you uncover needs that people may or may not be aware they have. How can we come to a deeper understanding of the situation? What are the clues in the picture or text? What are the needs of the person/group/user? Why did they behave that way? If that was you, what would you do? How could we find out what they need? What did you learn from making the prototype? What are the parts of the problem? What might a computer do? Ask lots of 'what if' questions.

Understanding the purpose of STEM

Defining

Defining is the process of synthesising the information that was created during the empathise stage for the purpose of looking for patterns and gaining insight to articulate what to focus on or the problem that will be solved.

This stage involves a significant amount of convergent thinking as it is a synthesis process (creatively piecing together the puzzle together to form whole ideas) with the aim of clearly articulating what to focus on or the problem to be solved.

The computational thinking strategies of abstraction and pattern recognition are particularly useful in this stage as the learner identifies what is important and what is not amongst the information gathered.

Example can-do statements:
- I can sort and classify ...
- I can compare and contrast ...
- I can arrange ...
- I can organise data and information.
- I can represent the data in different ways for different purposes.
- I can create charts and use other ways to visualise the data to help make sense of patterns and trends.
- I can identify the needs and wants of the end users.
- I can create a mind map to show relationships between information.
- I can sort and organise data and identify patterns in data.
- I can organise data and use that data to generate a graph.
- I can identify what is important and what is not.
- I can identify what is relevant to a topic and what is not.
- I can make generalisations based on the data I have collected, organised, sorted and analysed.

The skill of defining what to focus on is a core learning skill in multiple disciplines. It requires the learner to develop the capacity to be clear about what is being asked of them so they can then apply the appropriate strategy.

Mathematics:
- Teachers know that students can find worded problems much more difficult than when they are given a formula to solve. By developing their capacity to distinguish what is important and what is not in worded problems (a synthesising process), they will become better at choosing the most appropriate strategy.

English and HASS:
- The skill of inferring requires students to synthesise information from the text so they can understand or predict character or scene. This requires students to look for patterns and make meaning from what was written.

Science:
- Scientists find patterns and synthesise the data they have gathered so they can make predictions (hypotheses) about future outcomes. This enables them to focus experimentations on particular variables and exclude others.

Health and PE:
- Coaches in sport and dance synthesise information gathered from observations to identify what to coach someone on as they develop a skill. This can lead to the development of specific drills to build a skill.

Let's look at all the information we have gathered and see if we can find some patterns.

What does the picture tell us about what the author wrote?

What problem is the character in the story trying to solve?

Let's work on defining what problem the character is attempting to solve from the clues in the text.

Now that we have identified the key words and ideas what is the problem we are trying to solve?

We are in a define phase in solving this problem:
- What patterns can we see?
- What is important and what is not?
- What should we focus on?

The:
- [user ... (descriptive)] needs
- [need ... (verb)] because
- [insight ... (compelling)].

How might we:
- make TV more social, so youths feel more engaged?
- enable TV programs to be watched anywhere, at any time?
- make watching TV at home more exciting?

Continued ...

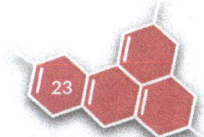

Igniting STEM Learning

Skill	Examples of where to use it	Examples of how to use it
Ideation Ideation is the process of generating a large quantity of ideas and filtering down the ideas into the best, most practical or most innovative ones to inspire new and better design solutions and products. This stage is about creativity and divergent thinking. It has the learner start to think outside the box, look for alternative ways to view the problem and identify innovative solutions to the problem statement they've created. Many possible solutions are explored in a short amount of time and unexpected connections can be drawn. There is no evaluation during this stage as that would shut down the divergent thinking. **Example can-do statements:**<ul><li>I can draw/sketch various possible solutions to a problem.</li><li>I can identify various strategies that I could use to solve a problem.</li><li>I can annotate my sketches/design to clarify the pros and cons of each.</li><li>I can compare and contrast features of existing products to provide new ideas.</li><li>I can describe how a design idea meets the needs of those who will use the solution.</li><li>I can use a variety of critical and creative thinking strategies (e.g. brainstorming, sketching, 3D modelling and experimenting) to generate innovative design ideas.</li></ul>	In ideation sessions, it's important to create the right type of environment to help create a culture with a curious, courageous and concentrated atmosphere. All judgement is deferred (there are no stupid ideas). In fact one must encourage weird, wild and wacky ideas. Teachers can use this process pedagogically in many day-to-day situations. However, students need to be explicitly taught:<ul><li>different strategies to generate new ideas without judgement</li><li>strategies to collect, categorise, refine and narrow the ideas.</li></ul>**Science:**<ul><li>Having students brainstorm potential outcomes of an experiment is creative practice. These predictions can be discussed and refined as they gather more information from experiments.</li></ul>**English and HASS:**<ul><li>Building on the skill of inferring (see the 'Defining' row in this table, page 23) students can then explain the motivation of a character in a narrative or a historical setting. This will deepen their ability to use figurative language such as allegories, similes, analogies, metaphors and more.</li></ul>**Digital and design technologies:**<ul><li>Brainstorming the features of a game or a product that meet a range of design criteria is an example of ideation. Students can explore a wide range of options and make new innovative connections as they formulate a potential solution.</li></ul>	What are some weird and wacky ideas to solve this problem? Draw at least five ideas that solve … What are some adjectives that could describe the situation/character? What are the pros and cons of each idea? Let's come up with as many ideas as we can. Fill in a PMI (plus, minus, interesting) template for each of your ideas. What are features we see elsewhere that could be useful here? Let's brainstorm possible ideas and solutions to this situation. What are some of the best features of the ideas we have seen? What is another way we can look at this problem that might give us some more ideas? How does each idea meet the needs of the users?

Understanding the purpose of STEM

Prototype–test–evaluation iterative cycle

The iterative cycle is a process of creating a model, simulation or scaled down prototype of the product; evaluating how well the product meets expectations, wants and needs; and providing feedback to refine/improve the model, simulation or scaled down prototype with the aim of identifying the best possible solution using minimal time and effort.

These stages involve a convergent thinking process where the various ideas generated in the previous stage are put together in some organised, structured way and feedback is used to refine and improve the product.

Note: Sometimes the learner discovers they need to return to an earlier stage as the prototyping and testing can reveal new problems, new ideas and new solutions.

Example can-do statements
- I can create …
- I can evaluate …
- I can refine …
- I can use feedback to …
- I can build models or representations (prototypes) of …
- I can repeatedly test the prototypes and use the results to continually inform improvements to …
- I can create a chart/graph and discuss its usefulness.
- I can collaborate to create and refine a product.
- I can create a program for a particular purpose and evaluate its effectiveness.
- I can evaluate the appropriateness of my own behaviour and conduct.
- I can seek and act on feedback.

The iterative process is one where students use formative feedback from self, peers and teachers to incrementally learn or improve.

Teachers will need to explicitly teach the processes of:
- building a model, creating a draft and having a go at skills
- reflecting on how well an attempt meets the expectations, criteria and desired outcome
- using feedback to identify actions/strategies to improve outcomes.

English and HASS:
- When writing, writers go through a drafting process. This process often involves multiple iterations of drafting text, reading it and evaluating it against criteria such as coherency and whether it fulfils its intention. Authors can even receive feedback from editors and readers to improve the quality of the written piece.

Science:
- The process of designing an effective science experiment to test a hypothesis involves multiple iterations. This iterative cycle ensures that the test is fair and valid.

General capabilities:
- Learning involves the progressive development of a set of skills. Skills such as critical and creative thinking, collaboration and self-regulation require learners to practice, receive feedback and refine their strategies and behaviour. This iterative process mimics the prototype–test–evaluation iterative cycle.

Health and PE, and the arts:
- Development of a skill in physical disciplines such as sport, art, cooking and so on follow the iterative cycles of practising, receiving and using feedback, and then refining one's strategies.

We are going to go through a drafting process to learn how to …

As we go through the prototype–test–evaluate process we want to learn from what works and what doesn't so we can improve …

Does the product meet the needs and wants we originally identified?

Now that we have tested the design, in what ways could it be improved?

How well does our prototype meet the design criteria?

What feedback would you give one another to improve your draft?

How could we use the rubric to improve our solution as we go through the iterative cycle?

The design thinking process is applicable in many learning areas. Using the language of the design process across the learning areas will allow for transferability of skills and thinking. For example, students will begin reading a text (and perhaps looking at the associated images) and will go through the empathising stage as they come to an understanding of what the author is describing or arguing. From discussions with each other and the teacher, plus any prior knowledge, they will recognise any patterns and identify the key words and ideas (define stage). The teacher may then pose a question, prompting the students to brainstorm possible answers (ideate stage). The teacher may then direct students to practise writing a response and refine their writing skill via a drafting process with formative feedback (prototype–test–evaluate iterative cycle).

SYSTEMS THINKING

Much like design thinking, systems thinking is embedded in both the digital technologies, and design and technologies curriculums. Systems are made up of a set of components that work together in a particular environment to achieve the overall objective of the whole. Systems can have sub-systems and may themselves be part of larger systems.

Systems thinking is the process of identifying and examining the interactions between different components (or sub-systems) of a system to understand how the components influence each other and the function of the entire system. In nature, ecosystems are an example of a system in which various elements such as air, water, movement, plants and animals work together to survive. Schools, classes, societies, landscapes, food webs, team sports and the human body can all be considered examples of systems.

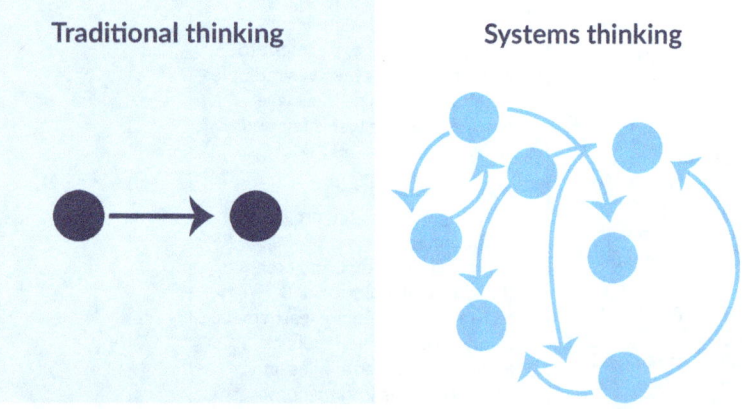

Figure 1.4: Traditional and systems thinking

Systems thinking is distinct from design thinking and is often associated with analysis – the process of breaking something down into its component parts to understand it. As the Australian Curriculum highlights, systems thinking 'helps people to think holistically about the interactions and interconnections that shape the behaviour of systems' (ACARA, n.d.-s, 'Structure: Systems thinking' section). Design thinking is more associated with the process of synthesis – using the understanding gained through analysis to create a solution. Table 1.6 unpacks systems thinking into a description of the process, example success criteria, examples of where the skill is used in different disciplines and examples of how it can be used.

Understanding the purpose of STEM

Table 1.6: Use of system thinking across disciplines

\multicolumn{3}{c}{**Systems thinking skills**}		
Skill	**Examples of where to use it**	**Examples of how you can use it**
Systems thinking Systems thinking is the process of identifying the different components (or sub-systems) of a system and identifying and examining the interactions between these components to understand how the components influence each other and the function of the entire system. **Example can-do statements:**<ul><li>I can produce a diagram that shows the interactions between different parts of a system.</li><li>I can create a flow chart of an algorithm.</li><li>I can identify the interactions between parts of the …</li><li>I can explain how and why … behaves as it does.</li><li>I can test and evaluate a prototype to understand how each part influences the others.</li><li>I can discuss the constraints on the solution/system.</li><li>I can compare the similarities and differences between two similar products/systems to help predict the function/purpose of each part.</li><li>I can identify patterns of behaviour over time.</li><li>I can identify possible causes of a problem.</li></ul>	**English:**<ul><li>Systems thinking is demonstrated by learners understanding how different language usage produces different effects and even how different text structures have different purposes.</li><li>Filmic analysis requires learners to examine the interactions between components such as lighting, music and camera angles and how they influence the viewer's perception.</li></ul>**The arts:**<ul><li>The analysis of art involves an understanding not only of the specific techniques used by the artist but also of trends and thinking at the time of production. An artist is not separated from the 'system' that they are part of and understanding that system leads to an understanding of the art.</li></ul>**Science and geography:**<ul><li>When designing experiments and making hypotheses scientists take into account how different components of a system (natural or human-made) can influence one another. Examples include the relationship between cells and body systems; deforestation and loss of species or landslides; and the increase in greenhouse gases and loss of ice at the north and south poles.</li></ul>**History:**<ul><li>Historical analysis using primary and secondary sources is a systems thinking process. The exploration of how different cultures influenced one another, the factors that led to a particular historical event and topics such as migration all require an understanding of the interactions between different parts of a system.</li></ul>	What are the key components of this system? What are the parts of an essay? Use TEEL or PEEL to write this essay. How do they influence one another? What are the possible causes of …? How would we work out the purpose of this system? How did this influence that?

27

There are extraordinary learning gains that can be made if teachers invest time in creating opportunities for their students to go through the computational, design and systems thinking processes in their learning. As John Spencer and AJ Juliani (2016) point out, design and systems thinking develops learners to be empathetic, be questioners, be curious and take creative risks, be critical and creative thinkers, make connections between ideas, to think about the bigger picture and the relationship between things, be problem-solvers and to work collaboratively with others towards a solution. Interestingly enough, many of these skills, behaviours and dispositions are captured by the general capabilities in the Australian Curriculum.

Perhaps the most valuable outcome that arises from focusing on the thinking frameworks is the mindset that is nurtured. Learners who have ingrained computational, design and systems thinking see the world differently. No problem is insurmountable. They bring clarity in the way they work through complexity to find a solution. They know themselves as capable learners. They are courageous and confident within themselves. These are the individuals who lead humanity forward.

Unfortunately, when schools and teachers focus on delivering the content of STEM rather than developing student thinking, the value and opportunity of the thinking frameworks within the Australian Curriculum are lost.

LAYING THE FOUNDATIONAL THINKING

One of the early steps to embedding an authentic STEM program is teachers and school leaders infusing the thinking frameworks into the way their school plans, delivers and assesses learning. To answer this challenge, it is important to step back to gain a deeper appreciation and understanding of what actually creates effective learning.

LEARNING IS BUILT ON HABITS

The brain has evolved over millions of years to be an efficient energy user. One of the major ways that the brain attempts to lower energy usage is by making almost any routine into a habit. In other words, anything that we do ritually will, over time, become a subconscious habit.

As Duhigg (2014) points out in *The Power of Habits*, this energy-saving short cut has a number of huge advantages:

> *An efficient brain requires less room, which makes for a smaller head, which makes childbirth easier and therefore causes fewer infant and mother deaths. An efficient brain also allows us to stop thinking constantly about basic behaviours, such as walking and choosing what to eat. (p. 18)*

We walk every day, but for the majority of us it is a completely subconscious activity. Biomechanically, the action of walking, putting one foot in front of another in such a way that we maintain balance while we move forward, is quite a complex ballet of motion and coordination. It requires the perfect timing and coordination of many of our body systems to enable it to occur. When babies are learning to walk, the action requires a high level of conscious focus from their brains. Over time, as walking becomes routine and a habit, the action of walking requires less and less attention from the brain until it becomes subconscious.

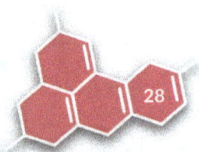

Understanding the purpose of STEM

While our ability to make routines subconscious habits is a valuable trait for thriving in an increasingly complex world, switching to automatic does have its drawbacks in certain areas. For example, human and primate brains are susceptible to optical illusions because our optic nerves exit our retinas at a particular place. This exit area has no photoreceptors and we physically cannot 'see' when light falls on this region of our eyeballs. Yet we do not experience having a blind spot at all. What happens is that our brains mentally fill in what should be there with its best guess, based on past experience as well as the constant scanning of our eyes. The result is that our eyes and our brains can be tricked – and not just by optical illusions.

How we learn and why we have particular biases, strengths, misconceptions, responses to situations and dispositions to learning are all shaped by the brain's attempt to minimise energy usage. As we grow and interact with the world around us, our brains build a mental schema. This schema is a personal framework, woven from our experiences and emotions, which is then reinforced over time. This mental schema underpins the way we understand and interpret reality, how we communicate, what we believe, our mindset in various situations, the way we learn and our conception of ourselves. It influences what makes us happy, the way we teach, the people we connect with and those we do not, how we organise (or don't organise) ourselves, and absolutely every interaction we have.

A mental schema is not a fixed framework and it does adapt and adjust as new learning takes place. As we experience new situations, new ideas and new emotions, the brain has the capacity to form new neuronal connections and pathways as well as reclassify experiences, emotions and knowledge to arrive at a refined mental schema of the world. If particular knowledge or experiences and their associated emotions are not reinforced by usage, then the connections to those neural pathways are not reinforced and eventually end up pruned away. The more that specific neural pathways and connections are used, the stronger the connections and pathways become – and the more likely it is that the brain will use those connections and pathways automatically in a situation. This is how we learn. It also allows us to re-train and reframe our responses, actions and habits as we age and when we perceive threat.

However, if our thinking, beliefs and understandings are not examined and challenged periodically, the schema we operate from can become so automatic that we believe our perception and habits are 'just who we are' and that we cannot change. While it is not actually physically true that our brain and mental schemas cannot change, it does take significant effort to overcome our beliefs and the automaticity of our habits.

The habits and practices of individual teachers and school leaders have been shaped by experiences such as how they were taught, the way their parents interacted with and taught them, the teaching practicum they experienced, what worked when they began teaching, what new approaches they learnt in professional development sessions and even what they noticed watching other teachers in action. Equally, since schools are designed by a community of human beings, a school's culture, structures, processes and policies systemically ritualise what is considered important (and what is not) and what is valued (and what is not). This includes what time school begins and ends, the length of lessons, whether bells ring to signal a change in lessons, when staff meetings are held, what is done during meetings, how parents are communicated with, the processes and language used to deal with 'disruptive' students, the approach to professional learning and development at the school, the instructional model, the pedagogical model and so on.

What is worth every leader, teacher and stakeholder involved in each school examining and reflecting on is this question: Does the current set of habits, beliefs, school structures and

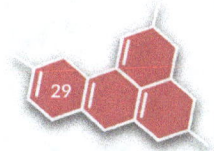

processes build the learning we wish to occur in our learning environment? This examination will enable teachers and school leaders to become more intentional in creating and ritualising new habits, strategies, school structures and processes that are aligned with the outcomes they want to achieve. In essence, when education researchers such as John Hattie (2009) identify high-effect size teaching strategies such as explicit teaching, learning intentions and success criteria, formative feedback and so on, they are identifying the specific habitual practices that make a difference to learning growth. The goal should be to consistently embed specific rituals, habitual practices and thinking frameworks throughout learning so that students internalise them and begin to think, view and interpret the world in particular ways.

DEVELOPING HIGHLY CAPABLE LEARNERS IS THE GOAL

If schools are preparing young people to be future ready in a world of rapid change, they must have a focus on developing a learning environment that nurtures young people to be problem-solvers, critical and creative thinkers, and collaborative and adaptable learners. Schools need to ensure they are embedding the rituals, practices and thinking that progressively develop students to be highly capable learners.

A key trait of highly capable learners is that they self-regulate their learning. While there are a number of frameworks describing self-regulated learning, Zimmerman and Moylan's (2009) model is one of the most influential. This cyclical model of self-regulated learning, illustrated in figure 1.5, outlines the three phases and respective processes of self-regulation (Zimmerman & Moylan, 2009):

1. The forethought phase
   Learners analyse the components of a task, set goals and plan strategies prior to commencing learning.
   Key processes comprise:
   - task analysis, where learners deconstruct the task and establish the strategies they will use
   - self-motivation beliefs, addressing the variables that generate and maintain the motivation to perform the task. This includes beliefs about capability, potential for success on the task and the relevance of the task to personal goals.
2. The performance phase
   Learners make use of planning from the forethought phase by implementing and remaining aware of the selected strategies while they are in use. They use self-observation and feedback to monitor their progress and motivation.
   Key processes include:
   - self-observation, where learners assess and regulate their behaviour and learning strategies for the purpose of remaining on track to achieve their goal or, if need be, alter their goal according to changed conditions
   - self-control, which is about maintaining concentration and interest using strategies such as time management, mental imagery, setting up the learning environment, self-praise and self-reward.
3. The self-reflection phase
   Learners evaluate and judge their performance against the standards established in the forethought phase against the selected goals and strategies. This phase requires learners to use observations and feedback to evaluate their results and performance and formulate causal attributions.

Key processes are:
- self-judgement, in which learners assess their performance against particular criteria and explain the reasons for success or failure
- self-reaction, where learners react to self-judgement and identify strategies and approaches to use in future (for example, learning strategies, effort or use of feedback).

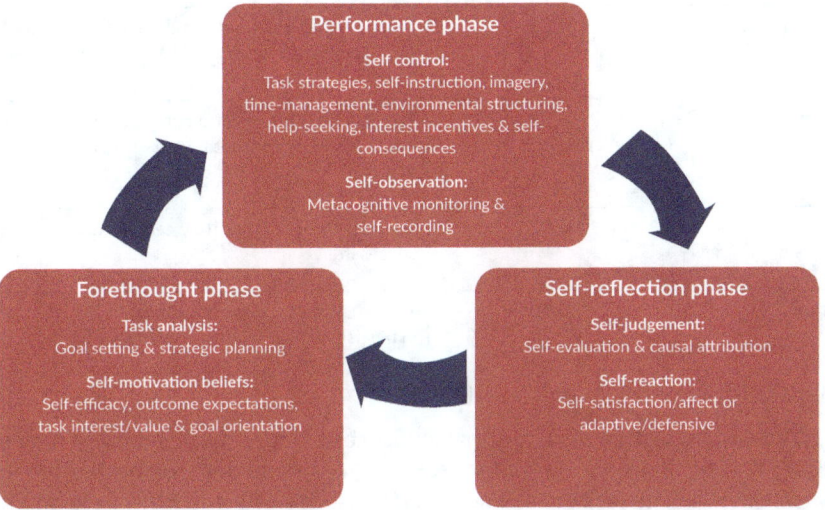

Figure 1.5: Zimmerman and Moylan's (2009) cyclical model of self-regulation
Source: Adapted from Zimmerman and Moylan (2009)

To develop students to be highly capable learners, schools need to explicitly teach and embed the rituals, practices and thinking that progressively develop students to be self-regulated. This includes skills in:
- task analysis and goal setting
- reflecting on and addressing their feelings and self-beliefs
- self-monitoring their behaviour and the learning strategies they are using
- using feedback to self-modify their behaviour and the learning strategies they are using
- reflecting on whether they achieved their goal or not and then refining their approach for future use.

These self-regulation skills are, unsurprisingly, not only central to the systems thinking, design thinking and computational thinking frameworks but also at the heart of the general capabilities within the Australian Curriculum.

DEVELOPING THE MOTIVATION AND MINDSET TO LEARN

Self-motivation beliefs are key to self-regulation. However, it has been rare for teachers and school leaders to discuss and address how the subconscious beliefs of learners and teachers influence student learning growth.

Igniting STEM Learning

Table 1.7: A selection of influences and effect sizes related to student achievement

Factor related to student achievement	Effect size	Description
Collective teacher efficacy	1.57	Teachers collaborate based upon the shared belief that their work will make a difference to student learning
Self-reported grades	1.33	Teachers find out what are the student's expectations and push the learner to exceed those expectations
Teacher estimates of student achievement	1.29	The teacher's beliefs and conceptions about a student inform their views about what students are able to achieve
Self-efficacy	0.92	A student's belief that they can perform a particular task successfully
Teacher credibility	0.90	The student's beliefs about teacher knowledge and expertise; as well as high relational trust

Source: Adapted from Hattie (2017) and Waack (2018)

Table 1.7 shows a selection of factors that influence student achievement and their effect sizes (Hattie, 2017; Waack, 2018). Evidence for Learning (n.d.) finds that feedback – the information given to a learner or teacher about a learner's performance relative to learning goals or outcomes – has an effect size of 0.70 and can have learning gains between three and eight months' progress depending on the area. The much larger effect sizes displayed in table 1.7 indicate that if a school explicitly supports students and teachers to reflect on and address their beliefs then there should be significant learning progress. The implication is that there must be opportunities across the planning, teaching, learning, assessment cycle where students and teachers reflect on their beliefs and mindsets, and for strategies to be put in place to have them move beyond any that hinder learning growth.

In summary, an effective learning environment is built upon rituals, practices and thinking that:
- develop highly capable learners who think from and use the skills, practices and habits of self-regulation
- have learners and teachers self-reflect upon and address their beliefs
- create opportunities for learners to use the computational, design and system thinking frameworks across all of their learning.

CREATING A MEANINGFUL PURPOSE FOR STEM IN YOUR SCHOOL

Sustainable STEM programs are built on a shared understanding of learning and how STEM fits into a school's vision and strategic goals. Ideally this chapter has provided enough insight for a design team to come to a deep understanding of the issues, needs and challenges involved in designing an authentic STEM program. The next step is for that design team to define a clear and inspiring vision and purpose for learning and STEM within their school.

The approach that will be used is that of a design brief. A design brief normally outlines the aims, deliverables and scope of a design project, including any products, timing and budget. It is from the brief that everything else flows. The design brief gives direction, provides purpose and clarifies what to focus on. It also provides a way to check whether the school is on track to achieve the desired outcomes.

The following two exercises will support the development of a design brief and guide the thinking and planning involved in designing an authentic primary school STEM program.

Exercise: Define 1

With the design team, use the following three prompts to produce a design brief for a STEM program at your school:
1. To design a program that ...
2. That meets the needs of ...
3. And has the benefits of ...

Figure 1.6 is an example of a design brief created in the style of the 'Define 1' exercise for a Catholic school with a highly culturally diverse group of students. The design team deliberately wanted to ensure that any STEM program they developed not only addressed the curriculum requirements but also honoured and supported the community to grow and learn together.

Design brief

To design a STEM program that:
- has students be curious and see the bigger picture, purpose and relevance of concepts being taught
- grows their capacity to be independent, self-regulated learners who can transfer their learning to new situations.

This program meets the needs of:
- gender and cultural diversity
- low cost
- engagement
- curriculum relevance (learning areas, general capabilities and cross-curriculum priorities)
- honouring the identity and past of the students and the school
- growing the confidence and competence of the students and teachers.

And has the benefits of:
- giving students agency, voice and leadership opportunities
- recapping some of the curriculum covered previously
- shifting the perception of staff, students and parents about what is possible
- creating an authentic through-line through the years that grows students as learners
- developing metacognition
- having a gradual release of responsibility where students learn to drive their own learning.

Figure 1.6: Sample design brief

> **Exercise: Define 2**
>
> Against the design brief created in 'Exercise: Define 1' (page 33), answer the following questions:
> - Which systems, policies, processes and roles are currently aligned?
> - Which systems, policies, processes and roles are not currently aligned?
> - What non-negotiable ideas and priorities could unite the school community as you design a STEM program to meet the design brief?

This second exercise allows a design team to assess where the school sits against the design brief at a given point in time. This will give an idea of potential actions to be taken to lay the groundwork for a sustainable STEM program. Some of the gaps that may be discovered in this process include:

- The school does not have whole-school learning structures in place to allow for learner-driven or learner-centred learning to occur.
- Teachers do not yet have the capacity to facilitate learner-driven or learner-centred learning.
- The school is constrained by the way the timetable is designed.
- The school is constrained by the available facilities.
- The school is constrained by teacher or parent beliefs and mindsets.
- The school does not yet have the curriculum documentation in place to be able to design transdisciplinary units.
- Teachers are not skilled in developing their capacity through mini action-research projects.
- Students have become passive learners over time and need to be empowered to be the drivers of their learning.
- There is a very shallow depth of understanding about self-regulation and the vision for learning in the school.

As the design team goes through these exercises, the next steps and non-negotiable priorities should become clear. In the next chapter, a systems thinking process will be used to identify how a school can begin to align itself to a design brief.

KEY POINTS

- Students come to your school with already existing habits, beliefs and learning practices they have developed over time. These influence their ability to learn – and many remain unexamined.
- Teachers and school leaders need to examine pre-existing habitual practices, structures and beliefs if they are going to design a STEM program that is sustainable, meets its purpose and nurtures future-ready learners.

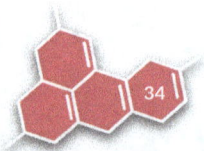

Understanding the purpose of STEM

- The process of examining the pre-existing beliefs and thinking will often highlight challenges that will require addressing, such as misconceptions about what STEM is, limiting teacher mindsets and the perceptions that STEM is simply yet another thing to do.
- STEM and the Australian Curriculum: Technologies can transform how learning in schools occurs if schools and teachers focus on embedding thinking frameworks with content as the vehicle for thinking and problem-solving.
- Computational, design and systems thinking are applicable in all disciplines and many teachers naturally apply the strategies, to differing extents, in their classes.
- Powerful learning is nurtured by being thoughtful about the specific rituals and habitual practices schools embed throughout their learning environment.
- To develop highly capable learners, schools need to ritualise the habits, practices and thinking that develop learners to be self-regulated. They also need to create opportunities for teachers and students to habitually self-reflect and address their beliefs about learning.
- Developing a sustainable STEM program requires the creation of a design brief that articulates the purpose of STEM in the school.

CHAPTER 2

Developing a whole-school skill and mindset map

When you have a vision for what a school can be, it has to permeate every pore of the school. Every process, every interaction, every system needs to be held to that process. And although there are pieces of the school that may be only tangential to the mission, it is important to go through the process of examining how the core vision of the school affects each part of the school.

(Lehmann & Chase, 2015, p. 20)

FROM DESIGN TO ACTION

Schools often begin enacting STEM by introducing clubs or activities at lunchtime or after school, establishing specialist subjects and maker spaces, or even participating in the ever-growing number of robotics, maths, computational thinking, science and engineering competitions. These approaches are all great ways to begin laying the groundwork for a sustainable STEM program. They start to orient teachers, students and parents to the possibilities and outcomes that a STEM program can deliver, help schools build a range of resources over time and can be used as a vehicle to address some of the gaps identified in the design brief-building exercises at the end of Chapter 1 (from page 33). The challenge for many schools will be moving from these groundwork-laying activities to an authentic STEM program that delivers the desired outcomes articulated in their design brief.

An example of the gap between an authentic STEM program and a 'laying the groundwork' approach was highlighted at an education system's STEM showcase. The aim of the showcase was to have students 'address real-world problems and demonstrate how students … take actions that matter' (Melbourne Archdiocese Catholic Schools, 2019, 'STEM MAD' section). There were some amazing project ideas, including:

- a sustainable feeding system that could be set up in a national park to support the survival of endangered yellow-tailed rock wallabies during the dry season
- a range of activities that could be used in the lemur enclosure at Melbourne Zoo to keep the lemurs cognitively challenged
- an app that people who experience depression could use to communicate with those who are closest to them so they can get support
- a microbial fuel cell that could be built to get rid of household waste and generate electricity
- a desktop activity centre for students who have attention deficit hyperactivity disorder (ADHD) to support them in self-regulating
- a child's peddle car that had been converted into an electric car driven by batteries
- a project to design material or clothing to get past heat sensor burglar alarms.

The students from every school shared that they learned an enormous amount about the topic they were investigating. They had become better at empathising (coming to a deep understanding of a challenge), which was a great step not only in learning about people but also in problem-solving. However, of the ninety-three project teams participating in that year's showcase, only two had built a working prototype having gone through the process of testing and revising their designs to make something that actually physically worked.

The discussions with those two teams about what they learned was very different to those with every other project team, who had only built models of their prototype. These students had dealt with the challenge of making their designs a working reality. They had to do an enormous amount of problem-solving and thinking to get their ideas to work. These students actually confronted the system aspects of their designs, and suddenly had to do the work of understanding the interrelated impacts of making design changes – many of them unexpected or unanticipated. They had learned more during the prototyping stage than in all the previous design stages combined. Both teams shared that they had learned a lot about themselves and how to overcome obstacles and challenges in the process of figuring out how to make their design a reality. This experience and growth of the learner is what STEM programs should be aiming for.

A school's goal might be to authentically nurture highly capable learners who are:

- resourceful, curious and adaptable, and have the ability to find quick and clever ways to overcome difficulties
- creative problem-solvers and systems thinkers
- data driven and capable of using evidence, data and context to inform their responses and decisions
- collaborative learners who work together to learn and address challenges
- empathetic – exploring and understanding the needs of people and situations.

However, this cannot be achieved without designing STEM learning that takes students through the entire design thinking process – from understanding to design to real-world prototype. Professor Bill Lucas (2018), an international adviser to the Victorian Curriculum and Assessment Authority (VCAA) and to the Organization for Economic Co-operation and Development (OECD) on creativity and critical thinking, proposes that the outcome of schooling is not only about students being capable but also about routinely deploying capabilities in a range of real-world settings. In his research, Lucas (2018) suggests that 'a young person who is disposed to routinely persevere in a variety of contexts is much more likely to succeed than one who has some good persevering techniques but frequently fails to apply these' (p. 8).

To have students routinely deploy their capabilities in a range of real-world contexts will require schools to invest the time, thinking and effort to design and plan the system of learning across the whole school to achieve it. It cannot be achieved by simply having STEM or digital technologies activities separate from the core learning within the school. As articulated in the quote that begins this chapter, STEM learning 'has to permeate every pore in the school ... every process, every interaction, every system' (Lehmann & Chase, 2015, p. 20). Without embedding the thinking and ways of learning that STEM encourages and promotes, schools will not nurture the highly capable learners I have described.

This chapter begins the process of designing an authentic STEM program that permeates, in the words of Lehmann and Chase (2015), a school's 'every pore'. It starts by outlining two aspects that are often overlooked when planning an authentic whole-school STEM program: the explicit progressive development of a learner mindset and the skills articulated by the general capabilities. Key to negotiating these aspects is a mindset and capabilities planning document, which will be introduced in coming pages. This will support teachers and design teams through creating a whole-school approach to nurturing particular mindsets and developing students through four of the general capabilities articulated in the Australian Curriculum.

THE IMPORTANCE OF A WHOLE-SCHOOL MINDSET AND GENERAL CAPABILITIES MAP

For their Future of Education and Skills 2030 project, the OECD (n.d.) gathered submissions from researchers and education systems around the world, exploring what an educational model that addresses the following two questions could look like:

> *How can we prepare students for jobs that have not yet been created, to tackle societal challenges that we can't yet imagine, and to use technologies that have not yet been invented? How can we equip them to thrive in an interconnected world where they need to understand and appreciate different perspectives and world views, interact respectfully with others, and take responsible action towards sustainability and collective well-being? ('OECD Future of Education and Skills 2030 project' section)*

Figure 2.1 (page 40) seeks to capture the relationships between knowledge, skills, attitudes and values with competencies that students will need to develop to thrive in a fast-changing, interconnected world (Lucas, 2018).

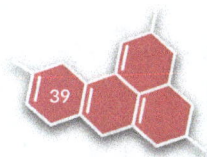

Figure 2.1: 'The Future of Education and Skills: OECD Education 2030 Framework'
Source: Lucas (2018, p. 8)

In this model, knowledge, skills, attitudes and values are seen as interconnected and interacting to produce competencies (which we call capabilities in Australia) in action. If a school is aiming to develop students to routinely deploy their capabilities in a range of real-world contexts and 'prepare students for jobs that have not yet been created, to tackle societal challenges that we can't yet imagine, and to use technologies that have not yet been invented' (OECD, n.d., 'OECD Future of Education and Skills 2030 project' section), the model implies that there should be a significant focus on developing student skills, attitudes and values as much as specific disciplinary, interdisciplinary and practical knowledge. This is exactly how the Australian Curriculum was structured, with eight learning areas (English, maths, science, health and physical education, humanities and social sciences, the arts, technologies, and languages), seven general capabilities (critical and creative thinking, digital literacy, ethical understanding, intercultural understanding, literacy, numeracy, and personal and social capability) and three cross-curriculum priorities (Aboriginal and Torres Strait Islander histories and cultures, Asia and Australia's engagement with Asia, and sustainability; see ACARA, n.d.-b).

However, as mentioned in Chapter 1, many teachers do not yet explicitly design learning across the year to progressively develop their students in the skills, attitudes and values that will make them highly capable, self-regulated learners. It is even rarer that schools have developed whole-school maps that articulate how teachers can develop the general capabilities and learner mindset (what I call the attitudes and values of a learner) across the years of schooling. If a school is aiming to nurture a particular set of capabilities and thinking in its students, there must be explicit structures and habits embedded in 'every process, every interaction, and every system' (Lehmann & Chase, 2015, p. 20).

NURTURING A LEARNER MINDSET

Mindset is the collection of thoughts and beliefs about how the world works that shape individuals' experiences of reality. It shapes the way an individual habitually thinks, feels and acts. Think of it as the operating system for a mind – working below the surface, controlling everything that happens. For example, as supported by Carol Dweck's (2008) research, students with negative views about their capability to do maths will invest less time and effort in improving their ability in maths over time. This view becomes a belief that is entrenched as they fall further behind in their learning of maths and struggle to understand new material, most of which relies on prior knowledge and skill. The belief becomes the reality. Students with positive views could see maths as enjoyable and engaging, and therefore put in the effort, seek feedback when they make mistakes and invest time in overcoming the gaps in their understanding.

Developing a whole-school skill and mindset map

One key outcome of a well-designed and thought-out STEM program is the mindset it nurtures in the learners. Great STEM learners are problem-solvers, creative and critical thinkers, resourceful, and curious. They strive to be empathetic and they take risks, fail, learn and try again. They work with others to learn and use evidence and data to inform their responses and decisions. As Yeager and Dweck's (2020) research has shown, learner mindsets can be nurtured through explicitly creating supportive learning environments.

My approach to developing student mindsets through whole-school planning arose when I coached a primary school over a number of years as they developed transdisciplinary units. The teachers at each year level often shared the challenging student mindsets and behaviours they faced as they attempted to run their units. In the younger age groups, teachers found they spent an enormous amount of time working with students to get them used to learning harmoniously in a community. At times, certain students threw tantrums or behaved in ways that upset others in the class. In the older age groups, teachers found that their students became very passive or behaved in a very cliquey manner as learners. As they explored the behaviour and mindsets that they wanted their students to develop, the teachers realised they had an existing structure that they were not using very effectively.

At the start of every school year the teachers created, sometimes in partnership with their students, a set of norms and agreements for learning and behaviour in their classes. These were often a mix of what the individual teachers found worked in the past and school-imposed agreements. Some teachers spent a significant amount of time thinking their way through what routines and practices they would establish to achieve the student behavioural and mindset outcomes they wanted, while others did not. What we discovered was that the teachers who were most successful at achieving the desired learning behaviours and mindsets in their classes were those who embedded explicit structures, routines and conversations in everything they did. They found that it often took up to two terms before students had internalised the desired learning behaviours and mindset. It was at this point that the leadership team recognised that it would make a difference if the whole school explicitly planned to nurture an empowering learning mindset progressively through the years of schooling.

A team of teachers from across the school then articulated a progression of 'mindset mottos' that built from Foundation through to Year 6 (see table 2.1 for examples). The intention was that every conversation, interaction and learning activity the teachers designed would be framed within the mindset motto for that year level. The thinking was that if the school approached developing classroom routines, curriculum planning, learning norms and agreements in this way, then students would gradually internalise specific thinking and mindsets consistent with becoming highly capable learners.

Table 2.1: Sample mindset mottos from Foundation to Year 6

	F	Year 1	Year 2	Year 3	Year 4	Year 5	Year 6
Mindset motto	Have a go and take care.	Have a go and manage my learning.	'Mistakes are my friend' and take on challenges.	Be a super learner.	Be the owner of my learning.	Drive my own learning and support others to learn.	Work together as a team to learn.

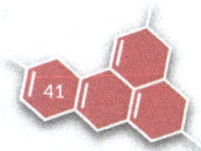

As shown in table 2.1 (page 41), the Foundation teachers created the mindset motto 'Have a go and take care'. Their cohort of students came from many different cultural backgrounds and a large number of them were displaying antisocial behaviours due to not having attended preschool programs. Their aim was to encourage their students to look after one another while they had a go at learning in a way that was new to them within a community of learners.

These teachers created a Term 1 transdisciplinary unit called 'Have a go and take care' that focused on the health and physical education curriculum and the personal and social capabilities. They designed various ways to introduce the mindset motto each week: they created routines and structures to reinforce the mindset, modelled and showcased the behaviour and skills they desired, and explored how they could refine the learning so that the mindset motto was encouraged. In Term 2 they designed a unit called 'My family and celebrations' that addressed the humanities and social sciences (HASS) curriculum and built on the personal and social capabilities. By Term 3 the teachers found that their students were more productive, so they began to set up learning activities to extend them. They then consolidated the work done in Terms 1 and 2 with two transdisciplinary units: one addressing science and HASS called 'Wild and domestic animals', and a design, creative thinking and science unit called 'Totally amazing toys'.

By the end of Term 1, the Foundation teachers noticed that students were starting to know their routines, have a go, learn the rules, and take care of themselves and each other. Their independence was improving and parents were 'helping' their children less. By Term 3, a personal-best system had been introduced to extend the students so they could begin to self-motivate and self-manage their own growth by going for their personal best in learning areas.

This thinking and planning was done at each year level with the aim to ultimately develop students to be highly capable, self-regulated learners. Naturally there were challenges and setbacks along the way, but teachers learned key lessons in overcoming these challenges. The first was that they needed to explicitly teach and model the self-regulation behaviour they wanted the students to develop. It was insufficient to just talk about it; they also had to walk the walk in their pedagogy – all their learning activities throughout the week had to highlight and model the behaviours and agreements established at the start of the year. The teachers also discovered that they needed to learn how to let go and develop a learning environment where the students could drive their own learning. Many of the teachers realised how much they drove the learning and how this was leading, over the years, to students becoming passive learners. Finally, the teachers realised that they needed to educate the parents about how to support their children in ways that were consistent with mindset, behaviours and agreements that were being established – otherwise the work they were doing would be undermined at home. This was done via newsletters, social media, parent–teacher meetings and explicit parent instructions on any homework sent home.

The progression of mindset mottos sampled in table 2.1 was useful to that particular primary school given the values and vision they created, the needs of their students and the outcomes they wanted to achieve. The following exercise begins the process of explicit thinking and planning that year-level and design teams should complete to nurture student mindsets and STEM thinking skills.

Developing a whole-school skill and mindset map

Exercise: Pre-planning 1

Using the template provided, and with reference to the design brief created in Chapter 1, consider and discuss the particular needs of your students and then collaboratively design a progression of mindset mottos from Foundation to Year 6. The mindset mottos should address what year-level teachers identify as the current needs of their students.

	F	Year 1	Year 2	Year 3	Year 4	Year 5	Year 6
What needs are you addressing?							
Mindset motto							

Reproducible available

Table 2.2 features a sample of the mindset mottos and needs to be addressed as articulated by the primary school I've been discussing in this chapter. The year-level teachers began the process of identifying a mindset motto by sharing and discussing their experiences of working with students in their year level. They reflected on what general attitudes and behaviours the students came into their classes with and reflected on the broad patterns of behaviour they saw students demonstrate regardless of cohort. The teaching teams then used this information to specify the needs they wanted to address. This empathising process allowed the teaching teams to then articulate a mindset motto that they felt would address the needs of their students.

Table 2.2: Sample Foundation and Year 1 needs to be addressed and mindset mottos

	Foundation	Year 1
What needs are you addressing?	The children, for the most part, have not been involved in large-group learning and can display behaviours that are antisocial or have difficulty managing their own learning.	Students lose some ground over the holiday between year levels, so we need to continue to reinforce the need to have a go and build on their capacity to self-manage their own learning.
Mindset motto	Have a go and take care.	Have a go and manage my learning.

Once all the year-level teaching teams have articulated the needs of their cohort of students plus their year-level mindset motto, the design or leadership team should reflect on the progression of needs and mindset mottos across year levels to see if any tweaking of wording should take place. The goal is to come to a shared understanding of how the mindset mottos can be used to progressively nurture a learner mindset across the school.

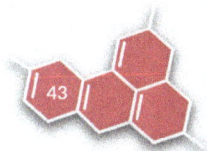

UNPACKING THE GENERAL CAPABILITY ASPECTS, PRACTICES, NORMS, AGREEMENTS AND STRATEGIES

Given that the desired outcome is to nurture a specific mindset and associated behaviours in students by the end of each year level, the next step is to backward plan. This involves identifying the key aspects of the general capabilities related to the chosen mindset mottos, the practices and routines to be turned into habits, the norms and agreements to be established and the possible strategies to be used.

Table 2.3 is an example of a mindset and capabilities planning document for Foundation and Year 1. This supports the steps teaching teams can take to rigorously plan to nurture their chosen mindset motto in their classes.

Table 2.3: Sample Foundation and Year 1 mindset and capabilities planning document

	Foundation	Year 1
What needs are you addressing?	The children, for the most part, have not been involved in large-group learning, display behaviours that are antisocial or have difficulty managing their own learning.	Students lose some ground over the holiday between year levels, so we need to continue to reinforce the need to have a go and build on their capacity to self-manage their own learning.
Mindset motto	Have a go and take care.	Have a go and manage my learning.
Key general capabilities aspects to develop	Personal and social capability: - understand themselves as learners - express emotions appropriately - understand relationships - communicate effectively. Ethical understanding: - various aspects.	Personal and social capability: - understand themselves as learners - develop reflective practice - work independently and show initiative. Ethical understanding: - various aspects. Critical and creative thinking: - pose questions - reflect on processes.
Habitual practices we want students to develop	- Having a go at new challenges - putting their hand up to ask questions - waiting their turn to ask questions - identifying how they feel - encouraging others - working with others in the classroom - actively listening.	- Having a go at new challenges - explaining what they have learned - improving their own work using feedback - asking for help when they need it - asking questions to find out more information - following steps to complete a task.
Norms and agreements	- 'We wait our turn when we want to ask questions.' - 'We can listen to others in our group.' - 'We listen to the entire message.' - 'We can encourage and thank others.' - 'We can show that we know how to work well and finish our work.'	- 'We stay on topic.' - 'We ask for help when we are stuck.' - 'I can challenge myself.' - 'I can share what I have learned.' - 'I can ask for feedback.' - 'I use the three-before-me strategy when I don't know what to do: look at others' work, ask a buddy, ask the teacher, have a go.' - 'I can ask questions to find out more information.'

Developing a whole-school skill and mindset map

Possible strategies	<ul><li>Explorative play in Terms 1–3</li><li>personal-best system from Term 3</li><li>investigative play in Term 4</li><li>discussing and modelling socialisation and good learning habits so the children can develop social awareness</li><li>some paired activities in Term 3 and 4 with anchor charts around how to be a good partner (each person says an idea; we listen to both ideas; we use both ideas to create one idea; if we disagree we can rock, paper, scissors or ask a friend to choose or ask the teacher).</li></ul>	<ul><li>Part explorative play in Term 1, then move into investigative play</li><li>simple PBL in Term 4</li><li>personal-best system</li><li>explicit teaching of self-management of learning</li><li>continue to build skills that lay the foundation for independent learning</li><li>use the 'No opt out' poster</li><li>James Nottingham's 'learning pit' activity</li><li>'Austin's butterfly' activity</li><li>cold calling</li><li>the Zones of Regulation™ programs.</li></ul>

KEY GENERAL CAPABILITIES ASPECTS TO DEVELOP

The Australian Curriculum: General Capabilities articulate learning continuums for the knowledge, skills, behaviours and dispositions that will assist students to live and work successfully in the twenty-first century. While the literacy, numeracy and digital literacy capabilities tend to be well-addressed in most schools, many teachers and schools still appear to be struggling in addressing the remaining general capabilities. Yet it is the learning continuums for critical and creative thinking, personal and social capability, ethical understanding and intercultural understanding that are the most useful for developing the thinking and mindset that highly capable (and STEM) learners demonstrate. These are the four capabilities that should be examined as teachers explore how they will nurture the desired mindset in their students. (To assist teachers in supporting students to drive their own learning, and to provide a structure for teachers to assess and gather evidence of progression, the learning continuums for the four capabilities have been deconstructed into a usable sequence of success criteria in Chapter 7.)

To fill in this section, the year-level teachers should use the information they gathered from empathising about the student needs to identify which of the skills within the four capabilities (critical and creative thinking, personal and social capability, ethical understanding and intercultural understanding) are most appropriate and related to the specific mindset they intend to develop across the year. Teachers can use the general capabilities learning continuum provided on the Australian Curriculum website to identify the skills (called sub-elements). Depending on the mindset motto and year level, teaching teams might identify a particular set of general capability skills for the first two terms and then, as their students increasingly demonstrate the internalisation of those skills, choose a set of general capability skills that builds on the first set. In the more senior year levels, the progression of skills could even be chosen from term to term. The intent of this thinking approach is for teachers to use their professional judgement of their cohort's progression to plan for the general capability skills that will make the greatest difference to nurturing the desired mindset and learning behaviours.

HABITUAL PRACTICES WE WANT STUDENTS TO DEVELOP

This section captures the practices and behaviours that the students will be required to demonstrate until they become habitual. The practices and behaviours are directly related to the identified general capability skills and mindset motto. Teaching teams should use the general capability continuum to assist in identifying these, choosing practices and behaviours that are developmentally appropriate and observable. The students and teachers should be able to quickly identify whether they are demonstrating the practice or behaviour. As can be seen in this section of the sample, the teaching team should articulate the behaviours they will observe in their classrooms when students are demonstrating the mindset motto and specified general capability skills.

NORMS AND AGREEMENTS

Starting the school year with classroom norms and agreements lays the foundation for student behaviour and mindset in the learning environment. Norms and agreements need to be discussed and used daily to guide interactions and behaviour. In the younger year levels, norms tend to be established by teachers in discussion with students. From Year 2 onwards, I would recommend that teachers co-design the classroom norms and agreements with students, guided by the mindset theme and appropriate general capabilities for their year level. Not only does this foreground student agency in the classroom; it also addresses elements of the civics and citizenship aspect of the HASS curriculum.

Some of the norms should align with the habitual practices you want the students to develop. For example, if you want students to develop the habit of waiting their turn to ask a question, norms such as 'We wait our turn when we want to ask questions' and 'We listen to the entire message' would be appropriate. Norms should be worded simply and clearly as an action. This means students can say them to their peers as part of developing the classroom learning culture.

POSSIBLE STRATEGIES

In this section, teaching teams speculate on the structures, routines and strategies they could use to support the students to internalise the desired norms, practices and behaviours. This could include thinking routines as suggested by Harvard's Project Zero (Harvard Graduate School of Education, n.d.), the strategies compiled by Doug Lemov (2014), the Leader in Me routines (FranklinCovey Co., n.d.), Habits of Mind (Boyes & Watts, 2009), de Bono's (n.d.) Six Thinking Hats, Kath Walker's (2011; Walker & Bass, 2011) play-based learning approach and many others.

Graphic organisers also help students internalise ways of thinking through consistent use. A quick search online for graphic organisers will result in a wide range of possibilities to consider for your context. For example, figure 2.3 is a graphic organiser created by the Victorian Curriculum and Assessment Authority (2008) that is great for considering a range of options to make an informed decision. Not only is it a useful tool that could address a range of general capability skills (such as negotiating and resolving conflicts and disagreements, using critical and creative thinking and so on); it is also a great way of developing design thinking.

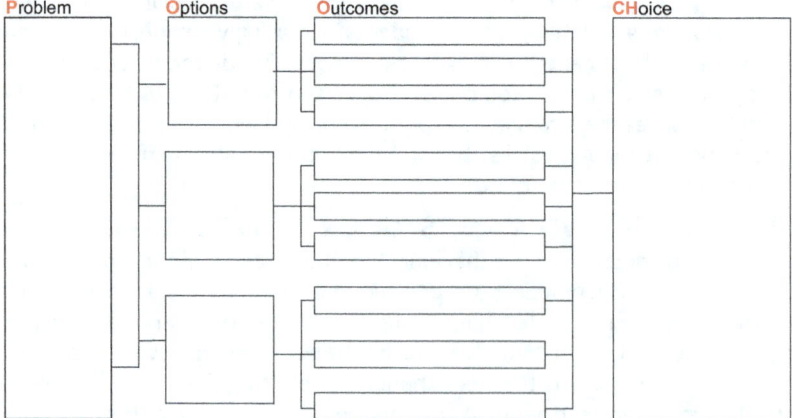

Figure 2.3: POOCH template

Source: Victorian Curriculum and Assessment Authority (2008)

Developing a whole-school skill and mindset map

Teaching teams can also design their own graphic organisers and pedagogical practices that focus on developing specific general capability skills. For example, I designed the research graphic organiser shown in figure 2.4 in partnership with a group of teachers who complained that their students struggled with research. The teachers wanted to shift students from cutting and pasting information when they researched to writing researched information in their own words. The research organiser begins with the existing habit (cutting and pasting), then requires the students to identify the key words and ideas from this source information (top-right box), to re-write the information in their own words (bottom-left box) and supply a reference to where they sourced the original information. Students were explicitly taught each skill as they used the research organiser, and teachers made completed research organisers mandatory whenever students were required to research as part of a project or unit. Over time this led to students developing the appropriate research skills.

Research organiser

Research question:

Cut and paste your source information here:	Key words in source information:
Rewrite source information in your own words:	Reference:

Figure 2.4: Research graphic organiser
Reproducible available

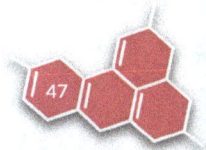

Igniting STEM Learning

Exercise: Pre-planning 2

Continue the thinking and planning work begun in the first pre-planning exercise by identifying the key general capabilities aspects to be developed at each year level, the habitual practices students should demonstrate, the norms and agreements to be put in place and possible strategies that can be embedded to develop the general capability skills and nurture the desired mindset.

	F	Year 1	Year 2	Year 3	Year 4	Year 5	Year 6
Key general capabilities aspects to develop							
Habitual practices we want students to develop							
Norms and agreements							
Possible strategies							

Reproducible available

I recommended that this process of pre-planning occurs in Term 4 in preparation for the following year. The most useful time tends to be towards the end of the term, during the period in which teaching teams are doing a handover of student information from one year level to the next. This allows teaching teams to share the progress that students have made across the year and identify the gaps they feel still need to be addressed. Teaching teams can then do the thinking and planning in preparation for the following year. In the first year of enacting this approach, this will take a significant amount of discussion and time. However, once the approach is embedded, teaching teams will only need to refine existing planning.

One of the major benefits of following this approach is that teaching teams start to think in terms of a whole-school system of learning. They begin to realise that each teacher and each year-level team is part of a system that is nurturing and developing highly capable learners. They aren't just teaching Year 1 or Year 5 students. They are not just working on improving the literacy and numeracy of a cohort of children. They are part of a concerted effort by their school to achieve its design brief for students – perhaps even preparing students for 'jobs that have not yet been created, to tackle societal challenges that we can't yet imagine, and to use technologies that have not yet been invented' (OECD, n.d., 'OECD Future of Education and Skills 2030 project' section).

Chapter 3 builds on the mindset and capabilities planning work completed in this chapter and supports year-level and design teams to create a whole-school curriculum map that allows for transdisciplinary and STEM units to be easily developed.

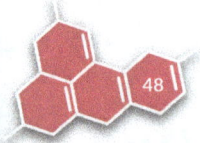

KEY POINTS

- Setting up STEM clubs or activities at lunchtime or after school, establishing STEM specialist subjects and maker spaces, and even participating in STEM competitions are great ways to begin laying the groundwork for a sustainable STEM program.
- However, schools cannot authentically nurture highly capable learners without designing STEM learning that takes students through the entire design thinking process, from understanding to design to real-world prototype.
- Preparing students to routinely deploy their capabilities in a range of real-world contexts require schools to invest the time, thinking and effort to design and plan a system of learning across the whole school.
- If a school is aiming to nurture a particular set of capabilities and thinking in their students, there must be explicit structures and habits embedded in 'every process, every interaction, and every system' (Lehmann & Chase, 2015, p. 20).
- Great STEM learners are problem-solvers, creative and critical thinkers, resourceful and curious. They strive to be empathetic and take risks, fail, learn and try again. They work with others to learn, and they use evidence and data to inform their responses and decisions.
- In practice, great STEM learners demonstrate a learner mindset and are skilled in the Australian Curriculum general capabilities.
- For a school to progressively develop a learner mindset, plus the associated general capability skills, each year-level teaching team needs to create a mindset and capabilities planning document. This document will capture the learning needs of their student cohort, an empowering mindset motto, associated key general capability skills to develop across the year, the habitual practices the students will demonstrate, the norms and agreements that need to be embedded, and the possible strategies that will be used.
- The design team can then produce a refined whole-school pre-planning document that reflects a shared understanding of how the school will nurture a learner mindset and develop students progressively through the Australian Curriculum: General Capabilities.
- This process of mindset and capabilities planning will enable teachers to start thinking from a systems perspective and understand how they are part of a system that is nurturing and developing highly capable learners.

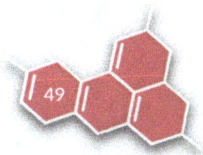

CHAPTER 3

Developing curriculum and learning ladder maps

The world is changed by our maps of the world. The way that we choose ... also shapes the map of our lives, and that in turn shapes our lives. I believe that what we map changes the life we lead. And I don't mean that in some ... you-can-think-your-way-out-of-cancer sense. But I do believe that while maps don't show you where you will go in your life, they show you where you might go. You very rarely go to a place that isn't on your personal map.

John Green, 'The nerd's guide to learning everything online'

THE PURPOSE OF DEVELOPING MAPS

Maps are amazing tools. They help organise and present information in a simple, visual way for the purpose of navigating. They bring clarity to complex information and make it easier to understand where you have been, where you are and where you are going. Maps can be used to highlight important features and identify potential roadblocks. When planning to achieve a particular outcome it is useful to create a range of maps at different levels of detail. For example, architects create a range of overall and detailed floor plans (or maps) that builders use to plan and resource the construction of a building. Similarly, authors and filmmakers create maps and storyboards of characters and situations, engineers create overall and detailed plans of complex structures. Designers do the same when they create a product, as do organisations when planning expansion. In any domain, when an individual or an organisation is intending to successfully achieve a particular outcome, both overall and detailed maps and plans are produced.

To achieve the outcomes articulated in the STEM design brief, schools will need to invest a significant amount of time and thinking to create curriculum and other associated maps that

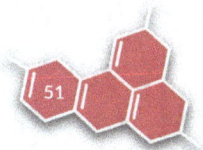

articulate how they plan to nurture and develop student knowledge, skills, thinking and capabilities progressively across the years of schooling. The process of creating these maps assists teachers to come to a deeper understanding of the curriculum and the various ways the different elements of each curriculum area can fit together in a useful and coherent manner. These maps should be used by teachers to ensure they not only address all the requirements of the Australian Curriculum, but also develop learning that routinely deploy student capabilities in a range of real-world contexts. The challenge for many schools and teachers will be in shifting their thinking and planning from developing learning based on individual curriculum areas to creating learning that is transdisciplinary.

Creating transdisciplinary learning units is a key part of breaking down the artificial curriculum and learning silos that have appeared in many schools during the implementation of the Australian Curriculum. Transdisciplinary units provide wonderful foundations for creating real-world contexts and embedding the key thinking frameworks more authentically. Strategically they can also free up the school timetable as they allow teachers to design learning and activities that reinforce particular knowledge, skills and thinking in different ways across multiple curriculum areas. This will naturally help students engage with their learning and encourage the realisation that the strategies they have learnt can be applied across all of their learning. Examples of such transdisciplinary STEM units include a Year 1 'Paddock to the plate' unit that addresses aspects of the history, geography, science, technologies and English curriculum areas; a Year 3–4 'Design a playground' unit that interleaves maths, English, humanities and social sciences (HASS), and design and digital technologies; and a Year 6 'Minecraft' unit on natural disasters that addresses science, geography and history, sustainable practices, and technology and design.

This chapter outlines the process of creating whole-school curriculum and learning ladder maps that will support the development of a coherent and authentic STEM program. It begins with a metaphor for learning that provides a contextual guide for the mapping process and for developing highly capable, self-regulated learners. Three levels of mapping are then proposed to support schools in their planning to achieve their design brief outcomes. Keeping with the design mentality, we will explore iterative planning processes that enable teachers and schools to design a whole-school learning ladder and a sequence of year-level curriculum maps. The thinking and planning in Chapter 3 lays the foundation for effectively planning transdisciplinary STEM units in coming chapters. It is also worth noting that while we focus here on developing STEM learning, the processes described are equally applicable to all curriculum planning.

LEARNING TO DRIVE AND DRIVING TO LEARN

Over the past few years, I have had the job of being a driving instructor for my two children. Each was quite different in their learning approaches and thinking, and each had different strengths and areas of development. One was very confident, while the other experienced doubt, at times, about their skill and decision-making powers. One was more willing to be thrown into driving challenges that were beyond their perceived level of experience while the other wanted a lot of structure. Interestingly, their behaviour and learning approaches as drivers appeared to be quite similar to how they approached learning in school.

During my time as the driving instructor, I gained a number of insights. An individual cannot learn to drive a car without driving a car. Neither being a passenger nor playing driving video games provides the necessary groundwork to be a highly capable driver. The real-world experience of driving a car forces the driver to be active in their learning; to observe, problem-solve, think critically, develop one's skill level and be responsible for one's own actions.

Developing curriculum and learning ladder maps

The goal of a driving instructor is not to have the learner driver pass their test. It is to develop the learner driver's knowledge, skills and thinking. The driving test is simply a milestone that a learner driver needs to achieve on the journey to becoming a safe, self-regulated and adaptable driver. Being a driving instructor also requires one to let go and extend trust to the learner driver. A driving instructor has very little control over the speed and direction of the car when driving begins. The only thing an instructor has control over is the situations they put the learner driver in. An instructor can guide the development of a learner driver by gradually increasing the challenge of activities and situations as the learner driver grows in competence and confidence.

While each learner driver had a different starting point and learned at a different rate, they appeared to go through similar broad phases of development. In the first phase they needed to build their knowledge and understanding of each aspect of driving a car and how and when to use it. The focus in the second phase was the deepening of driving skills and thinking through practising in progressively more complex situations with a greater number of cars, an increasing variety of driving conditions and at various speeds. The final phase involved refining their thinking by discussing and attempting more nuanced situations, such as drivers behaving out of the norm or rapidly changing traffic and driving conditions, so they could learn how to anticipate and respond to new situations as they arise.

Learning to drive is a useful metaphor that reframes the purpose of schooling and allows for new ways of thinking about what needs to be mapped so that students with different sets of skills, strengths and abilities can learn how to drive their own learning. The curriculum becomes the vehicle that the students (the learner drivers) use to learn how to drive. The teachers become driving instructors who partner with and support the students to develop their ability to drive their own learning. And the students are driving towards the destination of having gained the requisite level of knowledge, skills and thinking to be highly capable learners.

This metaphor allows teachers and school leaders to tackle traditional challenges in an empowering way. For example, if students are becoming increasingly passive as learners or even disliking school as they progress through their schooling, this could be a function of those students not having the agency or ability to drive their own learning (Benner et al., 2019). When the students are only passengers, they don't bring the same intentionality or forethought to driving their own learning. Over time this can lead some students to become dependent on their teachers to drive their learning, learned helplessness and even presumed incompetence (Weins, 1983). Returning to our metaphor, this could be overcome by the school systematically planning to provide students with the environment, learning opportunities and explicit strategies and thinking they need to be able to drive better.

The shift of the focus towards developing each and every student to be the driver of their own learning forces the examination of the underlying assumptions around teaching and learning and opens up some worthwhile questions. What could curriculum planning and lessons look like with this destination in mind? How could learning progress be planned and measured? Clearly knowledge would be one aspect to measure, but then what about the skills and thinking to apply that knowledge in a range of learning situations? What does gradual release of responsibility look like when students are the drivers of their own learning? As the OECD (2019) points out,

> *When students are the agents in their learning, that is, when they play an active role in deciding what and how they will learn, they tend to show greater motivation to learn and are more likely to define*

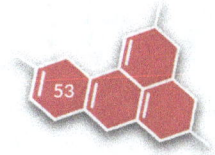

Igniting STEM Learning

> *objectives for their learning. These students are also more likely to have 'learned how to learn' – an invaluable skill that they can and will use throughout their lives. (p. 2)*

While these questions and more will be explored in more detail over the coming chapters, the concept of progressively developing each and every student to drive their own learning will shape the process by which teachers map and plan the learning that will occur.

THREE LEVELS OF MAPPING

A rigorous approach to developing a clear and progressive map of STEM learning across a school requires three levels of maps: a whole-school master map to guide whole-school thinking and planning, a map that year-level teachers use to guide their planning and thinking for the year, and a unit plan to map transdisciplinary STEM learning across a period of weeks.

WHOLE-SCHOOL MASTER MAP

A whole-school master map is a scope and sequence document that provides the big picture of how a school plans to develop students in the necessary knowledge, skills, thinking and capabilities from Foundation to Year 6.

Figure 3.1 outlines the structure of a whole-school master map for a school which has individual year levels. Within each year-level column, the 'Mindset and capabilities plan' field captures how the school is going to nurture the development of the students as highly capable, self-regulated learners (see Chapter 2 planning); 'Learning ladder' contains the progression of expected standards for a range of core STEM skills and resources that will be required at each year level; and the 'Curriculum map' charts how the curriculum areas will be integrated into transdisciplinary STEM units.

Foundation	Year 1	Year 2	Year 3	Year 4	Year 5	Year 6
Mindset and capabilities plan	Mindset and capabilities plan	Mindset and capabilities plan	Mindset and capabilities plan	Mindset and capabilities plan	Mindset and capabilities plan	Mindset and capabilities plan
Learning ladder	Learning ladder	Learning ladder	Learning ladder	Learning ladder	Learning ladder	Learning ladder
Curriculum map	Curriculum map	Curriculum map	Curriculum map	Curriculum map	Curriculum map	Curriculum map

Figure 3.1: Sample whole-school master map structure

Figure 3.2 is an alternative version of a whole-school master map for primary schools that operate with combined year classrooms or prefer to design learning to address curriculum areas over a two-year cycle. This two-year cycle structure has the benefit of giving teachers more freedom to design units that integrate curriculum areas more authentically or to more appropriately address specific events (for example, particular STEM competitions, National Science Day, the Olympics,

Developing curriculum and learning ladder maps

Anzac Day, school concerts, camps and so on).

Foundation	Years 1/2		Years 3/4		Years 5/6	
Mindset and capabilities plan	Year A mindset and capabilities plan	Year B mindset and capabilities plan	Year A mindset and capabilities plan	Year B mindset and capabilities plan	Year A mindset and capabilities plan	Year B mindset and capabilities plan
Learning ladder	Year A learning ladder	Year B learning ladder	Year A learning ladder	Year B learning ladder	Year A learning ladder	Year B learning ladder
Curriculum map	Year A curriculum map	Year B curriculum map	Year A curriculum map	Year B curriculum map	Year A curriculum map	Year B curriculum map

Figure 3.2: Sample whole-school master map structure, two-year cycle

Much like an architect's stylised drawing of a house, this type of whole-school mapping is deliberately broad-brushstroke planning with the aim of conveying how a school is bringing the curriculum, capabilities and learning together in a cohesive whole. Not only can it be used to ensure that all the required state or national curriculum content is addressed, but it also provides a useful tool for forward planning the growth of specific knowledge, skills, thinking and capabilities across the years of schooling. Further, it is highly beneficial for teachers moving between year levels, the induction of teachers new to a school and the transition of students from year to year. School leaders need to ensure that this sort of whole-school map is reviewed and refined each year to take in the lessons learned by teaching teams and adapt to changes in student capacity.

YEAR-LEVEL MAP

The aim of the year-level map is to capture how teaching teams plan to nurture the progressive development of knowledge, skills, thinking and capabilities across a specific year level. Continuing the building analogy, this is equivalent to a floor plan. This document includes the year level's mindset and capabilities plan, learning ladder, the curriculum areas mapped across terms and the transdisciplinary STEM units that will be delivered. Multiple transdisciplinary units can occur within a single term or may even straddle a series of terms, depending on the size of the unit or project undertaken. Figure 3.3 is an example of how a year-level map might be structured. The process of developing a learning ladder and year-level curriculum map is outlined in the next section.

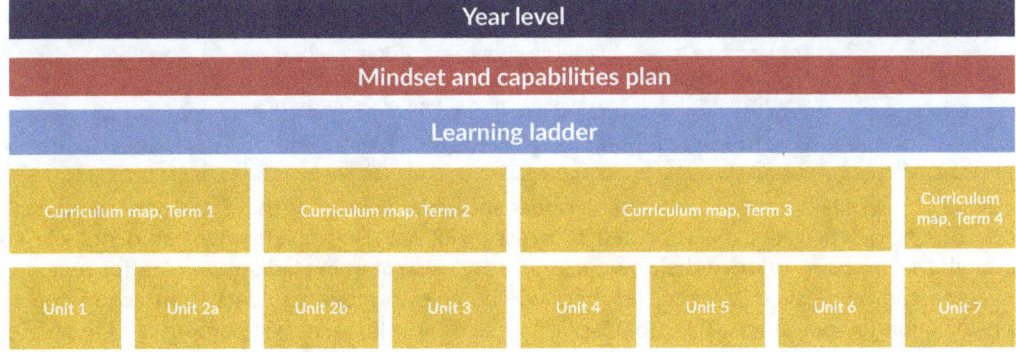

Figure 3.3: Sample year-level map structure

UNIT PLAN

This document is a detailed plan of teaching and learning for a transdisciplinary STEM unit. The planning document provides the detail of the curriculum that a unit will address, the assessment that will measure progress, the activities to be run, and the strategies and structures that will support the students to achieve the learning goals and drive their own learning. Chapters 4, 5 and 6 (from page 73) will explain how teaching teams can design transdisciplinary STEM units.

DEVELOPING A STEM LEARNING LADDER

The 'Learning ladder' row in the whole-school master map captures the progression of core skills, materials, equipment and resources that support students to become highly capable STEM learners. This could include practical skills, programming skills or the progression of specific digital and design technologies resources, materials and equipment. A STEM learning ladder is a useful map for teachers and schools to create because it ensures that there is a plan to provide students with the necessary exposure, practice and skills to tackle more complex STEM tasks and projects as they progress through their schooling.

Table 3.1 is an example of a learning ladder for two practical skills: using hand tools, and drawing and drafting. This was developed in response to a number of upper primary teachers sharing that their students struggle to use scissors or simple hand tools properly. Teachers cannot assume their students have learned these skills at home. If the expectation is that a school's upper-primary students are going to tackle STEM projects that require some level of practical skill (for example, a wearable fashion project in which students sew LEDs into items they create and then connect these to an Arduino using conductive thread), establishing a learning ladder for these skills will support teaching teams to ensure that students will be suitably prepared to encounter the project.

Table 3.1: Sample learning ladder for two practical skills

Learning ladder: Practical cross-curricula skills				
Year Level	**Foundation**	**Years 1/2**	**Years 3/4**	**Years 5/6**
Stage of development	**Acquire**		**Acquire and consolidate**	**Consolidate and apply**
Hand tools	Cutting and pasting Using scissors	Using a hammer, screwdriver, spanner and wrench, tape measure etc.	Using a Stanley knife, handsaw, pliers, sewing, knitting	Using simple electric power tools, chisels, soldering irons etc.
Drawing and drafting	Learning how to hold a pencil, draw straight lines	Drawing diagrams and patterns, sketching, measuring	Drawing 2D maps, drawing house plans, measuring Making Minecraft models	Tinkercad 3D printing 3D models/prototypes

One of the key features of the learning ladder shown in table 3.1 is the 'Stage of development' row. This field articulates the expected progression of learning development students will go through as they learn to drive their own learning. By using learning ladders to plan for repeated coverage and interleaved practice, teachers will be able to move students from acquisition to consolidation to application. The progressive stages of development will be unpacked in greater

Developing curriculum and learning ladder maps

depth in Chapter 5 when it is linked to a model of learning proposed by John Hattie and Gregory Donoghue (2016).

Since the Australian Curriculum: Technologies is central to developing STEM learners, schools should also develop digital and design learning ladders. These ladders are valuable because it is not unusual for schools to purchase the latest piece of technology or software without thinking through how and when it will be used to build student capabilities. In some cases, the technology ends up unused and in storage because it is not linked well to the curriculum, the person who knew how to use it has left or no one has invested time in learning to use the technology effectively. Digital and design learning ladders enable schools to think through the technology and physical resourcing requirements for embedding the digital and design technologies curriculums in an effective and progressive manner through the years of schooling. The learning ladders not only help schools to minimise poor financial purchases, but also support coherent future planning for when new technologies and approaches become available (for example, augmented and virtual reality, 3D printing, laser cutting and so on).

Table 3.2 is a draft learning ladder for digital technologies put together by a primary school STEM teacher. The teacher first examined the Australian Curriculum: Technologies documents to get a sense of what was required at each year level. This enabled her to identify a range of learning ladder topics in which she categorised the possible software, hardware and concepts that could be applied at each level. Finally, she explored what free and paid software could be most valuable, what technology the school already owns, and what software or technology that the school may need to buy.

Table 3.2: Draft digital technologies learning ladder

Learning ladder: Digital technologies				
Year Level	**Foundation**	**Years 1/2**	**Years 3/4**	**Years 5/6**
Stage of development	Acquire		**Acquire and consolidate**	**Consolidate and apply**
Focus	Language and movement		Software	
Cyber safety and digital communications	Common Sense Education F–2 Hector's World	Common Sense Education F–2 Hector's World	Common Sense Education 3–4	Common Sense Education 5–6
Programming	Programming a person using step cards Lightbot Jr (Term 4)	Programming a person using step cards ScratchJr LightBot	Scratch Minecraft Education	Scratch (creating games and animations) Minecraft Education
	Unplugged coding	Unplugged coding	GameStar Mechanic Hopscotch (block code) Kodable Code Combat (Python)	Python (written code) Code Academy (written code) Grok Learning

Continued ...

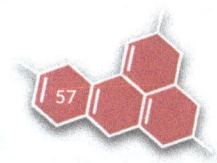

Igniting STEM Learning

Year Level	Foundation	Years 1/2	Years 3/4	Years 5/6
Stage of development	Acquire		Acquire and consolidate	Consolidate and apply
Focus				
Circuits	Makey Makey	Makey Makey	Makey Makey Squishy Circuits KodeKLIX®, littleBits (buy?)	Makey Makey Squishy Circuits KodeKLIX®, littleBits (buy?)
Robotics	Program BeeBots to move to a particular destination and write down simple coding using pictures/arrows/directional language (tie in with procedural texts)	BeeBots – program a dance, link to counting and number lines, addition, subtraction Dash & Dot	ProBot (buy?) Dash & Dot Blue-Bot®	ProBot (buy?) Sphero machines
	Lego® WeDo	Lego® WeDo	Lego® WeDo 2.0 Lego SPIKE™ Prime	Lego® WeDo 2.0 Lego SPIKE™ Prime
Hardware	Breaker space – students use tools to pull apart different household items and even computers (Need to ask parents to donate appropriate items that they would normally throw away into hard rubbish.)		Maker space – could use Lego blocks, blocks or planks iFixit.com – gets students to pull items apart and then put it back together (needs items donated for students to put back together) micro:bit, LittleBits, Arduino (buy?), 3D printers	
	Labelling a paper computer What is a website or the internet?	Make a computer (out of materials) What is the internet? – browsers, search engines, login, navigation Folders – what does this look like? (organisation)	Organising files into folders	Network routers etc. – map the home network
Data	Drawing data graph to given problem Taking pics with iPads/cameras	Wordle Downloading/uploading pics into different mediums Collecting general data	Google online Graphing/tables using different media Binary – explore using games	Binary – google presentations and games How computers work to convey ideas and information Validating information using data sources

Developing curriculum and learning ladder maps

Language	Laptop, computer, keyboard, mouse, monitor, systems unit, control, alt, delete, start, log off, log in, enter, software, technology, data	Year 1: Internet Explorer/Chrome, PowerPoint, Word, Photo Story, space bar, shift, caps lock, backspace, screen, delete, apps, tablet and iPad, patterns, algorithm Year 2: arrow keys, function keys, qwerty, tab, Excel, snipping tool, restart, charts, graphs, robot, password, cyberbullying	Peripheral, circuit board, pins, sensors, power supply, QR code, algorithm, names of visual programming blocks, sprite, feedback, iteration, if-then statements, debug, repeat-until statements, protocols, datasets, user input	Infographic, database, validation, digital system, Bluetooth technology, binary numbers, binary character table, pixels, debug, protocols, digital identity, blog, webpage, HTML, Python, Padlet, OneNote, storyboard, functional requirements, loops and repetition, flow chart, prototype, if-then statements, user input

Learning ladders can be designed to capture a progression of milestones for many other key STEM skills, including research skills, digital literacy skills and the ability to use software programs such as Word, Excel and PowerPoint. The Australian Curriculum website also provides useful downloads (see for example the science scope and sequence document at ACARA, n.d.-n) that can be used to create learning ladders that capture useful materials and equipment, online resources and potential links to digital and design technologies. Once designed, learning ladders should be used by year-level teaching teams to ensure that their planning, pedagogy and assessments develop their students in the identified knowledge, skills and thinking.

Igniting STEM Learning

Exercise: Learning ladder

As a design team, use the Australian Curriculum documents as a guide to identify what materials, equipment, resources and skill milestones are required in each year level. At a minimum, create learning ladders for practical skills, digital literacy, and the digital and design technologies curriculums (as set out in in the following template). Once these learning ladders are complete, audit what is currently done in each year level, using this information to refine the ladders and identify any activities, resources, materials and equipment that need to be introduced.

Learning ladder:				
Year Level	**Foundation**	**Years 1/2**	**Years 3/4**	**Years 5/6**
Stage of development	...	...	...	...
Focus	...	...	...	...

Reproducible available

DEVELOPING A YEAR-LEVEL CURRICULUM MAP

The final part of the mapping process involves year-level teaching teams developing a year-level curriculum map. This requires teaching teams to examine the national or state curriculum for their year level(s) and then map the curriculum across school terms to guide the development of potential transdisciplinary STEM units. In this mapping process there are no expectations that transdisciplinary units will address every aspect of the curriculum in a coherent fashion. It is quite normal in the first cycle of mapping and running transdisciplinary STEM units that certain curriculum topics may be planned as standalone units. However, teaching teams can strategically weave the design process (design and technologies processes and production skill), the language of computational and systems thinking, science inquiry skills, and even aspects of maths, English and digital technologies into most learning planned for each term.

Going through the mapping process, year-level teams should consider the natural flow of a school year as they make their choices for which curriculum areas to address in which units in which term. Figure 3.4 is a progression framework based on the learning to drive metaphor explored earlier in this chapter and the idea that the curriculum can be sequenced to take students more authentically through the acquisition, consolidation and application stages of development.

Developing curriculum and learning ladder maps

Term 1 Surface acquire	Term 2 Surface acquire and consolidate	Term 3 Surface consolidate and deep acquire	Term 4 Deep consolidate and transfer
Me **Laying the foundation I** Establishing routines, norms, agreements and habitual practices Diagnostic assessment of knowledge, skill and thinking Building the base of knowledge and skill **Curriculum focus:** ourselves as learners and human beings	**We** **Laying the foundation II** Continuing to build the base of knowledge and skill Using activities and challenges with clear bounds to develop skill and capacity in applying the problem-solving/design process **Curriculum focus:** how we fit together in community and society	**Us** **Practising** Using more complex activities and challenges with clear bounds to develop skill and capacity in applying the problem-solving/design process **Curriculum focus:** our impact on the world and each other	**All** **Applying** Open-ended problems where students apply everything they have learnt to a task that has no solution **Curriculum focus:** what we create and build, and how that links together and connects our world

Figure 3.4: Curriculum progression planning framework

In Term 1 students return from an extended holiday break, often to a new class with a new teacher and new peers. Normally teachers invest a significant amount of time in Term 1 laying the foundation for an effective learning environment. This process generally involves establishing routines, classroom norms and agreements, habitual practices and strong relationships. In some schools, teachers will also perform diagnostic assessments to get a clear idea of their students' stages of development in a range of areas. In the framework illustrated in figure 3.4, Term 1 has a 'Me' theme because, in practice, teachers naturally focus on the students getting to know themselves as learners with certain strengths and areas for development and run a range of activities to build student capacity to work as a learning community. It would therefore be strategic for the transdisciplinary STEM learning planned for Term 1 to focus on the personal and social capability, the civics and citizenship aspect of the HASS curriculum, the health and physical education curriculum, the knowledge aspects of the design and technologies curriculum, and maybe even elements of the arts curriculum.

By Term 2 students have begun to internalise the norms, agreements and routines. At this stage, students will mostly be operating and learning more collaboratively. The curriculum focus could now extend to having students explore and understand the local and Australian community (reflecting the 'We' theme). This represents a natural progression in thinking for students as the

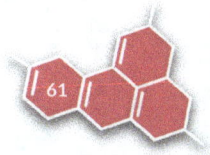

learning focus moves from them as a classroom of individuals to exploring their relationship to the local community and larger society. Transdisciplinary units could involve curriculum elements such as the geography, history or civics and citizenship aspects of HASS, science, the knowledge aspects of the digital and design technologies curriculum, the intercultural understanding capability and the First Australians histories and culture cross-curriculum priority.

By Term 3 students will have internalised the norms, agreements and routines and will be operating more effectively in collaborative-learning pairs or teams. This is often the term in which teachers see students begin to drive their own learning. At this point the curriculum focus can expand beyond the local and Australian context to have the students explore humanity's thinking about the world. The 'Us' theme of this term has students look through the lenses of science, geography, art, the ethical understanding capability, and the sustainability cross-curriculum priority to understand the world they inhabit. This is a great term to create transdisciplinary units, such as scientific and geographic investigations or smaller digital and design projects that have clear end points, to support students to consolidate their knowledge, skills and thinking.

During Term 4, to continue consolidating and even transferring their knowledge, skills and thinking to new situations, transdisciplinary units could involve students producing something. This is the term where they bring together everything they have learnt (reflecting the 'All' theme). Term 4 is a great time to do larger design projects that integrate science, economics, art and the production elements of the technologies curriculum. It is often also the term that primary schools have their concerts, musical productions and sports days, and these projects can be linked to the curriculum with students organising and driving them.

Table 3.3 samples a whole-school curriculum map content from Foundation to Year 6 based on the curriculum progression planning framework of figure 3.4. This map represents the first prototype whole-school mapping of a transdisciplinary STEM curriculum. The design team behind this map began with existing units as a broad framework for their thinking and explored how the units could be tailored or moved around in year levels to provide the coherent progression outlined in the planning framework. Literacy and numeracy were not specifically addressed in the map because, as is the case in most primary schools, it was timetabled separately. However, aspects of English and maths were, as much as authentically possible, embedded into the units that were being run (for example, the books that were required reading related to the transdisciplinary unit being run). The design team also cleverly linked the Year 5 and 6 camps to the transdisciplinary units for that term. This allowed for an authentic linking of the curriculum to real-world, hands-on experiences while still addressing the normal building of year-level relationships. The design team decided that some curriculum aspects had to be delivered as independent disciplinary units because they felt they could not do the specific areas justice in their first iteration of mapping transdisciplinary units. Furthermore, they did not address some of the specialist curriculum areas, the digital literacy general capability or the technologies curriculum. Instead, they left it to the year-level teams to work out in the next stage of planning.

Developing curriculum and learning ladder maps

Table 3.3: Sample whole-school curriculum map

Term, theme and Australian Curriculum areas	Term 1: Knowing me Health Personal and social capability	Term 2: Our community HASS (geography, history, civics) Aboriginal and Torres Strait Islander history and culture Intercultural understanding	Term 3: Our world Arts Science HASS (geography) Ethical understanding Sustainability Asia and Australia's engagement	Term 4: Innovation and action Technologies (design, digital) Science HASS (economics) Reflection and celebration
Foundation	Have a go and take care Health Personal and social capability	My family and celebrations Geography History Aboriginal and Torres Strait Islander history and culture Personal and social capability	Wild and domestic animals Geography Science, biological Science, earth and space	Totally amazing toys Technologies Science, chemical Science, physical
Year 1	Being safe and independent Health Personal and social capability	Paddock to plate Geography History Aboriginal and Torres Strait Islander history and culture Science, biological Science, chemical (standalone)	Mini-beasts Geography Science, biological Science, earth and space (standalone)	Transport Technologies Science, physical
Year 2	Super learners Health Personal and social capability Science, physical (standalone)	Then and now – local Geography History Aboriginal and Torres Strait Islander history and culture Civics Science, chemical (standalone)	Water for life Geography Science, biological Science, earth and space Science, chemical	Packaging and marketing Technologies Economics
Year 3	Keeping me healthy Health Personal and social capability	Then and now – greater Melbourne Geography History Aboriginal and Torres Strait Islander history and culture Built environment Victoria	Big blue marble Geography Science, biological Science, earth and space	Fabulous fabrics Technologies Economics Science, chemical Science, physical (standalone)

Continued ...

Igniting STEM Learning

Term, theme and Australian Curriculum areas	Term 1: Knowing me Health Personal and social capability	Term 2: Our community HASS (geography, history, civics) Aboriginal and Torres Strait Islander history and culture Intercultural understanding	Term 3: Our world Arts Science HASS (geography) Ethical understanding Sustainability Asia and Australia's engagement	Term 4: Innovation and action Technologies (design, digital) Science HASS (economics) Reflection and celebration
Year 4	Community life Health Civics Personal and social capability	Early Australian history Geography History Aboriginal and Torres Strait Islander history and culture Asia and Australia's engagement	What on earth! Geography Science, biological Science, earth and space Sustainability	Marvellous machines Technologies Science, chemical Science, physical
Year 5	Best foot forward Health Personal and social capability *Note: Cover drug education and building of healthy relationships. Start Term 2 work in Term 1.*	Our colonial past Geography History Aboriginal and Torres Strait Islander history and culture Asia and Australia's engagement Economics (one week; informed consumer) Science, chemical (first two weeks of term) *Note: Year 5 camp (goldfields).*	Being green on a blue planet Science, biological Science, earth and space Science, physical (last two weeks of term; light) Sustainability Economics (one week; work)	Imagine it – create it Technologies Economics (two-week unit; budgeting, classroom economy, advertising)
Year 6	Healthy minds, healthy body, healthy relationships Health Personal and social capability *Note: About being an adolescent, drug education. Culminates in Year 6 camp (team building).*	Democracy, migration, multiculturalism and diversity Geography History Civics Aboriginal and Torres Strait Islander history and culture Asia and Australia's engagement Science, chemical (first two weeks of term)	Natural disasters Sustainability Asia and Australia's engagement Geography Science, biological Science, earth and space	Mini-cars Technologies Economics Science, physical (electrical energy; standalone)

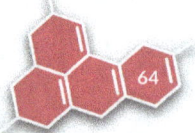

STEPS TO DEVELOPING A YEAR-LEVEL CURRICULUM MAP

Developing a curriculum map for each year level is not a complicated task, but it does take a significant amount of time to do well. Many schools already have year-long curriculum maps that ensure teaching teams cover everything as mandated. The following process is not about reinventing the wheel, but rather about bringing further rigour and thinking to the process so that schools can develop an authentic STEM program aligned to their design brief. The more rigour and detail that teaching and design teams bring to the process, the greater the opportunity for creative and authentic STEM learning. The best way of thinking about this process is as an iterative planning procedure that progressively adds more detail and gets clearer about how the curriculum can fit together in cohesive transdisciplinary units.

FIRST PLANNING ITERATION: DRAFT A WHOLE-SCHOOL CURRICULUM MAP

The first step in this iteration is to have a design team made up of teachers from each year level create a broadbrush map of the existing integrated, transdisciplinary or inquiry units in each term. The intent is to get a sense of what already is being delivered. This is the best place to start as unit planners should already be available to build a clear picture of what curriculum areas are addressed.

Once this draft map has been produced, the design team can tailor units or move them around in each year level to provide a coherent progression as outlined in figure 3.4 (page 61) and sampled in table 3.3 (page 63). During this process the design team should be able to articulate whole-school term themes and align these with the specific curriculum areas that will be addressed in each term by each year-level team. If the design team discovers that there are unaddressed curriculum areas or that new transdisciplinary units need to be developed, this should be noted in each year-level curriculum map. Table 3.4 shows an early draft version of this mapping process for three year levels in the curriculum map in table 3.3.

Table 3.4: Excerpt of an early draft the sample whole-school curriculum map shown in table 3.3 (page 63)

	Units			
Year 1	Health, happiness and belonging (belonging to groups etc.)	New unit (Keeping in touch?)	Fresh water	New unit (Shopping and packaging)
Year 2	Food and nutrition Me and healthy living	New unit (Victoria over time, Aboriginal and Torres Strait Islander history, built environment, Victoria)	Caring and sustainable environment unit to be redeveloped	New unit (Fabulous fabrics)
Year 3	Growing up – human body	New unit (Australia over time, history, Asia and Australia's engagement?) Countries and cultures unit to be redeveloped	Australian environment (biotic, abiotic, geography, adaptations etc.)	New unit (Energy and change, simple machines) – design focus

Once the design team has done its work, the whole-school map should be sent to year-level teaching teams to discuss and refine. The year-level teams' task is to add curriculum detail and work out what aspects should be addressed in which units, come up with potential unit names, identify links to already existing events and programs, and begin to grapple with how they can design

Igniting STEM Learning

learning that builds the acquisition and consolidation of knowledge, skills and thinking across the year. This process, which sees the design and year-level teams working in tandem, should continue until everyone believes they have a clear and useful curriculum map that they can all work to.

A benefit of this iterative design process is that teachers have cause to reflect on and come to a deeper understanding of the curriculum and how it can fit together to deliver learning outcomes. The Australian Curriculum is remarkably rich and interconnected across many curriculum areas. The interconnectedness and relationships between curriculum areas are often lost when each area is looked at in isolation. In following this process, teachers have remarked that they have far greater clarity about how the curriculum fits together and how they can be more effective in linking learning across the years.

Exercise: Curriculum mapping 1

Using the following template, follow the outlined process to design a whole-school curriculum map.

Term, theme and Australian Curriculum areas	Term 1: Theme Curriculum areas	Term 2: Theme	Term 3: Theme	Term 4: Theme
Foundation	Transdisciplinary unit Curriculum areas			
Year 1				
Year 2				
Year 3				
Year 4				
Year 5				
Year 6				

Reproducible available

SECOND PLANNING ITERATION: ADD YEAR-LEVEL DETAIL

Once the whole-school curriculum map has been agreed upon, the next planning iteration involves year-level teams fleshing out the detail of the curriculum areas and general capabilities to be addressed by each transdisciplinary unit. The most practical approach to doing this is for teachers to download the content descriptors for the entire curriculum relevant to their year level and then to assign the descriptors to the most relevant transdisciplinary unit. This can be done either digitally by using a word processor or by printing out the content descriptors and arranging them physically. Table 3.5 is an example of this transdisciplinary unit mapping, drawing on the Year 2 'Super learners' unit shown in table 3.3 (page 63).

Developing curriculum and learning ladder maps

Table 3.5: Sample transdisciplinary unit map

Curriculum area	Term 1: Super learners Health Personal and social capability
English	Investigate how interpersonal language choices vary depending on the context, including the different roles taken on in interactions. (AC9E2LA01) Use interaction skills when engaging with topics, actively listening to others, receiving instructions and extending own ideas, speaking appropriately, expressing and responding to opinions, making statements, and giving instructions. (AC9E2LY02)
Health and physical education	Describe their personal qualities and those of others, and explain how they contribute to developing identities. (AC9HP2P01) Identify and demonstrate protective behaviours and help-seeking strategies they can use to help them and others stay safe. (AC9HP2P05) Identify and explore skills and strategies to develop respectful relationships. (AC9HP2P02)
Digital technologies	Represent data as objects, pictures and symbols. (AC9TDIFK02) Follow and describe algorithms involving a sequence of steps, branching (decisions) and iteration (repetition). (AC9TDI2P02)
Literacy capability	Sub-elements to focus on: - Compose emergent texts for specific purposes. - Use appropriate language or dialect to interact with speakers of the same language. - Use appropriate volume for small audiences.
Personal and social capability	Sub-elements that could be addressed: - Develop personal awareness. - Participate in reflective practice. - Set goals. - Persevere and adapt. - Communicate. - Collaborate. - Practise decision-making. - Resolve conflict.
Critical and creative thinking	Sub-elements that could be addressed: - Identify, process and evaluate information. - Think about thinking (metacognition). - Transfer knowledge. - Draw conclusions and provide reasons. - Evaluate actions and outcomes.
Ethical understanding	Sub-elements that could be addressed: - Recognise influences on ethical behaviour and perspectives. - Examine values, rights and responsibilities, and ethical norms.
Digital literacy	Sub-element that could be addressed: - Create, communicate and collaborate.

Source: Adapted from ACARA (n.d.-e)

While the Year 2 'Super learners' unit in the original whole-school mapping (see table 3.3, page 63) was only associated with the health curriculum and the personal and social capability, the teachers expanded what they felt they could authentically address through the unit. This included English, the data knowledge and a production and process aspect of the digital technologies

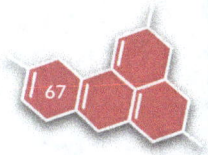

curriculum, and a range of sub-elements of the general capabilities. At this stage of planning, they weren't entirely clear about how they would address the range of general capability sub-elements, but they believed that such a unit would provide a natural structure to address them.

As year-level teaching teams go through this planning process, they may discover that content descriptors in certain curriculum areas have not yet been addressed. They should use this as an opportunity to explore whether those descriptors or general capabilities elements could be addressed by learning activities elsewhere or if there is a need for a standalone unit. In curriculum areas such as science, HASS and technologies there are descriptors for skills and understanding as well as knowledge. Understanding descriptors, like the cross-curriculum priorities, describe a lens through which units can be taught. These descriptors should be included as part of unit mapping. The descriptors for skill or production processes need to be repeated in units across multiple terms as they are developed through practice. Teaching teams should ensure that their year-level curriculum map reflects the building of those skills across the year.

Figure 3.5 is a photo of preliminary thinking and planning performed by a group of Year 3 and 4 teachers as they began mapping out how they could embed the technologies curriculum into pre-existing transdisciplinary units. The two year-level teaching teams decided to work together because they felt that they could develop more authentic transdisciplinary units if they planned for a two-year cycle of learning. They printed all the appropriate Year 3 and 4 descriptors for the digital and design technologies curriculum, cut them into separate descriptors and used a whiteboard table to do their mapping. The teachers initially placed the descriptors where they thought they would fit best in the units they were already running. They discussed the themes for each term, what specific curriculum areas and units might address those themes, whether to move certain content descriptors to Year 3 or 4 so that more authentic transdisciplinary units could be designed, how they could use the language and thinking frameworks from the technologies curriculum throughout each year level, and what activities could be designed so students would repeatedly use the process and production skills across multiple units.

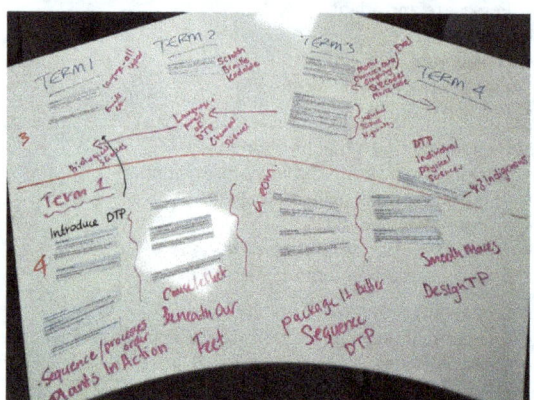

Figure 3.5: Preliminary thinking and planning for Years 3 and 4 curriculum mapping

Prior to beginning the mapping process in figure 3.5, the teachers had avoided enacting the technologies curriculum because they felt it was yet another thing to do. While their school did have a STEAM lab and students in each year level visited the lab for activities, the teachers felt that STEAM and the technologies curriculum were a specialist responsibility. The prevailing belief was that they did not know much about coding or design, so how could they include it in their planning.

Developing curriculum and learning ladder maps

By the end of the session the teachers had a greater understanding of how they could embed the technologies curriculum into what they were already doing and felt more confident that they could create transdisciplinary STEM learning. Interestingly, as they went through the mapping process the teachers began to see how they could create stronger links to the learning occurring in other specialist areas such as the arts, language, science and physical education.

Exercise: Curriculum mapping 2

Using the transdisciplinary unit mapping completed in Exercise 1, download the content descriptors for the entire curriculum and general capabilities relevant to your year level and assign the descriptors to the most relevant transdisciplinary unit using the following template. The goal is to put together a detailed map of how the curriculum will be addressed across the year with transdisciplinary STEM units and standalone activities.

Curriculum area	Term 1	Term 2	Term 3	Term 4
Unit name				
English				
Mathematics				
Science				
HASS				
The arts				
Health and PE				
Digital technologies				
Design and technologies				
Languages				
Literacy capability				
Numeracy capability				
Personal and social capability				
Critical and creative thinking				
Intercultural understanding				
Ethical understanding				
Digital literacy				

Reproducible available

THIRD PLANNING ITERATION: COMPLETE YEAR-LEVEL AND WHOLE-SCHOOL MAPS

Once each year-level teaching team is happy that their curriculum map captures all the content descriptors and that there is a coherent progression and opportunity for transdisciplinary STEM learning throughout the year, there is one more refinement process required. The final step is then for the design team to gather all the year-level curriculum maps and refine the whole-school curriculum map.

Exercise: Curriculum mapping 3

If they have not yet done so, each year-level team should refer to their learning ladder as well as their mindset and capabilities plan (developed in Chapter 2) and refine their map to ensure that it is aligned with the thinking and planning in those two documents. Once this step is completed, the design team should gather every year-level curriculum map and create the final whole-school curriculum map using the whole-school master map structures set out in figures 3.1 and 3.2 (pages 54 and 55).

Some of the questions that the design team might ask when going through this refinement process include:

- Is there a clear progression of knowledge, skills, thinking and mindset through the years? If not, what refinements can be made?
- Does the design of the whole-school curriculum map provide a clear map for the school leadership and the teaching teams to use? If not, how could it be improved?
- Does the whole-school curriculum map allow the school to achieve its design brief? If not, what refinements can be made?
- Does the whole-school curriculum map support the development of highly capable learners? If not, what refinements can be made?
- How will the year-level and whole-school maps be refined each year?

COACHING ON THE MAPPING PROCESS

The iterative process to create year-level and whole-school curriculum maps is essentially a design process. The planning iterations bring the design and year-level teaching teams to a deeper understanding of the structure of the Australian Curriculum and the interrelationships between all the curriculum areas.

Teachers may feel overwhelmed in the first planning iteration as there seems to be a lot of curriculum to address. At this stage, design and year-level teaching teams should be reminded that it will all become clearer as they go through the planning process. In the second and third planning iterations, teachers will begin to identify authentic links between the descriptors in various curriculum areas and naturally start to speculate about transdisciplinary STEM units that will achieve multiple learning outcomes. During these stages teachers will have rich professional discussions as they use their various understandings and curriculum expertise to come to a shared understanding of learning flow through a year. Over time the deeper insights gained will allow for greater creativity in designing learning.

While the first time through the mapping process is time-intensive and challenging, the evaluation and refinement process that follows after the resulting units have been run for a year is comparatively quick and easy. This evaluation and refinement process leads not only to simpler

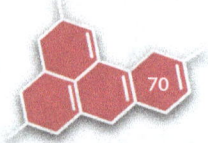

and clearer documentation, but also to teachers developing greater mastery of the curriculum. With year-level and whole-school curriculum maps, schools will find it easier to respond to curriculum changes dictated from external sources, for teachers to move between year levels and for teachers new to the school to be effective quickly. The next chapter begins the process of designing transdisciplinary units based on year-level curriculum maps.

KEY POINTS

- Creating transdisciplinary learning units is a key part of breaking down artificial learning silos and developing learning that routinely deploy student capabilities in a range of real-world contexts.
- To be able to do this effectively, schools need to invest the time and thinking to create curriculum and other associated maps that articulate how they plan to nurture and develop student knowledge, skills, thinking and capabilities progressively across the years of schooling.
- The goal of developing students to drive their own learning reframes the purpose of schooling and allows for new ways of thinking about what needs to be mapped.
- A rigorous map of STEM learning across a school requires three levels of mapping: mapping to guide whole-school thinking and planning; mapping that year-level teachers can use to guide their planning and thinking for the year; and unit planning that sets out transdisciplinary STEM learning across a period of weeks and terms.
- An iterative curriculum-mapping process supports teachers to come to a deeper understanding of the structure of the Australian Curriculum and interrelationships between curriculum areas. As a result, schools will find it easier to respond to curriculum changes dictated from external sources, for teachers to move between year levels and for teachers new to the school to be effective quickly.
- The greater rigour applied to the mapping process, the easier teachers will find designing creative and engaging transdisciplinary STEM learning opportunities.

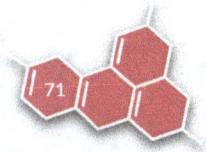

CHAPTER 4

First steps in planning transdisciplinary STEM units

A goal without a plan is just a wish.

Antoine de Saint-Exupéry, The Little Prince

BACKWARD PLANNING

The idea of backward planning has existed in building, engineering and design for millennia. The designer begins with the end goal (a pyramid, an aqueduct, a road, a house, a car or a product) and then works out what needs to be done to achieve that goal. In education, the process of backward planning was introduced in the late 1940s by Ralph W Tyler (1949) when he suggested that teachers could create a statement of objectives so that instructional activities could be planned and developed in a way likely to attain these objectives. More recently the term *backward design* was introduced to curriculum design by Grant Wiggins and Jay McTighe (1998). Figure 4.1 represents the flow of the three stages of backward design as identified by Wiggins and McTighe (1998).

Stage 1 Identify desired results. → **Stage 2** Determine acceptable evidence. → **Stage 3** Plan learning experiences and instructions.

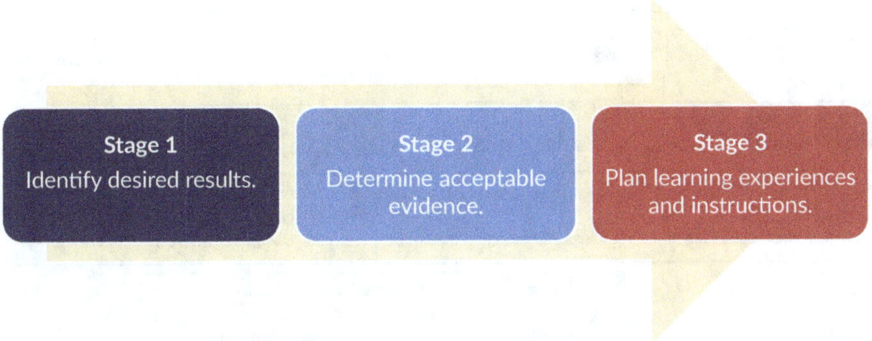

Figure 4.1: Flow of the three stages of backward design
Source: Adapted from Wiggins and McTighe (1998)

In Stage 1 of the backward design process teachers consider the required state or national curriculum expectations and the specific needs and developmental goals for their students (Wiggins & McTighe, 2011). This first stage involves teachers becoming clear about the long-term learning priorities for their students and identifying what knowledge teachers want students to acquire, what meaning they want students to make and what transfer of learning that teachers would they like students to have. In Stage 2 Wiggins and McTighe (2011) recommend that teachers consider the assessment evidence that needs to be collected to demonstrate that students have achieved the desired learning outcomes. From considering this, teachers will be able to design a range of assessment methods including the use of observations, rubrics, tests and culminating assessment tasks. The third stage involves teachers thinking about their teaching and feedback methods, sequence of lessons and resource materials to achieve three goals: transfer, meaning making and acquisition (Wiggins & McTighe, 2011).

As a framework for designing, planning and sequencing curriculum and instruction, the backward-planning process fits well with developing students as drivers of their own learning, and creating rich, real-world STEM learning. It helps teachers create logical teaching and learning progressions that move students coherently toward achieving specific and important learning objectives. Backward planning is well researched and has been used effectively to develop transdisciplinary STEM learning (McTighe & Seif, 2003; Rider-Bertrand, 2017). The challenge is to not use backward planning so precisely that the students experience a loss of personalisation. The aim is for students with different starting points and different strengths and areas for development to be able to progress their learning in meaningful and empowering ways (Heick, 2019).

This chapter introduces a process of backward planning to identify the learning destination for a transdisciplinary STEM unit based on the curriculum map for each term. We begin with extracting learning intentions and success criteria from the state or national curriculum. This approach not only helps teachers come to a deep understanding of the curriculum but also develops teacher capacity in elements of the computational thinking framework. This is followed by an explanation of how teachers can define a logical sequence of key understandings to create an authentic purpose for students (and teachers) to engage with the curriculum content. This sequence of key understandings forms the basis for teaching in a unit. In support of this goal, the process of creating questions aligned to the key understandings and possible culminating rich task assessments is also explored. The thinking and planning performed throughout this chapter lays the foundation for designing authentic transdisciplinary STEM assessment tasks, as we will move on to in Chapters 5 and 6.

A SIMPLIFIED BACKWARD-PLANNING PROCESS

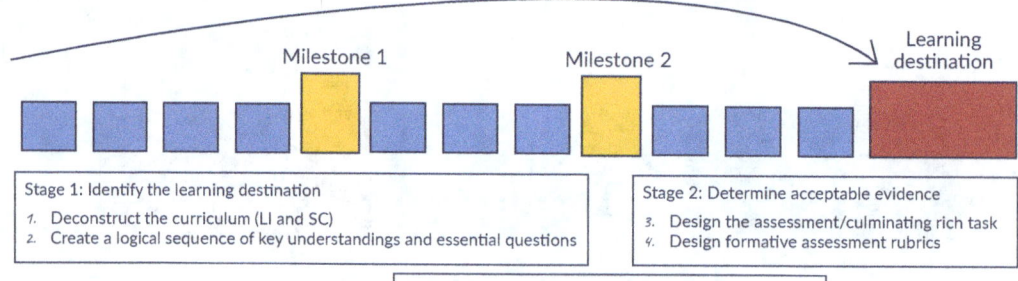

Figure 4.2: Simplified visualisation of the backward-planning process

Aligned with the stages and thinking set out in Wiggins and McTighe's (1998) concept of backward design, figure 4.2 illustrates a simplified variation on the backward-planning process for teachers designing STEM learning. The intention of this simplified approach is to let teachers focus on the processes and thinking of backward planning without necessarily going into all the detail involved in the Understanding by Design® framework from which this concept is drawn.

This backward-planning process is carried out over three distinct stages made up of a total six individual steps. Before we begin to unpack this in greater detail, here is a short overview.

STAGE 1: IDENTIFY THE LEARNING DESTINATION
The steps in this first stage support teachers to begin rigorously defining the learning destination (denoted in figure 4.2 by a magenta rectangle) of the transdisciplinary unit they are planning.

STEP 1: DECONSTRUCT THE CURRICULUM
Teachers use the curriculum content descriptors and elaborations to identify what they want students to know and be able to do by the end of the unit in this step. This involves creating concrete and observable learning intentions and success criteria written in language appropriate to the year level. This can include learning intentions and success criteria from the general capabilities or other useful social-emotional behavioural standards.

STEP 2: CREATE A LOGICAL SEQUENCE OF KEY UNDERSTANDINGS AND ESSENTIAL QUESTIONS
In this step teachers articulate a logical sequence of key understandings that they will use to frame the learning and teaching that occurs within the unit. This sequence addresses the meaning they would like students to make and the lasting understandings that students should take away from the unit. The essential questions for the transdisciplinary unit will proceed from these key understandings.

STAGE 2: DETERMINE ACCEPTABLE EVIDENCE
In the second stage, teachers finish defining the learning destination and articulate how students will demonstrate having achieved the desired learning outcomes.

STEP 3: DESIGN THE ASSESSMENT OR CULMINATING RICH TASK
This step involves designing a culminating rich task assessment or a sequence of assessments where students can authentically demonstrate their knowledge, skills and thinking. The aim is to create assessments that are real, practical and have meaning beyond students' day-to-day school experiences.

STEP 4: DESIGN FORMATIVE ASSESSMENT STRUCTURES
Formative assessment structures are critical to developing student capacity to self-assess and give, receive and use feedback to improve. They can highlight the expectations and desired outcome quality, show students and teachers what to look for as they collect evidence of learning, and indicate their next learning steps. Formative assessment structures can be derived from the curriculum or co-designed in learning conversations with students.

STAGE 3: PLAN LEARNING EXPERIENCES AND INSTRUCTION
In the final stage, teachers backward plan to set out the steps (denoted in figure 4.2 by blue boxes) to be completed and milestones (denoted by yellow rectangles) to be reached in order for students to achieve the desired learning outcomes.

STEP 5: CREATE A CHECKLIST OF STEPS
This checklist outlines the steps that teachers believe students need to take to achieve the culminating rich task assessment or sequence of assessments effectively and successfully. The checklist allows teachers to develop a coherent teaching plan and think through the link between the logical sequence of key understandings, the assessments, and the learning experiences and instruction. This is also the stage in which deliverable assessment milestones are established.

STEP 6: PLAN LEARNING EXPERIENCES AND INSTRUCTION
In this final step, teachers build on the thinking and planning from the first five steps to plan learning experiences and instruction.

DEVELOPING STUDENT AGENCY
While the six steps of backward planning are used by teachers to plan transdisciplinary STEM units, students can also be supported to use the backward-planning process to become more skilful at planning and driving their own learning. For example, teachers could pre-plan Steps 1–5, and then discuss and co-design learning experiences and instruction with their students. Alternatively, teachers could provide a culminating rich task and support the students to create a plan (a checklist of steps) before co-designing learning experiences and instruction with them. They could also replace Step 4 by providing students with various high-quality examples of the final product and co-create formative assessment structures. Teachers could even start with the curriculum map for the transdisciplinary unit and support students through the entire backward-planning process. By involving students in the process of planning to achieve the goals of their learning teachers will develop student voice, agency and leadership.

IDENTIFYING THE LEARNING DESTINATION
The remainder of this chapter unpacks the process of identifying the learning destination, Stage 1 of backward-planning, which is broken down into two key steps: deconstructing the curriculum and creating a logical sequence of key understandings and essential questions. Having covered Steps 1 and 2 here, Chapters 5 and 6 will detail Steps 3 and 5 respectively, while Step 4 will be addressed in Chapter 7. We will not address planning learning experiences and instruction (Step 6) in detail as this process is highly dependent on individual schools' instructional models.

STEP 1: DECONSTRUCT THE CURRICULUM
Learning begins with defining a goal. We identify what success looks like, have a go and then evaluate the result in a feedback design cycle that reduces the distance between the learner and the desired goal. In physical pursuits like sport and other physical activities, the goals and what success looks like is often quite clear. Further, learners in these situations tend to receive prompt feedback about whether they have achieved their desired goal. They know quite quickly if they have kicked a ball through the goal, drawn the picture accurately or set up the circuit to receive power when they flick a switch. The cycle of having concrete and observable goals, clarity about what success looks like and prompt feedback helps learner progress towards success relatively quickly.

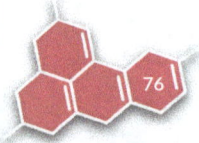

In more intellectual pursuits, which covers most of the curriculum that is taught to students, the goals or what success looks like are not necessarily clear. This is why it is necessary for teachers to deconstruct the curriculum, identify learning goals and articulate what success looks like in a way that is behaviourally concrete and observable to students.

The process of deconstructing the curriculum is beneficial in several ways. First, it develops teachers' capacity for computational thinking. The curriculum can be considered a complex system that needs to be broken down into smaller parts so that it is more manageable and easier to understand (decomposition). Teachers can find the patterns, order and links within the curriculum so that they can make sense of what is being asked given the background and stage of learning development of their students (pattern recognition). This clarity and sense-making creates the opportunity for rich professional discussions in which knowledge and thinking is shared so the team can come to a common understanding of what is important to focus on with students and what may not be (abstraction). Writing learning intentions and success criteria as concrete and observable behaviours in level-appropriate language provides clarity and direction for students and creates a foundation for them to drive their own learning. It answers the three essential questions that students have when driving their learning: 'Where am I going? How am I going? and Where to next?' (Hattie & Timperley, 2007, p. 88). Finally, creating and using learning intentions and success criteria develops of a learning culture of systemic and effective feedback. Feedback is often only provided by teachers and can suffer from a lack of timeliness. When each and every learner is aware of the goals of learning and what success looks like, it is possible to develop learners' capacity to feed up, feedback and feed forward to themselves and their peers. Supporting students to give, receive and use feedback develops their capacity as the owners of their own learning and is important to developing the skills and thinking required for self-regulation and collaboration (Wiliam, 2017).

Deconstructing the curriculum into learning intentions and success criteria does take some time to do effectively. The idea is to have year-level teaching teams collaboratively articulate sequences of success criteria that capture what they believe is important for students to know and be able to do from each content descriptor and its elaborations. The success criteria format is: I can [verb] [what teachers want students to know or be able to do]. For example, 'I can control a robot in play.' Once success criteria have been created, the learning intention (or intentions) around which the success criteria can be coherently collated should be clarified. Learning intentions should be articulated with this opening: 'We are learning to …' (Department of Education and Training, 2017, p. 13). Table 4.1 (p. 78) includes two examples of learning intentions and success criteria using these formats, created from deconstructed curriculum descriptors and elaborations.

Table 4.1: Two examples of curriculum deconstruction

Descriptor and elaborations	Learning intention and success criteria
Years F–2 Digital technologies – Knowledge and understanding: Digital systems Foundation: Recognise and explore digital systems (hardware and software) for a purpose (AC9TDIFK01) - recognising digital systems that they interact with at home and school, for example smartphone, laptop or programmable toy - playing with (with guidance) and using different digital systems to explore what they do for a purpose, for example the class speaking to an expert via videoconference - recording, with permission, audio or video of local community members' stories to share in class, for example sharing cultural stories of First Nations Australians - taking photos, with permission, to share with others, for example close-up photos of First Nations Australians' material culture, such as woven mats or baskets revealing intricate detail - making a model of a digital system, using it in a role-play scenario and describing its features, for example a cardboard box with a keyboard and screen with app icons. Year 1–2: Identify and explore digital systems and their components for a purpose (AC9TDI2K01) - exploring digital systems to better understand how they are used to provide communities with essential services, for example looking at the systems and components that allow First Nations Australians in communities classified as remote to watch their favourite television shows - naming and using digital systems that they interact with at home and school, for example using a touchpad to move the cursor on a laptop, or the keyboard to type a simple message on a tablet - using different digital systems to explore what they do and how to use them, for example selecting the camera icon allows them to take photos of things that are a familiar shape.	We are learning to recognise and use digital systems for a purpose. I can: - **connect** the major parts of a device – computer, iPad, phone - **take** a photo on my iPad to use during play - **control** a robot in play - **label** the major parts of a computer - **identify** the hardware and software I am using - **capture** data – image, video, audio - **upload** the captured data to Google Drive or camera roll - **use** the uploaded data in a presentation - **discuss** the hardware, software and peripheral devices I am using and how they are working together.
Year 4 Mathematics: Space Create and interpret grid reference systems using grid references and directions to locate and describe positions and pathways (AC9M4SP02) - interpreting a grid reference map of a familiar location of interest, such as a map of the showgrounds, a food festival, a botanical garden, a park in the local area or a train station, and writing instructions using grid references for a friend to find them at a specified location - recognising that a spreadsheet uses a grid reference system, locating and entering data in cells and using a spreadsheet to record data collected through observations or experiments - comparing and contrasting, describing and locating landmarks, people or things in a bird's eye picture of a busy scene, such as people in a park, initially without a transparent grid reference system overlaid on the picture, and then with the grid overlaid; noticing how the grid helps to pinpoint things quickly and easily - using different sized grids as a tool to enlarge an image or artwork.	We are learning to create a grid reference map using scale, legends and directions so we can interpret places and positions of objects in the map of our classroom. I can: - **draw** and **label** different areas in the classroom - **locate** classroom objects (e.g. desks, chairs) on a map - **create** a legend (key) - **interpret** the location of objects and places using the completed map.

Source: Adapted from ACARA (n.d.-k, -n)

Most teachers can use Bloom's taxonomy verbs to generate success criteria with little effort (Anderson et al., 2001). To be consistent with the given curriculum descriptors and elaborations, the success criteria sampled in the first deconstruction in table 4.1 features mostly lower-order verbs from Bloom's taxonomy, while two higher-order verbs were used in the Year 4 deconstruction. A more rigorous and evidence-based approach would be to use SOLO (structure of observed learning outcomes) taxonomy verbs that represent a model for progressive levels of complexity, quality and understanding (Biggs & Collis, 1982). The process of developing learning intentions and success criteria is non-linear and involves discussions and refinement. It is an iterative process in which teachers make sense of what curriculum descriptors and elaborations are asking, what learning could look like for students and what success criteria are necessary and sufficient to address each descriptor.

Recognising that many teachers do not necessarily have the background in digital technologies to be able to effectively make sense of or deconstruct the curriculum, the Australian Government created the Digital Technologies Hub (www.digitaltechnologieshub.edu.au) to provide teaching teams with scope and sequence learning plans for standalone digital technology units from Foundation to Year 10. Each learning plan includes a key focus, what to teach, supporting resources and assessment advice, and a deconstruction of the content descriptors and elaborations using the SOLO taxonomy. One of the great features of the deconstructed descriptors collected on the Digital Technologies Hub is that the link to the ways of thinking (computational, design and systems) is identified.

Table 4.2 is an example curriculum deconstruction for a full transdisciplinary STEM unit. The unit originally existed as a Year 5/6 science unit in which students created a sundial to explain why earth experiences day and night, and was redesigned as a STEM unit with the inclusion of mathematics: measurement, digital technologies: knowledge and understanding, and design and technologies: processes and production skills. An interesting feature of this deconstruction is the inclusion of a column that has teachers list the potential misconceptions, misunderstandings or roadblocks to learning that students commonly have when learning about particular descriptors or concepts. When students learn a new concept, they often have pre-existing beliefs, assumptions or misconceptions that could interfere with their capacity to learn. By noting these, teachers can design specific success criteria and embed classroom discussion and questioning to ensure that such misconceptions and roadblocks are cleared up and removed as a barrier to learning. Such conceptual change processes have been shown to have a large positive effect on student learning in a number of curriculum areas (Kennedy, 2018).

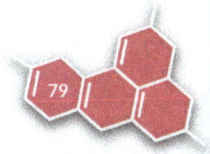

Table 4.2: Sample curriculum deconstruction for a Year 5/6 transdisciplinary STEM unit

Unit: Earth and space sciences STEM **Year:** 5/6 **Term:** 3 **Week:** 9		
Descriptor and elaborations	**Potential misconceptions and roadblocks to learning**	**Learning intentions and success criteria**
Year 6 Science: Science inquiry – questioning and predicting Pose investigable questions to identify patterns and test relationships and make reasoned predictions (AC9S6I01): • posing investigable questions to identify patterns, such as: 'What type of material is the best conductor and what is the best insulator?' • posing investigable questions to test relationships, such as: 'Will more salt dissolve in warm water than in cold water?' • discussing and refining questions to enable scientific investigation • making reasoned predictions about the physical conditions that will result in the largest mould colonies growing on bread • making reasoned predictions about electrical circuit function based on a picture or diagram of a circuit.	• Students are unable to identify research questions independently. • Students are reluctant to research things that they are naturally curious about. • The predictions students make are the truth.	We are learning to investigate scientifically and make reasoned predictions so we can explain why earth has regular changes such as day and night. I can: • identify investigable questions that 'I wonder' about night and day (or earth's rotation) • write a list of investigable questions with others that we want to research • discuss and select questions to research • make reasoned predictions about the answers to our selected questions • discuss the validity of the predictions using my prior knowledge.

First steps in planning transdisciplinary STEM units

Year 6 Science: Science understanding – earth and space sciences Describe the movement of Earth and other planets relative to the sun and model how Earth's tilt, rotation on its axis and revolution around the sun relate to cyclic observable phenomena, including variable day and night length (AC9S6U02): • exploring simulations of the solar system such as a pocket solar system to appreciate the distances and relationships between the sun and planets • recognising the role of gravity in keeping the planets in orbit around the sun • using 3D models or role-play to model how earth's rotation on its axis causes day and night • using virtual simulations or real-time views of earth from space to explore why different regions on earth, such as the South Pole, experience long periods of sunlight or darkness over the cycle of one revolution of earth around the sun • using 3D models to explore how the tilt of earth points one hemisphere towards the sun and the other away at different times of the year, and predicting how this affects the amount of sunlight on the surface of different regions on earth • researching First Nations Australians' understandings of the night sky and its use for timekeeping purposes as evidenced in oral cultural records, rock paintings, paintings and stone arrangements.	• The sun shines during the day and the moon shines at night. • The sun and the moon are on different sides of the earth and the earth rotates facing one and then the other. • The sun goes around the earth. • The sun moves to cause day and night. • A day is the time it takes the earth to move around the sun. • A day is the time it takes for the sun to move around the earth. • Night occurs when the moon covers the sun. • Night occurs when clouds cover the sun.	We are learning to explain why earth has regular changes such as day and night. I can: • ==define== what rotation means • ==demonstrate== rotation through role-play • ==research== the answers to our 'I wonder' questions • ==model== three different-sized balls to ==explain== how they appear similar in size • ==create== a model of earth and sun (complete with axis, based on research) • ==discuss== the relative sizes and movement of the sun and Earth • ==demonstrate== the effect of Earth's rotation • ==refine== my model to include the moon • ==discuss== the relative size and movement of the moon • ==create== a booklet about my investigation • ==discuss== how Aboriginal and Torres Strait Islander peoples explained earth's regular changes.
Year 6 Science: Science inquiry – planning and conducting Use equipment to observe, measure and record data with reasonable precision, using digital tools as appropriate (AC9S6I03): • selecting and using instruments with the correct scale for measuring data with appropriate accuracy, such as a multimeter • recording data in tables and diagrams or electronically as digital images and spreadsheets • discussing why precision is important in measurement, and the possible effect of low precision on investigation findings • recording data using standard units, such as volt, ampere, gram, second and metre, and developing the use of standard prefixes for metric units such as kilo- and milli- • using digital tools such as digital thermometers or soil moisture probes to collect data over time and record data in spreadsheets.	• Students don't know how to record their observations accurately. • Students don't include units of measurement in their recordings. • Students don't make repeat measurements of observations.	We are learning to construct a sundial, and make and record our observations accurately and with precision. I can: • ==monitor== the shadow created by the sun • ==create== a sundial • ==use== the provided table to ==collect== data (length in centimetres and time location) • ==make repeated measurements== as I collect data • ==discuss== why precision is important to my measurements • ==include== the appropriate units of measurement in my table • ==observe and draw== the patterns made by shadows.

Continued ...

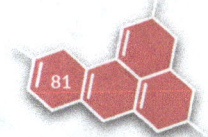

Descriptor and elaborations	Potential misconceptions and roadblocks to learning	Learning intentions and success criteria
Year 6 Science: Science inquiry – processing, modelling and analysing Construct and use appropriate representations, including tables, graphs and visual or physical models, to organise and process data and information and describe patterns, trends and relationships (AC9S6I04): - exploring how different representations can be used to show different aspects of relationships, processes and trends - representing circuits using virtual simulations or circuit diagrams and indicating the direction of electricity flow - using line graphs to show changes in growth over time under different physical conditions - developing a physical model of the sun and earth using objects or role-play to describe their relative positions when a place on earth is in day or night - organising information in graphic organisers to describe patterns and trends. **Years 4 Digital technologies: Knowledge and understanding – data representation** Recognise different types of data and explore how the same data can be represented differently depending on the purpose (AC9TDI4K03): - describing different types of data and how they can be used, for example numbers, letters, symbols and pictures - explaining how the same data can be represented in different ways and why some representations are better than others in certain contexts, for example four vs 4 vs IV vs |||| vs quatre, and that numerals are better for calculation than words - explaining that the same information can be represented differently, for example the term *stop* can also be represented with an octagon-shaped red sign or a hand icon - identifying rock paintings and other cultural expressions to understand that images are used to encode and represent ethnobotanical knowledge, for example the representation of plant use in the Kimberley cave paintings and ancient engravings including important data on medicinal and food plant classification and their usable parts. *Note: consolidation and transfer of Year 4 data representation content descriptor*	- Students don't realise that data can be categorised. - Students don't know how to use Excel. - Students don't know how to identify patterns or trends.	We are learning to represent and use data appropriately in a range of different ways. **Science** I can: - identify the different categories my data can be organised into - accurately arrange my data in a table with appropriate columns and rows - enter my collected data into an Excel spreadsheet. **Computational thinking** I can: - accurately organise data in Excel - use the organised data to generate a chart/graph - use Excel to order my data in different ways for different purposes. **Computational and design thinking** I can: - discuss the patterns I notice in my data - represent the same data in a range of different ways and justify selecting one particular way over others - create a presentation that explains my investigation and explains why earth has regular changes such as day and night.

First steps in planning transdisciplinary STEM units

Year 5 Mathematics: Measurement **Choose appropriate metric units when measuring the length, mass and capacity of objects; use smaller units or a combination of units to obtain a more accurate measure (AC9M5M01):** - recognising that some units of measurement are better suited to some tasks than others; for example, kilometres are more appropriate than metres to measure the distance between two towns - deciding on the unit required to estimate the amount of paint or carpet for a room or a whole building; justifying the choice of unit in relation to the context and the degree of accuracy required - measuring and comparing distances, such as jumps or throws using a metre length of string; for example, then measuring the part metre with centimetres and/or millimetres; explaining which unit of measure is most accurate. **Solve practical problems involving the perimeter and area of regular and irregular shapes using appropriate metric units (AC9M5M02):** - investigating problem situations involving perimeter; for example, 'How many metres of fencing are required around a paddock, or around a festival event?' - using efficient ways to calculate the perimeters of rectangles, such as adding the length and width together and doubling the result - solving measurement problems, such as 'How much carpet would be needed to cover the entire floor of the classroom', using square metre templates to directly measure the floor space - creating a model of a permaculture garden, dividing the area up to provide the most efficient use of space for gardens and walkways, labelling the measure of each area, and calculating the amount of resources needed; for example, compost to cover the vegetable garden. **Estimate, construct and measure angles in degrees, using appropriate tools including a protractor, and relate these measures to angle names (AC9M5M04):** - using a protractor to measure angles in degrees and classifying these angles using angle names; for example, an acute angle is less than 90°, an obtuse angle is more than 90° and less than 180°, a right angle is equal to 90° and a reflex angle is more than 180° and less than 360° - estimating the size of angles in the environment using a clinometer and describing the angles using angle names - using a ruler and protractor to construct triangles, given the angle measures and side lengths - using a protractor to measure angles when creating a pattern or string design within a circle.	- Students don't measure accurately. - Students use inconsistent units of measurement. - Students choose an inappropriate metric unit when measuring. - Students don't know the relationships between length, perimeter and area. - Students struggle with working out the perimeter and area of irregular shapes. - Students don't know how to use a protractor. - Students struggle to estimate and construct angles in practical problems.	*These descriptors will be addressed throughout the unit and will be consolidated through the creation of the earth–moon–sun model and the sundial activity.*

Continued ...

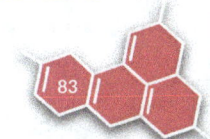

Igniting STEM Learning

Descriptor and elaborations	Potential misconceptions and roadblocks to learning	Learning intentions and success criteria
Years 5/6 Design and technologies: Processes and production skills – investigating and defining Investigate needs or opportunities for designing, and the materials, components, tools, equipment and processes needed to create designed solutions (AC9TDE6P01): - investigating the importance of complementary parts of working systems by deconstructing the components, structure and purpose of products, services or environments, for example labelling a diagram of a robotic weeder or vacuum cleaner and explaining the function of parts - testing a range of materials, components, tools and equipment to determine the appropriate technologies needed to make products, services or environments, for example the materials for a product such as a rubber-band-powered vehicle or item of protective clothing.	- Students do not follow the design process when developing the earth–moon–sun model or the sundial and so the quality of their products is poor. - Students use materials that they know or find easiest without testing what might be suitable. - Students don't create detailed drawings of their design prior to building a model.	We are learning to follow the design process as we create the earth–moon–sun model and the sundial. **Investigating and defining** I can: - **test** a range of materials I could use to build the model/sundial - **select** the materials I am going to use - **explain** why these materials are suitable - **test** a range of techniques and tools that could be used to build the model/sundial - **explain** the techniques and tools that will be used and why they are suitable.
Years 5/6 Design and technologies: Processes and production skills – generating and designing Generate, iterate and communicate design ideas, decisions and processes using technical terms and graphical representation techniques, including using digital tools (AC9TDE6P02): - generating a range of design ideas for products, services or environments using prior knowledge, skills and research, for example a security system for a community garden, a product made from a repurposed item of clothing, a permaculture vegetable patch or a healthy meal for a family picnic - representing and communicating design ideas using modelling and drawing standards including the use of digital tools, for example including scale, symbols and codes in plans and diagrams; using pictorial maps and aerial views; and using digital mapping applications or infographics to present research and ideas to others - developing and using models to iterate and improve design ideas, for example using modelling applications to design the layout and features of an enclosure for a chosen animal.	- Students don't evaluate their designs and use the feedback to improve their designs. - Students don't plan or manage their time. - Students think that making something once is enough and don't refine their products. - Students think they should get it right the first time.	**Generating and designing** I can: - **draw** a range of possible model/sundial designs - **label** each possible model/sundial design showing the pros and cons of each design - **create** a labelled and scaled drawing of the chosen model/sundial - **annotate** the drawing to explain its features - **modify** the drawing based on feedback.

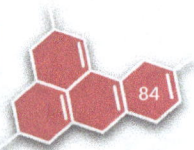

First steps in planning transdisciplinary STEM units

Years 5/6 Design and technologies: Processes and production skills – producing and implementing Select and use suitable materials, components, tools, equipment and techniques to safely make designed solutions (AC9TDE6P03): - matching material and joining techniques to the design intention, for example accurately and safely cutting and sewing the fabric pieces to make a community banner or joining components to produce an electric circuit - choosing appropriate materials, tools, equipment and techniques for a specific purpose, for example when safely and hygienically preparing food, cultivating garden beds or constructing electronic products.		**Producing** I can: - ==safely use== the appropriate tools to make a model/sundial - ==accurately measure and make== each aspect of a model/sundial - ==work cooperatively== with others to build the model/sundial.
Years 5/6 Design and technologies: Processes and production skills – evaluating Negotiate design criteria including sustainability to evaluate design ideas, processes and solutions (AC9TDE6P04): - deciding on design criteria collaboratively for a designed solution, for example including an environmental sustainability criterion such as product should be recyclable - iterating and modifying design ideas based on evaluation to improve solutions, for example modifying the sensitivity of sensors in the design of an automated light.		**Evaluating** I can: - ==collaboratively identify== design criteria for the model/sundial - ==evaluate and improve== the design based on feedback.
Years 5/6 Design and technologies: Processes and production skills – collaborating and managing Develop project plans that include consideration of resources to individually and collaboratively make designed solutions (AC9TDE6P05): - setting milestones for production processes and allocating roles to team members, for example using a cloud-based or server-based document or spreadsheet to list tasks, deadlines and roles for team members working on a project collaboratively, including setting document sharing permissions with selected people - identifying the human resources, materials, tools and equipment that will be needed to make the designed solution as part of the project plan and specifying when these will be needed, for example access to a wildlife expert at the planning stage and scheduling access to shared tools when building a habitat for local animals - planning production steps needed to produce a product, service or environment using digital tools, for example making a flow chart or using a digital planner to record the sequence of tasks and deadlines needed to complete a project.		**Collaborating and managing** I can: - ==list== the sequence of steps to take to make the model/sundial - ==set== milestones for the production of the model/sundial - ==allocate== roles for each team member - ==identify== what materials, tools and equipment are needed to make the model/sundial - ==manage== time to produce the model/sundial on time.

Source: Adapted from ACARA (n.d.-k, -m, -q, -r)

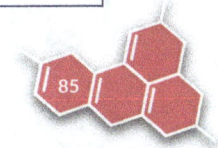

Igniting STEM Learning

Exercise: Deconstruct the curriculum

Building on the work completed in the second curriculum mapping exercise in Chapter 3 (page 69), as a teaching team use the following steps and template to deconstruct the curriculum in the style of the sample shown in table 4.2 (page 80; more samples are available via the downloadables).

1. In the first column enter each descriptor and all its elaborations using your state or the national curriculum. While there is no intent that teachers deliver each and every elaboration they should be included to support the professional discussions and thinking during the process of developing clear learning intentions and success criteria.
2. Identify any potential misconceptions, misunderstandings or roadblocks to learning that students commonly have when learning about this particular descriptor or concept.
3. Articulate a sequence of success criteria (use the sentence starter 'I can' followed by an appropriate verb) and then the learning intention(s) (use the sentence starter 'We are learning to') that captures what the teaching team believe it is important for the students to know and or able to do from the information in columns one and two.
4. The final column provides space for teachers to not only capture the activities they already run that address the learning intentions and success criteria but also brainstorm other possible activities that could address them. This column could be used to collect all the possible great activities that could be run and even could contain hyperlinks or the interschool folder names where the activities may be found. It is included in the template since teachers automatically tend to think of activities as they generate the success criteria.

Unit:
Year:
Term:
Week(s):

Descriptor and elaborations	Potential misconceptions and roadblocks to learning	Learning intentions and success criteria

Reproducible available

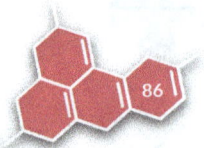

STEP 2: CREATE A LOGICAL SEQUENCE OF KEY UNDERSTANDINGS AND ESSENTIAL QUESTIONS

An oft-heard refrain from students is 'Why are we learning this?' – and teachers often reply, 'Because it is in the curriculum!' While this is an accurate response, it isn't necessarily a useful one.

Learning that is perceived by students as intrinsically purposeful is a factor in developing them to have a mastery goal orientation and growing their capacity to be highly capable learners. This leads students to try and learn new skills and to be task and learning focused, and supports the development of intrinsic motivation and self-efficacy (Carpenter, 2007). When learning devolves into delivering on a task or an assessment to receive an external reward such as a grade or approval by others, the environment is one of performance or goal orientation, with students focusing on the end goal rather than the learning (Ames & Archer, 1988). As Hattie and Donoghue (2016) highlight, 'when students learn how to gain an overall picture of what is to be learnt, have an understanding of the success criteria for the lessons to come and are somewhat clear at the outset about what it means to master the lessons, then their subsequent learning is maximised' (p. 6). It is therefore important for teachers to develop learning that is purposeful to students.

This is the purpose of developing a logical sequence of key understandings. The understandings teachers typically create are often a hotchpotch of unconnected ideas that they would like students to gain from participating in the learning. However, by going through the process of defining a logical sequence of understandings, teachers will be required to think deeply and create an authentic, thoughtful purpose for engaging with the curriculum. The understandings should reach through to students' existing understandings and motivations and become a factor in providing them with a 'why', a purpose for learning.

There are three other benefits of defining a logical sequence of key understandings. First, it becomes much easier to develop essential or big questions that will drive learning. Second, the sequence of understandings creates a logical guide for the teaching program and allows the linkage of concepts across multiple curriculum areas. Finally, the summative assessment (or culminating assessment task for the unit) arises from the learners applying their knowledge, skill and thinking in responding to the final (or overall goal) understanding in the sequence.

CREATING A LOGICAL SEQUENCE OF KEY UNDERSTANDINGS

Table 4.3 (page 88) is an example of a logical sequence of key understandings for a standalone Year 5 science unit. This unit addresses the Year 5 chemical sciences content descriptor (AC9S5U04) and the Year 5 'Science as a human endeavour' aspect of 'Nature and development of science' (AC9S5H01), and consolidates specific 'Science inquiry skills' (AC9S5I01, AC9S5I02, AC9S5I04, AC9S5I05, AC9S5I06; ACARA, n.d.-m).

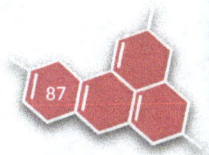

Igniting STEM Learning

Table 4.3: Sample logical sequence of key understandings for Year 5 science unit

Learning intention and success criteria	Key understandings
We are learning to use the scientific method to discuss how scientific theories change and improve over time.	
▪ I can draw diagrams of the different states of substances. ▪ I can describe the observable characteristics of the states of matter.	We use observation to create scientific theories.
▪ I can show evidence that gases have mass and take up space. ▪ I can explain how and why different substances change with heating and cooling.	Theories must be able to be tested.
▪ I can explain why not all substances act consistent with the observable characteristics we identified.	Scientific theories change and improve when new evidence contradicts the theories.

The first key understanding given in table 4.3 is quite general as this is often the stage in which teachers begin 'tuning in' the students to a topic. This key understanding enables teachers and students to discuss prior knowledge and explore how scientific theories often begin with individuals observing particular events and phenomena and trying to explain why they occur. Though it is linked to two success criteria that focus on observations already, the teacher might add further success criteria such as 'I can discuss how Aboriginal and Torres Strait Islander peoples used their stories to explain the world', 'I can explain how Aboriginal and Torres Strait Islander peoples used observation of the night sky to assist with navigation' and 'I can explain how observations lead to scientific theories'. These additional success criteria will ensure that the learning is framed inside the broader context of the scientific method.

The second key understanding logically follows and builds on the first. Once students recognise and understand that scientific theories arise from individuals, no matter the culture, trying to explain why particular events and phenomena occur, then their teacher can highlight the requirement of a fair test and have students plan and conduct experiments. In this way, the 'Science inquiry skills' and even the mathematics curriculum – for example, 'plan and conduct statistical investigations by posing questions or identifying a problem and collecting relevant data; choose appropriate displays and interpret the data; communicate findings within the context of the investigation' (AC9M5ST03; ACARA, n.d.-k) – can be addressed in a coherent and purposeful way. During this part of the unit, students could perform a range of experiments, gather evidence, visualise and interpret it, and come up with scientific explanations. This would consolidate their understanding of science inquiry skills while addressing chemical science content.

The final key understanding in this example brings the sequence to a logical conclusion and highlights the purpose of learning in this unit: as new evidence becomes available, new theories are created to better explain all the gathered evidence. In addition to being a fundamental truth of how science works, this can be used as a springboard into a scientific investigation where students create experiments to test their theories on other substances and accomplish most of the Year 5 achievement standard.

Designing the sequence of key understandings to progress logically in this way makes learning much more engaging and transferable for students because it supports them to understand the world around them. For teachers, the learning shifts its focus from the chemical science content to the scientific method using the chemical science content as an example. Unsurprisingly this

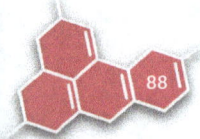

First steps in planning transdisciplinary STEM units

sequence of understandings can be used to frame other science and transdisciplinary STEM units. The sequence of understandings approach also supports the creation of activities that will take students through the acquiring, consolidating and transfer stages of learning.

Creating a logical sequence of understandings for a transdisciplinary STEM unit requires teachers to be much clearer about what they really want students to understand from the unit. Table 4.4 shows one possible logical sequence of key understandings for the Year 3/4 earth and space sciences unit featured in table 4.2 (page 80). In this transdisciplinary situation, the teachers used only the learning intentions (not success criteria) to design their sequence of key understandings. This sequence emphasises a logical progression of big-picture thinking and processes with the transdisciplinary curriculum knowledge acting as the vehicle for the learning. The understandings highlight the importance of students learning the scientific method and the design process as strategies for explaining the world around them. The teachers were then able to authentically link the assessment tasks they had in mind to create a purposeful unit.

Table 4.4: Sample logical sequence of key understandings for a Year 5/6 transdisciplinary STEM unit

Learning intention and success criteria	Key understandings
We are learning to investigate scientifically and make reasoned predictions so we can explain why earth has regular changes such as day and night.	1. Humanity has been observing and attempting to explain the world around us since ancient times. 2. This led to the development of the scientific method as a rigorous way of explaining the reasons for changes in the world.
We are learning to explain why earth has regular changes such as day and night.	3. The scientific method can be used investigate and explain why earth has regular changes such as day and night.
We are learning to construct a sundial and make and record our observations accurately and with precision.	4. We can use the design process to create high quality models and experiments to find evidence to support our explanations.
We are learning to represent and use data appropriately in a range of different ways. We are learning to follow the design process as we create the earth-moon-sun model and the sundial.	5. The more we understand the scientific method and the design process the better we can explain the world around us. **Culminating assessment task:** Students will use the design process to build an earth-moon-sun model and a sundial so they can learn the scientific method and begin to explain the world around them.

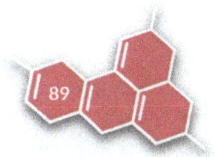

Exercise: A logical sequence of key understandings

Using the learning intentions and success criteria that were created in the previous exercise (page 86) teaching teams should use the following template to create a logical sequence of understandings for their planned transdisciplinary unit. The backward-planning approach set out in these steps and the examples shown in tables 4.3 and 4.4 (pages 88 and 89) can be used to guide planning. Further examples can be found in the downloadables.

1. Start at the end and answer this question: 'What do I want the students to understand by the end of this unit?' Remember that this understanding highlights the purpose of learning in the unit.
2. Once this final understanding is articulated, consider what students need to understand if they are to achieve this final understanding by the end of the unit.
3. List sufficient key understandings that logically lead to the final understanding.
4. Review and refine the sequence of key understandings to ensure that they progress logically and are consistent in their use of language and any achievement standards.

This process requires teachers to grapple with what will be an authentic and meaningful sequence of learning for students. As in previous exercises, key understandings should be written in age-appropriate language.

Learning intention and success criteria	Key understandings
We are learning: • I can • I can • I can	

Reproducible available

DESIGNING QUESTIONS TO DRIVE LEARNING

Once the logical sequence of key understandings has been articulated, teachers should design questions related to these understandings. These classroom questions are 'instructional cues or stimuli that convey to students the content elements to be learned and directions for what they are to do and how they are to do it' (Cotton, 1988, p. 1). By designing questions related to the key understandings, teachers spur critical and creative thinking and support students to drive their own learning within the unit.

McTighe and Wiggin (2013) recommend that teachers design essential questions to 'stimulate thought, to provoke inquiry, and to spark more questions, including thoughtful student questions, not just pat answers' (p. 3). Their thinking is that by using essential questions as part of their pedagogical approaches, teachers signal to students that learning is more than simply acquiring

First steps in planning transdisciplinary STEM units

knowledge and skills; it is about making meaning. They propose that a question is essential if it meets the following seven defining characteristics:

1. *Is open-ended; that is, it typically will not have a single, final, and correct answer.*
2. *Is thought-provoking and intellectually engaging, often sparking discussion and debate.*
3. *Calls for higher-order thinking, such as analysis, inference, evaluation, prediction. It cannot be effectively answered by recall alone.*
4. *Points toward important, transferable ideas within (and sometimes across) disciplines.*
5. *Raises additional questions and sparks further inquiry.*
6. *Requires support and justification, not just an answer.*
7. *Recurs over time; that is, the question can and should be revisited again and again. (McTighe & Wiggins, 2013, p. 3)*

The International Baccalaureate® Middle Years Programme takes a different approach, suggesting that teachers create three levels of questions: factual, conceptual and debatable (International Baccalaureate Organization, 2014). Factual questions encourage recall and comprehension and are focused on knowledge, evidence and skill. They tend to be seeking a specific answer (a single one or a range) and often start with *what* or *which*. Conceptual questions encourage analysis and application and are focused on exploring the big ideas that connect facts and topics as well as contradictions. They can look at the relationships between elements and are phrased as open-ended questions which often have multiple correct answers. Conceptual questions might start with *how might* or *why would*. Debatable questions encourage synthesis and evaluation by having students discuss and explore significant ideas and issues from multiple perspectives. These questions may start with *to what extent, do, is, should* and so on, and may result in opinions being formed or judgments being made.

My recommendation is that teachers be guided by both approaches as part of preparing to lead the learning that will occur. As Kathleen Cotton (1988) points out, when teachers plan for and employ higher cognitive questioning with an increase in waiting time, there are a range of benefits, including students developing greater interest and motivation to become actively involved in lessons. Students also develop critical thinking skills and inquiring attitudes, which allow them to have insights into the relationships between concepts and content. It also stimulates students to pursue knowledge on their own. Guided by this, table 4.5 (page 92) lists possible questions that could be generated to support the key understandings shown in table 4.3 (page 88) for a Year 5 science unit.

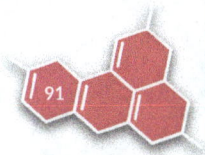

Table 4.5: Possible questions for a Year 5 science unit

1. We use observation to create scientific theories.
    • Factual: What is the definition of a theory?
    • Factual: What is the process that scientists go through as they come up with a theory?
    • Conceptual: Why is it important to understand how matter changes state?
    • Debatable: Are observations necessary to create a scientific theory?
2. Theories must be able to be tested.
    • Factual: What features make a theory useful?
    • Factual: What makes a test valid?
    • Conceptual: How do they prove that their theory is valid?
    • Debatable: Should theories be testable to be accepted?
3. Scientific theories change and improve when new evidence contradicts the theories.
    • Factual: What happens to scientific theories when new evidence becomes available?
    • Conceptual: How do we know whether a scientific theory is valid or not?
    • Debatable: To what extent do scientific theories change over time?
Essential question: How is the scientific method similar or different to superstition?

The aim is not to create perfect questions, but to design questions that provoke thinking and challenge students to unpack the understanding. Once the factual, conceptual and debatable questions have been articulated, an overarching essential question should be much easier to propose.

> ### Exercise: Questions to drive learning
>
> For each key understanding, design a series of factual, conceptual and debatable questions. Be sure to think about questions that will:
> - provoke students to think more deeply about the understanding in question
> - encourage students to recall and connect facts and topics
> - have students justify an opinion.
>
> Once these questions have been articulated, propose an overarching essential question for the unit.

SPECULATING ON CULMINATING ASSESSMENT TASKS

As I've mentioned, one of the benefits of creating a logical sequence of key understandings is that it becomes easier to speculate on possible culminating rich tasks. The culmination of learning should be where the students demonstrate they have gained the knowledge, skills and thinking by applying what they have learned to a real-world task arising from the final (or overall goal) understanding in the sequence.

Table 4.6 features eight sample sequences of key understandings for units from Foundation to Year 6. Each includes an example of a culminating rich task that is linked to the final key understanding.

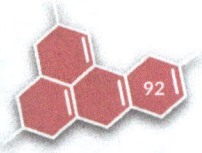

First steps in planning transdisciplinary STEM units

Table 4.6: Sequences of key understandings and possible culminating tasks

Foundation transdisciplinary STEM unit (science, literacy, numeracy, digital technologies)	Year 1 transdisciplinary STEM unit (HASS, digital technologies, health and PE)
1. Things can be sorted based on certain attributes. 2. We can sort things in our world into living, non-living, and once living. 3. Living things have certain attributes necessary for their survival. 4. Living things use these attributes and their environment to survive. **Culminating assessment task:** Students create a garden bed environment where local living things can thrive.	1. The food we consume comes from a variety of sources. 2. The food undergoes different processes on its journey to your home. 3. These processes have an impact on the environment, the food quality, and the nutrition of food, and these processes have changed over time. 4. To make good and responsible choices about what and how we consume, we need to understand where our food comes from and what processes it goes through. **Culminating assessment task:** Students create skits that show how to make responsible food choices.
Years 1/2 transdisciplinary unit (literacy, HASS, science)	**Year 3/4 transdisciplinary STEM unit** (music, HASS, general capabilities)
1. Stories, dance and artwork communicate messages. 2. We all have our own stories which communicate messages. 3. These shared stories make up our culture. 4. We can communicate our messages through art, stories and dance. **Culminating assessment task:** Students communicate a message through storytelling using art, dance or another medium.	1. Music has the power to stimulate strong emotions and tell stories. 2. Pitch, tone and tempo produced by different instruments are used to set scenes and create different feelings and emotions. 3. There is a process that composers go through to use music to tell stories and create particular emotions. 4. As musicians and composers the more we understand how music causes emotions and the process which composers use the more we can use music to communicate stories and evoke emotions and feelings. **Culminating assessment task:** Students create a soundtrack to a storybook for Foundation students.
Year 4 mathematics unit (digital technologies – data representation, numeracy, digital literacy, mathematics)	**Years 4–6 transdisciplinary STEM unit** (design and technologies, science, critical and creative thinking capability)
1. We base many of our decisions on data. 2. We can represent data in different ways. 3. Some ways of representing data are easier to interpret and use than others. 4. Being able to represent and interpret data is important because we then can make informed decisions. **Culminating assessment task:** Students use data to make an informed decision about mobile phone plans.	1. Engineering is used to solve real-world problems and build our future. 2. Engineers use science combined with the design process to solve problems and create new designs that benefit humanity. 3. As part of the design process engineers test their ideas cheaply and quickly by making prototypes using a variety of materials and techniques. 4. The more we understand the design process and how to prototype our ideas, the more effective we will be at solving problems. **Culminating assessment task:** Students use science and the design process to solve a real-world problem.

Continued ...

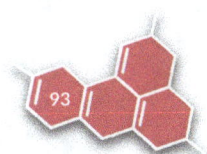

Igniting STEM Learning

Year 5 transdisciplinary STEM unit (technologies, physical science, mathematics)	Year 6 transdisciplinary STEM unit (HASS, mathematics, English, digital technologies – data representation)
1. Inventors and designers recognise what needs development. 2. They then identify the key criteria to address their design ideas. 3. They follow the design process to achieve their goals. 4. The first step of the design process is to investigate and design to meet a brief. 5. The second step is to use tools and techniques safely to produce and modify your design. 6. The final step is to evaluate and modify your product until it meets the brief. 7. There is a process that inventors and designers go through to have ideas become reality. **Culminating assessment task:** Students design and build a robot that can go through an obstacle course using light sensors.	1. Geographically, Australia is a close neighbour to the Asian region. 2. Australia and Asia have many interconnections – trade, tourism, aid, education, migration and environment. 3. Australia is a nation of migrants from Asia and the rest of the world. 4. Some migrants have come by choice and some have been forced to migrate to survive. 5. Our perception of migrants and refugees is influenced strongly by the media – positively and negatively. 6. Regardless of how migrants came to Australia, and their perception in the media, they have positively contributed to the Australian lifestyle, economy and social development. **Culminating assessment task:** Students create an expo that showcases the positive impact of migration to Australia.

Exercise: Culminating assessment tasks

Using the learning intentions, sequence of key understandings and the questions that have been generated through the exercises in this chapter, speculate on possible culminating assessment tasks. The goal is to come up with a range of possible options that will have students apply the knowledge, skills and thinking they have acquired during the unit.

At this stage of planning, this is purely a brainstorming exercise. Chapters 5 and 6 will provide more information about designing the appropriate level of culminating assessment tasks.

COACHING ON THE FIRST STAGE OF BACKWARD PLANNING

As with learning any new skill, teaching teams will generally find the first few times they go through these processes – of identifying the learning intentions and success criteria, articulating a logical sequence of key understandings, generating a range of questions and speculating on possible culminating assessment tasks – to be time-consuming and challenging. The processes demand that the teachers develop their capacity in thinking and planning function in ways that, though quite automatic to computational, design and system thinkers, may not be normal to them.

The Stage 1 backward-planning processes help teachers consolidate their capacity in the computational thinking skills of decomposition, pattern recognition and abstraction. The processes also require teachers to think about the bigger, systemic learning picture and how curriculum knowledge can be used as a vehicle for students to think about the interrelatedness of ideas and concepts beyond just the knowledge content. Over time, and with practice, teachers will become more skilled and find the processes easier and quicker.

The most effective way of approaching the two steps detailed in the first stage of backward planning is iterating through the processes multiple times. A first draft of the learning intentions and success criteria gives teachers insight into the possible logical sequence of key understandings. As teachers become clearer about what they want students to understand, they also become clearer about what they want students to know and be able to do. This can lead teachers to refining the learning intentions and adding success criteria that they had not originally thought of. Each step informs the other, so teachers should iterate through both until they feel they have addressed not only what the curriculum requires but also the lasting understandings they want the students to gain. The clarity gained from these two steps sets teachers up for Stages 2 and 3 of the planning process and designing authentic assessment tasks, which will be addressed in greater detail in coming chapters.

KEY POINTS

- Backward design of curriculum typically involves identifying the learning destination, determining acceptable evidence and planning learning experiences and instructions. These three stages can be broken down further into a simplified planning process of six steps:
    1. Deconstruct the curriculum into learning intentions and success criteria.
    2. Create a logical sequence of key understandings and essential questions.
    3. Design the assessments or culminating rich task.
    4. Design formative assessment rubrics.
    5. Create a checklist of steps.
    6. Plan the learning experiences and instruction.
- The process of deconstructing the curriculum develops teachers' capacity in elements of computational thinking, provides clarity and direction for students and teachers, and allows for the development of a learning culture of systemic and effective feedback.
- Identifying any potential misconceptions or roadblocks to learning about a concept as part of the deconstruction process allows teachers to design success criteria and conceptual change learning that support students to overcome beliefs and assumptions that could interfere with their capacity to learn.
- Learning that is perceived as intrinsically purposeful by students is a factor in developing their goal orientation towards mastery and growing their capacity to be highly capable learners. This leads students to try and learn new skills and be task and learning focused and supports the development of intrinsic motivation and self-efficacy. This is the intent for developing a logical sequence of key understandings.
- Developing a logical sequence of key understandings makes it easier to develop essential questions that will drive learning, creates a logical flow for a teaching program, and supports the development of authentic culminating tasks related to the bigger picture understanding teachers want students to achieve.
- The iterative process of developing learning intentions, success criteria and a logical sequence of key understandings will become easier and quicker as the teachers become more skilled.

CHAPTER 5

Beginning small with bounded STEM projects

The man who moves a mountain begins by carrying away small stones.

Confucius

BEGINNING SMALL

Planning and running authentic STEM learning and projects is no small feat. Given the rigour of the approach that has been outlined so far, it would take an enormous investment of time for teachers to significantly redesign current rich tasks or create entirely new STEM assessment tasks. Teachers need to design, plan and lead STEM learning and projects while they themselves are in the midst of learning about the technologies curriculum, thinking frameworks and general capabilities, at the same time as assessing STEM learning and developing students to drive their own learning – all in addition to everything else they are responsible for day-to-day in a classroom. And teachers aren't the only ones on a learning journey; so are students. STEM learning and projects mostly fail because students do not have the necessary background knowledge or skill to meet task requirements. Lastly, school systems and processes aren't necessarily aligned to develop highly capable learners with a STEM mindset. Timetables, assessment requirements and the design of school reports are three examples of school structures that can either support or constrain STEM learning.

Given these factors, the best way to start embedding authentic STEM learning is to reshape already existing units so they include smaller STEM activities and tasks. I call these bounded STEM activities and projects because they have clearly defined outcomes, timelines and end points. The curriculum deconstruction work performed in the Chapter 4 will aid in this reshaping (illustrated in figure 5.1, page 98).

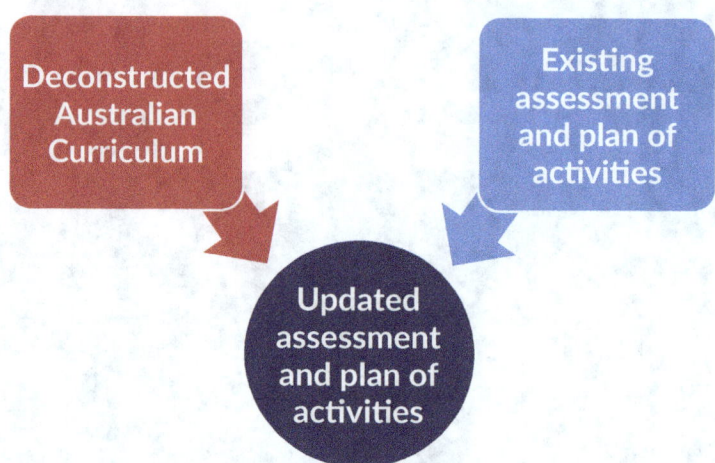

Figure 5.1: Enhancing existing learning plans and instruction

The primary benefit of this approach is that it lessens the planning work for teachers because they already have an existing teaching and learning plan to work from. As teachers enact the reshaped units they can go through an iterative prototype–test–evaluate process with the aim of learning what to focus on as they run activities; what is important and what is not; what to manage with students to ensure they achieve a desirable outcome; what to assess; how and when to let go so students own their learning; and how to build student confidence, thinking and skill. This first phase of embedding bounded STEM learning into existing units is fundamentally a 'learning by doing' phase. By beginning small, teachers and students can focus on acquiring and consolidating the knowledge, skills and thinking of STEM rather than necessarily producing a high-quality end product.

This chapter explores the thinking and planning process for creating bounded STEM learning and projects. It begins with a model of learning that can be used to guide teachers' thinking as they reshape or design the progression of STEM assessment tasks and learning activities across a year. This model of learning builds on the learning to drive metaphor discussed in Chapter 3 and will provide a context for designing and assessing learning. We also step through a backward-planning process supporting teachers to create smaller purposeful STEM tasks or bounded STEM projects that will enable students to acquire and consolidate their knowledge, skills and thinking. Finally, a two-stage planning process is outlined to assist teachers in designing learning activities and instruction while they support students to learn the design process and how to plan to achieve a goal.

CONCEPTUAL MODEL OF LEARNING

The designing of culminating rich STEM tasks and planning of learning activities and instruction must take into account that students will have different strengths and areas for development in their knowledge, skills and thinking and that their learning will progress with varying rates and paths (Ostroff, 2012). Teachers might normally approach this situation by differentiating the content, process and product (Tomlinson & Eidson, 2003). The challenge is that when the teacher is the driver of learning, the process of monitoring, managing and providing what each student needs at their individual phase of development is rather daunting and time-consuming. Unsurprisingly,

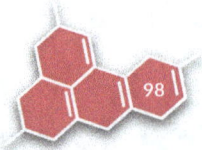

the strategies teachers typically use to differentiate for the large variance in student capacity in their classes has been shown to not always be effective (Berry, 2015; Griffin, 2012). However, the effectiveness of differentiation improves when teachers grow the capacity of students to drive of their own learning, take ownership of their learning and begin to self-differentiate (Tomlinson, 2008).

The conceptual model of learning proposed by Hattie and Donoghue in 2016 provides a useful tool for thinking about what students need at different stages of the learning process. In the model, shown in figure 5.2, each student begins the process of learning something new with a particular set of knowledge, skills and thinking (labelled skill), disposition to learning (will) and motivation to learn (thrill). Students will go through stages of acquisition and consolidation of new knowledge, skills and thinking as they progress through the phases from surface learning to deep learning and then to transfer. This progression of learning and knowing success influences each student's disposition and motivation to learn.

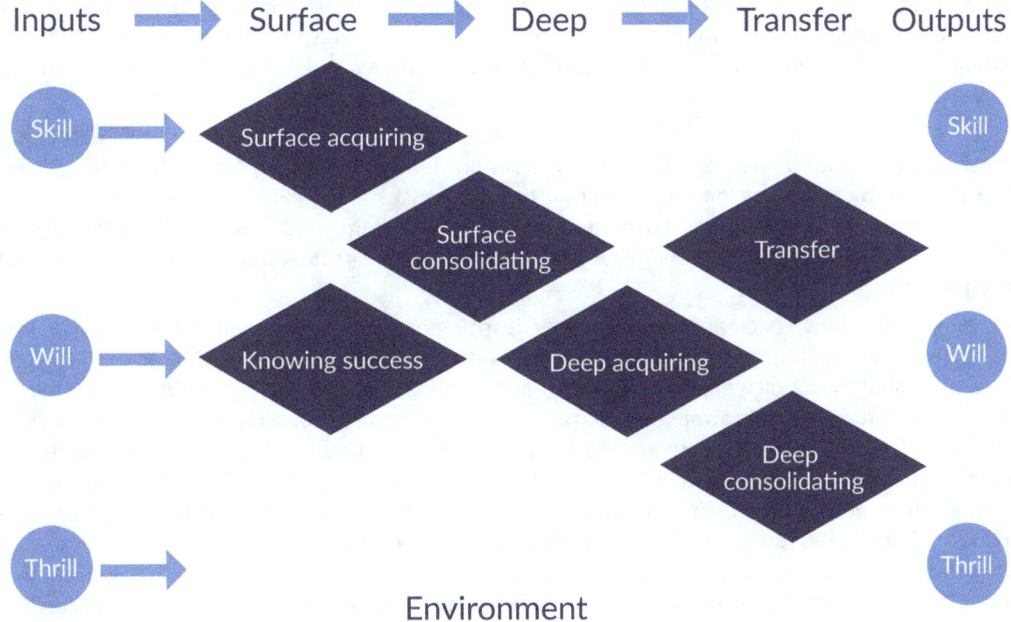

Figure 5.2: The conceptual model of learning
Source: Adapted from Hattie and Donoghue (2016)

Hattie and Donoghue's (2016) conceptual model of learning is consistent with the learning to drive metaphor established in Chapter 3 in that it provides the evidence base for the phases of learning that students go through to be able to drive their own learning. The conceptual model of learning can be used to guide teachers in the strategies they should use and the types of STEM activities and assessment tasks they should design as students move from the surface-learning phase to the deep-learning phase to transferring their learning to other situations and problems.

THREE PHASES OF LEARNING

During the surface-learning phase, in which students develop the capacity to encode new knowledge so it can be retrieved at appropriate moments, acquisition strategies can include learning the subject matter vocabulary as well as organising, summarising, underlining and taking notes of lesson content. Students can consolidate this knowledge through interleaved and deliberate practice while seeking, interpreting and using feedback to improve the accuracy and quality of their work.

To move students into the deep-learning phase, learning should focus on acquiring and consolidating metacognitive and self-regulation skills. Metacognition growth requires students to become aware of their strengths and areas for development around the subject knowledge, skills and thinking as well as what learning strategies they could use, and why and when to use those strategies (Schraw & Dennison, 1994). Growth in self-regulation involves students knowing how to plan, implement, monitor and evaluate the effectiveness of their learning strategies. Students should even know what to do when they do not know what to do (Hattie & Donoghue, 2016). During this phase, teachers should design learning and use pedagogy that deliberately has students learning from their peers and teaching one another, and involves a high level of self-regulation and critical thinking.

Transfer of learning occurs when students realise that the strategies they have learnt in a certain situation can be applied to a second situation. Teachers can support students to transfer their learning by engaging them in detecting the differences and similarities between situations and problems they have already encountered and new problems and situations (Marton, 2006). Hattie and Donoghue (2016) draw heavily from Marton in their understanding and placement of transfer within their model.

Learners will move back and forth between learning phases while acquiring and consolidating their knowledge, skills and thinking; for example, a learner might see the need to acquire specific surface vocabulary or skill while consolidating deep learning (Hattie & Donoghue, 2016). The model can also explain why certain strategies such as inquiry- and problem-based learning, which is where most transdisciplinary STEM learning falls, have such low effect sizes. Most inquiry- and problem-based learning would be situated in the deep-learning and transfer phases of the conceptual model because they require the application of deeply learned knowledge, skills and thinking. Schwartz and Bransford (1998) found that understanding something deeply requires a learner to have well-differentiated knowledge structure. Yet teachers often attempt inquiry- and problem-based learning before their students have sufficient content knowledge and skill to make connections. Further, Hattie (2017) points out that much of teacher practice appears to over-emphasise surface knowing to the detriment of deep learning. These findings imply that teachers need to be thoughtful in planning learning activities and strategies to more effectively take students through the phases of learning so that they have what they need to be successful in transdisciplinary STEM projects.

MOVING THROUGH THE PHASES OF LEARNING

To lay the appropriate foundation for the acquisition and consolidation of new knowledge and skill, a STEM learning unit should begin with students undergoing a diagnostic assessment of their current level of subject knowledge, skill and thinking. This enables teachers to establish appropriate routines and structures for interleaved retrieval and practice with the goal of developing students to be confident that they understand and value what they are learning. This could look like exploring and discussing the unit learning intentions, success criteria and any assessment rubrics so that students have a common understanding of what successful learning will look like. Not only will this build both surface and deeper understandings; it will also increase motivation and reduce possible anxiety (Hattie & Donoghue, 2016). Learning activities and feedback processes during the surface-learning phase should be mostly focused on developing the capacity of students to know what to and how to do it.

As students come to know what to do and how to do it, learning activities and associated formative feedback processes can shift beyond surface knowing and doing towards acquiring and consolidating deeper learning. At this stage, students should not only be expected to deliver quality products, but also be supported to think about and discuss the effectiveness of their learning strategies and relationships between ideas, and to grow their metacognitive capacity to adapt and learn. Learning activities should focus on students applying their learning. As they learn, students should be encouraged by their teachers to engage in productive failure, use feedback to revise their thinking and the learning strategies they are using, and make predictions of what could work in different contexts. The aim is to have students solve problems more efficiently, while acquiring more sophisticated understandings of the newly learned knowledge and skills, and any connections to their prior knowledge, skills and thinking.

PLANNING LEARNING THROUGH THE YEAR

As discussed alongside the curriculum mapping process in Chapter 3, STEM learning can be sequenced in a way that authentically takes students through the acquisition, consolidation and transfer stages of development. First shown in Chapter 3, the curriculum progression planning framework illustrated in figure 5.3 shows the type of STEM learning that would fit Hattie and Donoghue's (2016) conceptual model of learning.

Term 1 Surface acquire	Term 2 Surface acquire and consolidate	Term 3 Surface consolidate and deep acquire	Term 4 Deep consolidate and transfer
Me **Laying the foundation I** Establishing routines, norms, agreements and habitual practices Diagnostic assessment of knowledge, skill and thinking Building the base of knowledge and skill Curriculum focus: ourselves as learners and human beings	**We** **Laying the foundation II** Continuing to build the base of knowledge and skill Using activities and challenges with clear bounds to develop skill and capacity in applying the problem-solving/design process Curriculum focus: how we fit together in community and society	**Us** **Practising** Using more complex activities and challenges with clear bounds to develop skill and capacity in applying the problem-solving/design process Curriculum focus: our impact on the world and each other	**All** **Applying** Open-ended problems where students apply everything they have learnt to a task that has no solution Curriculum focus: what we create and build, and how that links together and connects our world

Figure 5.3: Curriculum progression planning framework

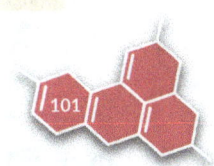

Igniting STEM Learning

Moving through this progression framework, STEM learning in Term 1 focuses on building the base of STEM knowledge, skill and thinking as teachers lay the foundation for an effective learning environment. Teachers should plan to run short, hands-on STEM activities so that students can iterate quickly through the design cycle and experience failure, feedback and success in a concrete and practical way. The goal is for students to begin to internalise the language, processes and strategies associated with the computational, design and systems thinking frameworks.

The marble run design brief shown in figure 5.4 is one such STEM activity. Simple to resource and quick to run, this activity is a great way to introduce the design or science-inquiry process. The simplicity of the activity allows teachers to focus on students learning the vocabulary, processes and strategies rather than producing a product. It can also address a diverse range of learning goals at different year levels. When run in Foundation to Year 2, the marble run can be used to introduce using equipment (like scissors) safely, practise working together, talk about the concept of time, use digital technology to take and upload photos and much more. In Years 3 and 4, the activity can be used to teach measurement, shapes, angles, the design process, working collaboratively, problem-solving strategies, collecting and presenting data, and engineering principles such as forces and materials. In Years 5 and 6 teachers can link the marble-run to budgeting (by putting a price on the resources used), decimals, volume, area, perimeter, prisms, chance, friction, designing algorithms, testing hypotheses and exploring the interrelationship between different design elements.

Figure 5.4: Marble run design brief
Reproducible available

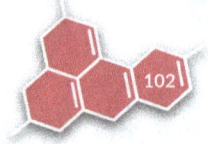

The marshmallow structure design brief (figure 5.5) and the 100-cup tower design brief (figure 5.6) are two more design challenges that support students to learn the design process and to begin acquiring and consolidating STEM knowledge, skills and thinking. They have the same qualities of being simple STEM activities that are easily resourced and quick to run, yet can be used to introduce a rich variety of transdisciplinary curriculum topics.

Design brief: Marshmallow challenge

Aim: Use the materials provided to create a tall structure.

Goal: Design and build the tallest freestanding structure, measured from the foundation surface to the top of the marshmallow.

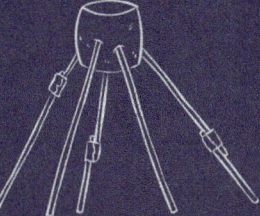

Materials:
- 20 sticks of spaghetti
- one metre of tape
- one metre of string
- one marshmallow
- measuring tape.

Considerations:
- The entire marshmallow must be on top. (Cutting or eating the marshmallow disqualifies the team.)
- Feel free to break up the spaghetti, string or tape.
- Use as much or little of the materials as you want.
- The structure must not be suspended, supported or held onto in any way when the time runs out.
- You have 15 minutes to complete your prototype.

Figure 5.5: Marshmallow structure design brief
Source: Adapted from Wujec (2010)

Reproducible available

Igniting STEM Learning

> **Design brief: 100-cup tower challenge**
>
> Aim: Use 100 cups to construct the highest tower in 10 minutes that does not fall down without intervention.
>
> Goal: Use the cups to create a strong structure that can be measured in terms of height and stability.
>
> **Materials:**
> - 100 large plastic cups
> - 100 small plastic cups
> - measuring tape.
>
> **Considerations:**
> - The tower will be measured from the lowest point of the lowest cup to the highest point of the highest cup.
> - The tower can only be built from the cups provided (no external reinforcing materials).
> - The tower must be freestanding (not leaning against or suspended from anything). You will need to step away from and not be in contact with the tower while it is being measured for height and stability.
> - The tower can only be built using one size of cup (no mixing of sizes).
> - Use as many or few of the provided cups as you want.
> - You have 10 minutes to complete your tower.
>
> **Some questions:**
> - Does it matter where or on what surface you build your tower?
> - Does the size of the cups make a difference?
> - Does the way you stack the cups matter?

Figure 5.6: 100-cup tower design brief
Reproducible available

During Term 2 and early Term 3, teachers can start planning and running bounded transdisciplinary STEM assessment tasks. These tasks should have the students practise the processes, strategies and thinking they learned from the shorter hands-on STEM activities and apply them to real-life transdisciplinary topics. During this phase of learning, students will begin deepening their understanding of computational, systems and design thinking while acquiring and consolidating their subject-specific knowledge. The formative feedback cycle inherent in the design process assists students in growing their capacity to collaborate and drive their own learning. Figures 5.7–9 are examples of these sorts of transdisciplinary STEM assessment tasks

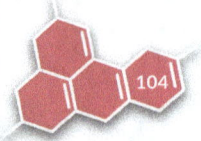

designed for various year levels. They all have clearly defined outcomes, timelines and end points, meaning they are also bounded STEM-rich tasks.

Paddock to plate

Integrated unit, Year 1, Term 2

Throughout Term 2 you will be discovering the processes food goes through in its journey from the paddock to your plate.

The processes that our food goes through have changed over time. These processes have an impact on the environment, food quality and nutrition. If we are to make good, responsible choices we need to understand where our food comes from and what processes it goes through.

Culminating task: Assessment requirements

To demonstrate your understanding of the processes food goes through to get from the paddock to the plate you will be creating and sharing a flow chart showing the process of an ingredient from one of your favourite dishes.

Your flow chart must include:
- the main steps taken in order by your ingredient to go from the paddock to the plate
- labelled pictures
- any interesting facts
- headings.

You will be sharing the flow chart with your class in the week beginning 3 June. The final 'Paddock to plate – food day' will be on Friday 7 June. Parents are most welcome.

Support material:

You will be provided with checklist and a rubric.

Figure 5.7: Year 1 'Paddock to plate' task

Fabulous fabrics

Year 3, Term 2–3

Design your own gift.

Task: During this term you will be designers who will be designing a gift made from fabric to give to a special friend.

To understand how fabrics are used for different purposes we must understand the process they go through from raw material to product.

You will be learning about and following the design process to design and build your gift.

You will be showcasing your gift on the due date to parents and other classes. On that day you will need to present your display book including sketches, drafts designs, fabric chosen and why, and your gift. Be ready to share your design and the process you took to make it.

Date handed out: 20 June

Date due: 5 August

Figure 5.8: Year 3 'Fabulous fabrics' task

Can you really play?

Mathematics is applied in many ways in the building industry. One major way is when builders and architects work together to design proposals to bid for upcoming building contracts. Decision-makers create design briefs to capture the needs and conditions that any proposals must meet. Builders and architects then use maths to work out what they can do to meet a design brief financially and logistically. They then persuade decision-makers by highlighting all the benefits and opportunities of their proposal.

Throughout this term you will be developing your skills as builders and architects by designing a playground and persuading decision-makers to choose your design proposal. This task is to be done in pairs. You must check each other's workings.

Culminating task: Assessment requirements

To demonstrate your understanding of measurement, you will be required to create a design that best suits the needs of students and present a design proposal to the principal.

- Use the attached checklists to guide you in the steps you will take to submit a proposal to the principal. The proposal generally takes the form of a letter and must contain the following elements:
    - neat, scaled diagram (including a key) of your chosen design
    - cost of playground, including equipment, mulch etc.
    - site chosen and area needed to build the playground
    - justification of your choice of equipment and layout.

  This proposal must be a formal piece of work.

- You are also to create a short (no longer than 2 minutes) persuasive presentation that highlights the benefits and opportunities of your proposal. Make sure you practise this with your family and friends before the presentation date.

This is a creative task and will require you to not only complete the assigned tasks, but also to *think outside the square!*

Support material:

You will be provided with a playground planning handbook, a planning checklist and a formative rubric that all must be completed and submitted at the end of the unit. Remember it is your job to provide evidence that you have completed each checklist item and achieved the required progression points for each skill.

Audience:

You will present to the Year 5 and 6 students and the principal.

Presentation date:

All presentations will occur on 24 August.

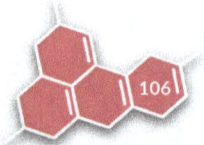

Beginning small with bounded STEM projects

> **Presentation ideas:**
>
> How you present is up to you, just make sure it is creative, engaging and informative for your audience. It is important to have materials and resources to support you. Below is a list to prompt some ideas:
>
> - poster
> - diorama
> - collage
> - model
> - rap
> - multimedia
> - graph
> - list criteria
> - podcast
> - advertisement
> - photography
> - newspaper.
> - video
> - play or musical
> - short film
> - construction
> - puzzle
> - factual booklet
> - pamphlet
> - poems
> - webpage
> - mimes
> - music
>
> Good luck with your research, planning and design! Make sure you use your time wisely and work on this assessment throughout the term. We look forward to seeing your finished products!

Figure 5.9: Year 6 'Can you really play?' task

As the students grow in confidence and ability to drive their own learning and use the appropriate STEM language, processes and strategies, teachers can begin to transition the bounded transdisciplinary STEM assessment tasks to include open-ended elements. The aim is to provide guided opportunities for students to acquire more sophisticated understandings of their newly acquired knowledge and skills. For example, the Year 3 'Fabulous fabrics' task (figure 5.8, page 105) could be extended to have students discuss and explain the sustainability of the gift they designed. They could explore throwaway fashion or create gifts by recycling or reusing materials. The Year 6 'Can you really play?' task (figure 5.9) could have students researching potential playground equipment and suppliers rather than simply being provided a playground-planning handbook. Further open-ended extensions could involve having students use CAD software and print 3D models; identify potential safety issues and include design elements to minimise risk; investigate the characteristics and properties of a range of materials and explain how chosen materials increase safety or reduce the wear of the equipment; or even create art to be installed as part of the playground to highlight the history of the area and the diversity of cultures represented in their school.

Figure 5.10 is an example of a robotics assessment task designed to take Year 5/6 students through the phases of learning across two–three terms. The assessment task begins with a bounded design challenge in which the students learn not only how to use specific technology (LEGO EV3s), but also to apply the thinking frameworks and aspects of the technologies curriculum to solve a progressive sequence of mini challenges. The final element of the first challenge is a limited open-ended task requiring students to apply design and coding processes and strategies to have their robot navigate a similar but unseen course. The second challenge is an open-ended challenge in which student teams research real-life examples of the uses of robotics and design their own

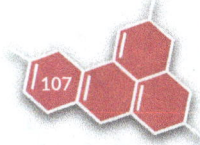

problem or situation to solve. The intention is for students to consolidate their learning and grow their capacity to adapt, learn and transfer their knowledge, skills and thinking to a different situation. Along the way, the teacher guides students in their choices, has discussions about the similarities and differences to previously solved problems and has students grapple with the effectiveness of their learning strategies.

Robotics Academy Program: Rescue me!

Robots are often portrayed in movies as quite intelligent but also threatening to humans. In industry robots aren't necessarily as smart as in the movies but they are most used to replace human effort in repetitive boring work. In recent years robots have been used in disaster response situations – searching for lost individuals in tough terrains, or going places where people or dogs can't go. Robots can (and have) been used in many ways to meet a perceived need to make our lives safer and easier.

When engineers and programmers design solutions they first identify the needs of their clients and the problem they are facing. They then break the problem down into smaller groups and use design thinking to collaboratively problem-solve and create solutions using a series of ordered steps. The more that we use the skills and thinking of engineering and programming the more effective we are in coming up with solutions for future problems.

For the Robotics Academy Program you will be developing your robotics and coding knowledge and skills by being a group of robotic engineers and programmers who are building robots using the available parts and to help out with situations where humans cannot go. Your goal is to design and program a robot to be helpful in the community or tackling human problems.

Culminating task: Assessment requirements

By the end of the Robotics Academy Program you will be involved in two challenges.

1. Firstly you will be building and programming an EV3 to go through four tasks. These tasks are designed to lead you through the thinking and planning to build your knowledge and skills necessary for the second challenge. The four tasks are:
   - **Movement**
     Navigate a known course with known obstacles and no need for sensors. Robots will have to maneuver around obstacles on a flat surface to explore basic skill and tinkering.
   - **Follow the line**
     Use sensors to stick to the path defined by a line.
   - **Colour recognition**
     Use sensors to distinguish between red, green and blue (for example, find water in a green area while avoiding toxic red areas).
   - **Unstructured challenge.**
2. The second challenge will involve you researching problems or situations where robots could be used to help in the community or for a particular human problem. You will then create a robotics solution to this problem or situation and showcase your solution.

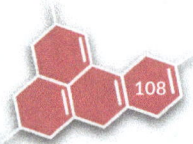

Support material:

You will be provided a planning checklist, a range of templates and resources, and a formative rubric. These will need to be completed and submitted at the end of the unit to demonstrate your growth in knowledge, skills and thinking throughout the unit. An online design portfolio will be set up to support your collection of the evidence of your thinking and planning.

Due date and audience:

There are two performances as part of this project.
1. The first performance will be in Term 2, Week 9. At this performance you will test your EV3 robot rover and its programming in an unstructured obstacle challenge. The event will be held 7–9 pm 16 June at the Cultural Centre. Your parents, family members and school staff and students are most welcome to attend. In Week 8 you will have the opportunity to test on a prototype obstacle course in readiness for the challenge course in Week 9.
2. The second performance will be in Term 3, Week 9. At this performance you will showcase your robotics solution to the problem or situation you identified at the start of Term 3. The performance will be part of a STEM showcase we will be holding at the school on 7 September. The showcase will be open to your parents, school staff and students, the school board and interested community members. We also intend to invite the local newspaper to the event.

Figure 5.10: Year 5/6 robotics design task

One thing worth noting is that when schools start to embed STEM learning into everyday learning approaches, the goalposts shift over time. As students start to internalise what to do and how to do it through deliberate practice and using feedback, transdisciplinary STEM assessment tasks such as figures 5.8 and 5.9 (pages 105 and 106) could be run earlier in the year. More challenging tasks and units of learning could then be designed for Term 4. Figure 5.11 is an example of an open-ended assessment task from a school that had embedded STEM learning into their learning approach for a number of years.

Igniting STEM Learning

Excellence Academy: A sustainable future for the valley

In the Lockyer Valley demand for usable water exceeds the supply. Some of the issues that have led to this situation include the following:

1. lack of regular and reliable rainfall to renew the aquifer (underground) and waterways (surface – could also be caused by poor placement of catchment for regional dams (Lake Clarendon, Bill Gunn Dam)
2. when dams get low they become filled with blue-green algae and are not usable
3. salinity of underground water in certain areas due to geology
4. population growth requiring greater supply
5. efficiency of irrigation practices
6. potential water quality issues due to run-off and other contaminations.

Your task is to prepare an environmental assessment report that makes recommendations to the Lockyer Valley Council to assist them in making a decision about how to sustainably manage the water supply in the Lockyer Valley.

Culminating task: Assessment requirements

To demonstrate your knowledge and understanding you will be working in groups of two or three. You will choose one of the six listed issues to investigate and will be required to create an environmental assessment report and recommendations for the Lockyer Valley Council on that issue.

Your report must include the following:
- description of the issue
- map of the area being investigated
- data and statistics that demonstrate the issue – primary and secondary data
- analysis and discussion identifying the potential short- and long-term effects of this issue
- research and analysis showing potential solutions to the issue from a range of sources
- recommendations for the Lockyer Valley Council.

Support material:

Each team will be provided a checklist, skill rubric and a range of templates and resources. You will also be given a guide to inform your report format, flow and structure. You will have access to experts from the Lockyer Valley High School and UQ Gatton to support you in developing your knowledge and skills.

Due date and audience:

Your report will be due 21 October. The final report to the Lockyer Valley Council will be a collation of each team's report and will be presented to the council 29 November.

Figure 5.11: Years 4–6 environment sustainability design task

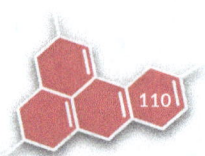

Teachers can find a wide variety of easily resourced and quick-to-run bounded STEM projects and activities online. There are also many great STEM-project books, such as Todd Stanley's *10 Performance-Based STEM Projects* series, the *Year-Round Project-Based Activities for STEM* series by various authors and Tracy Edmund's *STEM: Engaging Hands-On Challenges Using Everyday Materials* series. These series are useful for teachers because they provide supporting templates, structures, rubrics and links to various related curriculum areas. There are also a range of digital technologies challenges mapped to the Australian Curriculum on the Australian Computing Academy website (https://blog.aca.edu.au). Some of these can be run in one lesson and others go over several weeks. The Australian Government's Digital Technologies Hub (www.digitaltechnologieshub.edu.au) also lists a range of competitions and challenges from around the world that are great to use to develop student capacity around computational and design thinking (Australian Government Department of Education, n.d.-b).

STEP 3: DESIGN THE ASSESSMENT OR CULMINATING RICH TASK

Chapter 6 will explore developing open-ended transdisciplinary STEM assessment tasks like the environment sustainability design task of figure 5.11 (page 110), but first I will explain the process of designing bounded transdisciplinary STEM assessment tasks that allow for student choice and progressively support students to drive their learning. This covers how teachers can reshape existing units and learning into meaningful STEM assessment tasks (Step 3 of the simplified backward-planning process set out in Chapter 4, from page 74), and the two-stage process for creating a checklist to guide students through their learning (Step 5). Chapter 7 will address Step 4, the design of formative assessment structures for STEM activities and projects.

Some teachers may want to skip over identifying the learning destination, which we covered in Chapter 4, and go straight to creating STEM assessment tasks. This is not recommended, even if teachers are only re-shaping existing units. The rigour involved in deconstructing the curriculum (Step 1) and creating a logical sequence of key understandings (Step 2) has been shown to consistently open up new possibilities for learning activities and assessment tasks that can address multiple curriculum areas.

DESIGNING BOUNDED TRANSDISCIPLINARY STEM ASSESSMENT TASKS USING THE GRASPS MODEL

One of the simplest approaches to designing authentic assessment tasks is planning with the GRASPS (which stands for *goal, role, audience, situation, product* and *standards*) model outlined by Wiggins and McTighe (2005).

In this model, G stands for *goal* – a simple, clear statement that outlines the purpose for the assessment task. It communicates to the students what they are working on and why. The goal is a measurable demonstration of the final key understanding for the unit. R, which stands for *role*, connects students to an authentic role or career. The intention of this field is to have students start to explore what it means to be a scientist, investigator, detective, engineer, designer, programmer, digital artist, researcher, fashion designer and so on. A for *audience* articulates who students will present their product or performance to. In the younger year levels it is appropriate for the audience to be made up of students' parents and guardians. As students grow in experience, the audience should involve other classes, the entire school community, the school principal and even external experts. Choose an audience that will require students to stretch themselves when they present.

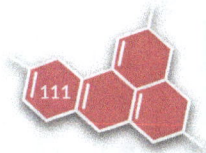

The *situation*, represented by S in the acronym, paints the background picture and context for the culminating task and can be taken directly from the logical sequence of key understandings created in Chapter 4. When transforming the plan into a one-page assessment sheet, teachers may add statistics and other information to further flesh out this field. *P* stands for *product/performance* and describes the measurable elements students need to produce to demonstrate their completion of the task. The clearer these are articulated for students, the better that students will understand what they need to do and the easier it is to plan learning activities. Finally, *S* for *standards* is where teachers articulate the quality of expected products. This could include formative assessment (for example, design portfolios, storyboards, self-reflections and so on). Normally standards and success criteria will be captured in rubrics, checklists and other documents.

Wiggins and McTighe's (2005) intention with the GRASPS model is for assessment tasks to be designed as performance assessments that simulate problems and situations beyond the normal school environment while giving students some choice in the product they deliver. The model also provides students with sufficient opportunities to cycle through the design, prototype, evaluate and refine stages and enable students to demonstrate the knowledge and skill they have acquired (Hansen, 2011).

The transdisciplinary STEM assessment tasks depicted in figures 5.7, 5.8 and 5.9 (pages 105–7) were all designed using the GRASPS model. Table 5.1 shows preliminary planning using the GRASPS model that formed the basis for the one-page assessment descriptions shown in those figures.

Table 5.1: Preliminary planning using the GRASPS model

Task	Year 1 'Paddock to plate' task	Year 3 'Fabulous fabrics' task	Year 6 'Can you really play?' task
Goal Goal, problem, challenge or obstacle for the task	To demonstrate understanding of the process food goes through to get from the paddock to the plate	To demonstrate understanding of how fabrics are used for different purposes and the design process	To demonstrate understanding of measurement and persuasion
Role Role of the students in the scenario and what they are being asked to do	Investigators	Designers	Builders and architects
Audience The target audience the students will be presenting to	Presentation to the class on one day and parents on another as part of a 'Paddock to plate' food celebration day	Presentation to parents and other classes	Presentation to the school principal and the Year 5 and 6 students

Beginning small with bounded STEM projects

Situation Context and explanation of the situation	Logical sequence of key understandings: 1. The processes that our food goes through to get to our plate have changed over time. 2. These processes have an impact on the environment, food quality and nutrition. 3. If we are to make good, responsible choices, we need to understand where our food comes from and what processes it goes through.	Logical sequence of key understandings: 1. Different fabrics are made from different raw materials. 2. Each fabric has different characteristics. 3. These characteristics come from the processes used to make the fabric and the raw materials. 4. To understand how fabrics are used for different purposes, we must understand the processes they go through from raw material to product.	Logical sequence of key understandings: 1. Mathematics is applied in many ways in the building industry. 2. Design briefs are used to capture the needs and conditions that any proposals must meet. 3. When builders put together a proposal, they use maths to work out what they can do to meet a design brief financially and logistically. 4. They then persuade decision-makers by highlighting the benefits and opportunities of their proposal.
Product/ performance The product or performance that needs to be created and its larger purpose	Create and share a flow chart of the journey from paddock to the plate for one ingredient from a favourite dish. The flow chart must include: - the main steps, in order, the ingredient takes from paddock to plate - labelled pictures - any interesting facts - headings.	Design and showcase a gift made from fabric to give to a friend. The showcase will involve presenting the: - gift - display book with sketches, drafts and designs - fabric chosen and why.	Create a playground design proposal and promotional pitch to be presented to the school principal and the Year 5 and 6 students. The proposal must contain the following elements: 1. a neat, scaled diagram (including a key) of the chosen design 2. the cost of the playground (including equipment, mulch etc.) 3. the site chosen and area needed to build the playground 4. a justification of the choice of equipment and layout. This proposal must be a formal piece of work.
Standards The specific standards for success that must be met and how the work will be judged	Captured in a checklist and rubric provided to students (and parents)	Captured in a checklist and design rubric provided to students	Captured in a planning checklist and formative rubric

Table 5.2 is an example of planning for a Year 5/6 digital technologies unit using the GRASPS model. In the year prior to developing this plan, the teacher ran a digital technologies unit that involved students playing and reviewing four different computer games to get a sense of the qualities that made a great game. They then created a design brief for a game they could design and modified existing Scratch game code to create a new game. While the unit was fun and engaging, the product quality was not very high. The teacher felt that she needed to bring a lot more structure and rigour to her planning so her students could develop the necessarily knowledge, skills and thinking to deliver high-quality games. Using the first two steps of the backward-planning process, the teacher clarified what she wanted students to know and be able to do by the end of the unit. She then created formative templates using the logical sequence of understanding success criteria to grow students' capacity to code and think computationally. The GRASPS model planning enabled the teacher to see how to include cross-curriculum topics such as English, mathematics, persuasive writing and ethical understanding into the unit planning. Figure 5.12 samples the subsequent one-page assessment task the teacher created for the unit.

Table 5.2: Preliminary GRASPS model planning for a Year 5/6 digital technologies assessment task

Goal Goal, problem, challenge or obstacle for the task	Essential question: Are games engaging and fun because they are violent or are there other features that make games worth playing? To produce a fun, non-violent video game for children/young adults using Scratch 3.0/GameMaker that won't upset parents. It must be engaging, fun, violence-free and user-friendly, have a theme and tell a clear story.
Role Role of the students in the scenario and what they are being asked to do	You are a group of programmers who are developing non-violent video games.
Audience The target audience the students will be presenting to	Students will create a 'Gamers' arcade' to showcase their games to the school community (look to invite some gamers/game creators as guest judges). The 'Gamers' arcade' will be held in […] – dates and times to be confirmed based on the school calendar.
Situation Context and explanation of the situation	A large survey of children between 12 and 17 years of age found that 97% are video game players who have played in the last day and that 75% of parents checked the censor's rating on a video game before allowing their child to purchase it. Some research finds that violent video game use is correlated with, and may cause, increases in aggression, while other research argues that there are no such effects of violent video games. It is well known that many Australian parents dislike the number of violent video games that their children play.
Product/ performance The product or performance that needs to be created and its larger purpose	Students will storyboard, design and code their game in small groups using Scratch 3.0/GameMaker. Students will research and play a range of non-violent games and identify the features that make for an engaging/fun game. Students will self- and peer-assess their games based on a rubric that they will create alongside their teacher. Students will create an advertising campaign to persuade other students to play their game.
Standards The specific standards for success that must be met and how the work will be judged	Co-design a rubric for the game elements with students. Have a second rubric that captures the processes and production skills (design thinking) and the quality of the advertising campaign. Students will reflect (self and peer) after the 'Gamers' arcade' against the focus skill areas and rubrics, and explain what they would do differently. Students will share their games with one another and note the different ways they did their programming. What was the difference between coding in Scratch 3.0 and coding in GameMaker?

Beginning small with bounded STEM projects

Code Academy Program: Get ready to play, gamer!

A large survey of children between 12 and 17 years of age found that 97% are video game players who have played in the last day and that 75% of parents checked the censor's rating on a video game before allowing their child to purchase it. Some research finds that violent video game use is correlated with, and may cause, increases in aggression and other research argues that there are no such effects of violent video games. Regardless of the research it is well known that many Australian parents dislike the number of violent video games that their children are playing.

For the Coding Academy Program you will be developing your coding knowledge and skills by being a group of programmers who are researching and then developing non-violent video games. Your goal is to design and program a game that is engaging, fun, violence-free, has a theme, tells a story, and is user-friendly

Are you ready?

Culminating task: Assessment requirements

By the end of the Coding Academy Program you will be involved in three phases in this project:

- First you will research and play a range of non-violent games and identify the features that make for an engaging/fun game. From this you will, with your teacher, create a rubric that will allow you to assess how any future video game meets the desired criteria.
- In the second phase you will storyboard, design and code your game in small groups using Scratch 3.0/Game Maker. During this phase you will self- and peer-assess your game based on a rubric you created in the previous phase.
- In the final phase of the project you will create an advertising campaign to persuade other school students to play your game. The games and advertising will be showcased to the Malvern Valley school community at a 'Gamers' arcade' held in Term 4.

Support material:

You will be provided a planning checklist, a range of templates and resources, and formative rubrics. These will need to be completed and submitted with your design portfolio at the end of the academy project.

Due date and audience:

Video game rubric due: 5 August

Storyboard and game due: 14 October

'Gamers' arcade' event: 23 November

The audience for the first two assessments will be your peers in the Code Academy Program. The audience for the 'Gamers' arcade' will be all students and staff, plus your parents and families.

Figure 5.12: Year 5/6 digital technologies assessment task sheet
Source: Adapted from Pollard (2020)

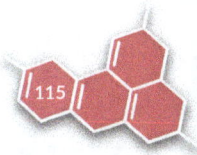

Exercise: Assessment task plan

Use the GRASPS model, set out in the following template, to plan a STEM assessment task.

Goal Goal, problem, challenge or obstacle for the task	
Role Role of the students in the scenario and what they are being asked to do	
Audience The target audience the students will be presenting to	
Situation Context and explanation of the situation	
Product/performance The product or performance that needs to be created and its larger purpose	
Standards The specific standards for success that must be met and how the work will be judged	

Reproducible available

Having completed the GRASPS model template, use this preliminary planning to write a one-page assessment document like those shown in figures 5.7–11. Possible section titles and fields include:

1. culminating task title
2. situation
3. assessment requirements
4. support materials
5. audience and due date
6. presentation ideas.

Further GRASPS model and assessment document examples are downloadable.

STEP 5: CREATE A CHECKLIST OF STEPS

Once the STEM assessment task has been written, the next action in the backward-planning process (see page 74) is to develop a checklist of steps. This checklist of steps outlines the actions a teacher believes students need to take to achieve the STEM assessment task effectively and successfully. Using the driving metaphor, the checklist represents explicit directions for the route one would take to drive from point A to point B. This checklist should be shared with students to guide their planning, and teachers should use it to develop a coherent teaching plan and think through the link between the logical sequence of key understandings, the assessments and the learning experiences and instruction.

There are several benefits to creating a checklist of steps. First, it supports teachers to sequence their teaching and the learning activities across the whole unit. When creating authentic STEM tasks, teachers often experience a lack of certainty of what needs to be taught and when. The process of articulating the checklist of steps requires teachers to consider the actions they want the students to take and therefore the learning activities and actions they need to design so that the students can take those actions.

The checklist also provides a planning structure that students can use to determine what to work on and their next step. Teachers can include milestone deliverables at various points in the checklist and thus monitor and support the quality of the work that is produced. The checklist is a great tool to keep students on task and to highlight potential areas of development for students if they get stuck at any step.

Finally, the checklist can be used to develop students in the process of planning to achieve a goal. To begin with, teachers can put the checklist up in class and use it to model the process of planning for an entire class. As students become accustomed to the planning process, they can use the checklist as individuals or as a part of a collaborative team to support their own planning and actions. Once they reach the stage of knowing what to do and how to do it, students can be supported to co-design a checklist of steps with their teacher. This develops their capacity to be self-regulated learners and addresses the planning requirements in the general capabilities and the technologies curriculum.

THE PROCESS OF CREATING THE CHECKLIST

Creating the checklist of steps involves two stages. In the first stage teachers use a design-process template to unpack the list of activities and actions that will support students to develop the necessary knowledge, skills and thinking to successfully accomplish the STEM assessment task.

Table 5.3 (page 118) is a completed design process template for the Year 5/6 digital technologies assessment discussed earlier (see pages 114–5). The benefit of using this template is that it forces teachers to consider what activities will align with each phase of the design process. This ensures that the design process is at the heart of any STEM unit. It is recommended that teachers broadly map the teaching and the learning activities to their calendar to get a sense of timing across the whole unit.

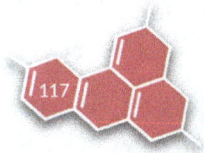

Table 5.3: **Design process template for a Year 5/6 digital technologies assessment**

Design phase	Approx. time to complete	Checklist steps
Empathise Includes research	Term 2, Weeks 2–10	1. Week 2 • Brainstorm the design constraints and understand the challenge. 2. Weeks 3–5 • Be immersed in coding programs Scratch, Blockly, Hour of Code etc. (block and written). • Brainstorm the key skills needed to create a game. 3. Weeks 6–8 • Attend coding incursion to further develop coding skills. 4. Weeks 9–10 • Investigate the history of gaming and game designs. • Play a variety of games. (What games did they enjoy most? Why? How can incorporate that in their own games?)
Define Includes mind-mapping	Term 3, Weeks 1–2	5. Weeks 1–2 • Identify the key aspects involved in designing (storyboarding) and creating (coding) a game.
Ideate–prototype–test	Term 3, Weeks 3–10 Term 4, Weeks 1–6	6. Weeks 3–10 (Term 3); Weeks 1–6 (Term 4) • Students to co-design rubric to assess their games. • Storyboard and code the game. • Use the design thinking process to develop and iteratively refine the coding. • Test games (self- and peer-assessment using the rubric designed in Week 3). • Create an advertising campaign to market their game.
Deliver Preparing for and delivering presentation	Term 4, Weeks 7–10	7. Week 7 • Run a mini arcade for robotics students in preparation for the 'Gamers' arcade'. • Receive feedback from the robotics group and make any necessary changes. 8. Weeks 8–10 • Present at the 'Gamers' arcade' community events. • Reflect on learnings.

Exercise: Design process template

Use the following design process template to create a rough draft of the sequence of activities and actions for the unit.

Things to consider while filling in the template:

- At each specific design phase, what actions or activities could take place that would be consistent with that phase's purpose?
- Have we embedded the appropriate iterative cycle of activities and actions that will result in the progressive development of student knowledge, skills and thinking?
- How many lessons or teaching weeks could each step authentically take?

Further examples of completed design process templates can be downloaded.

Design phase	Approx. time to complete	Checklist steps
Empathise Includes research		
Define Includes mind-mapping		
Ideate–prototype–test		
Deliver Preparing for and delivering presentation		

Reproducible available

The second stage of creating a checklist of steps sees teachers use a completed design process template to flesh out a more detailed sequence of action steps to be given to students. The aim is to provide a clear and simple plan so that students (and possibly their parents) know what actions need to be taken to produce a high-quality product or performance.

Table 5.4 (page 120) is a checklist of steps that was created for the Year 1 'Paddock to plate' unit (figure 5.7, page 105). The teaching team had many vibrant discussions about what steps should and shouldn't be included. They realised that they had to break down the steps so that it would be sufficiently clear to the Year 1 students (and their parents) what had to be done and by when. This included actions to address prior knowledge or skill that children may not have had. The teaching team also captured (in square parentheses) the actions they had to take so that students could deliver on each articulated checklist step. The resulting checklist captures learning activities, templates to be designed, graphic organisers to be used, times for explicit teaching to be done and much more.

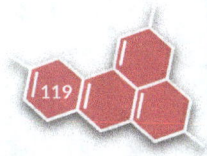

Igniting STEM Learning

Table 5.4: Checklist of steps for the Year 1 'Paddock to plate' unit, with teacher notes in square brackets

Paddock to plate Year 1 transdisciplinary unit checklist		Starting date	
Steps you need to take to complete your STEM assessment task		Date to be completed	Done
1	Identify your favourite food made at home and get a copy of the recipe. [Put in homework sheet.]		
2	Choose one of the main ingredients used to make your favourite food. [Done in class.]		
3	Prepare a list of questions about the ingredient you want to know more about. [Activity: Work with students to formulate questions.]		
4	With a parent or guardian's help, find information that can be used to answer your questions. Use the T-chart provided to organise your questions and information. [Have guide to send home, model it in class.]		
5	Ask your parents, guardians or grandparents about what is different about how they got their food when they were children. [Homework task: Venn diagram – do a refresher.]		
6	Show your T-chart to your teacher and get it approved before moving on. [Mini-conference with students about understanding of t-chart.]		
7	Identify the important steps for your ingredient to get from the paddock to the plate. Highlight them on your T-chart. [Done in conference, model organising information with students.]		
8	Sequence the important steps into order from paddock to plate. Add any interesting facts in each of the steps. [Model organising information with students.]		
9	Create a flow chart of the process the ingredient went through from paddock to the plate. [Model flow chart.]		
10	If you have interesting facts add them to the flow chart.		
11	Practice sharing the process shown in your flow chart with at least two other students in your class. Answer any questions asked of you. [Model the W questions with students.]		
12	Practise sharing the process shown in your flow chart at least three times with your parents or guardians. Answer any questions asked of you. [Put in homework sheet, guide to parents and guardians.]		
13	Share the process shown in your flow chart with the whole class on your designated day. Answer any questions asked of you.		
14	With your parents help, make your favourite food. Bring the food on the 'Paddock to the plate' food day to share.		

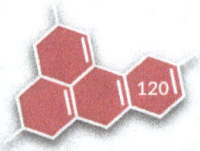

Beginning small with bounded STEM projects

Exercise: Checklist of steps

Use the completed design process template to create a checklist of steps that will inform students of what actions need to be taken to produce a high-quality product or performance.

Things to consider while filling in the template:
- Do students have the necessary prior knowledge or skill to take each step? If not, are there other prior steps that need to be articulated?
- Are there associated actions or activities that need to occur? Do you need to model an activity? Do you need to design a graphic organiser or template for students to use? For home-based activities, do you provide some guidance for how parents and guardians can support their child?
- Knowing the strengths and areas of development of the students in your class, are there any other steps that could be included?

Further checklist examples can be downloaded.

Unit title		Starting date	
Steps you need to take to complete your STEM assessment task		Date to be completed	Done
1			
2			
3			
4			
5			
6			
7			
8			
9			
10			
11			
12			
13			
14			

Reproducible available

The planning process and templates outlined in this chapter support teachers to both create new STEM assessment tasks and reshape already existing units into transdisciplinary assessment tasks that have clearly defined outcomes, timelines and end points. In following this approach, teachers will have more certainty about the flow of learning through a unit and will automatically embed the design process as part of their planning. This beginning-small approach enables students to acquire and consolidate the necessary knowledge, skills and thinking to tackle open-ended

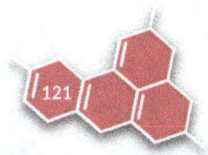

STEM challenges. In the next chapter we will examine and discuss how teachers can design these more substantial open-ended STEM assessment tasks so that students can apply and transfer their knowledge, skills and thinking to solving real-world challenges.

KEY POINTS

- The best way to start embedding authentic STEM learning is to reshape already existing units into smaller, bounded STEM assessment tasks that have clearly defined outcomes, timelines and end points.
- The conceptual model of learning proposed by Hattie and Donoghue (2016) provides insight into what students need at different stages of the learning process and can be used to guide the planning of STEM learning that will enable students to acquire and consolidate the necessary STEM knowledge, skills and thinking.
- The first goal teachers should aim for is having students build a base of STEM knowledge and skill as they internalise using the processes and strategies associated with the thinking frameworks. Shorter hands-on STEM activities will draw out the processes and learning strategies while engaging students.
- Wiggins and McTighe's (2005) GRASPS model is a great way to design STEM assessment tasks that simulate problems and situations beyond the normal school environment. The information captured in GRASPS model planning can then be used to create a one-page assessment document.
- Teachers should then create a checklist of steps outlining the actions students need to take to achieve the STEM assessment task effectively and successfully. This checklist supports students to determine what to work on and what their next step is, helps teachers to sequence teaching and learning activities, and teaches students how to plan to achieve a goal or outcome.

CHAPTER 6

Getting real-world with open-ended STEM projects

What we have got is whole generations of people helping children to pass exams ... But to really fire children's imaginations you need teachers who don't give them answers but give them questions. There's a dictum in primary education: when a child asks a really good question, don't answer it. Give them the information to work it out, so they can think: 'By God, I've got it!' That's how the brain works.

John Abbott, as quoted by Fran Abrams, 'When the lights go on', The Guardian

GETTING REAL-WORLD

If a school's goal is to develop young people to be problem-solvers, critical and creative thinkers and collaborative, adaptable learners, involving them in open-ended transdisciplinary STEM projects is crucial. Authentic open-ended STEM projects challenge students and teachers to use the knowledge, skills and strategies they have begun to internalise and apply them to real-world challenges and situations. Open-ended learning compels students to step out of the comfort zone created by a structured educational environment where they often end up doing things they already know how to do or reinforcing skills they already know how to use (Nottingham, 2017). In the process, students begin to make connections and extensions beyond surface knowing and doing, and deepen their capacity to self-regulate, collaborate, problem-solve and be creative.

Further, well-designed open-ended STEM projects can ignite young people's curiosity and thinking and empower them to be change-makers. Organisations such as Young Change Agents, STEM4Innovation, Engineers without Borders, BrainSTEM and ChangeMakeHer were

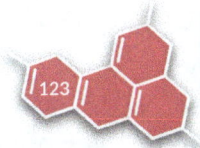

Igniting STEM Learning

founded with the belief that young people can apply their STEM knowledge, skills and thinking to solving real-world challenges. When students are involved in real-world STEM projects that are meaningful to them, they develop themselves as resilient, capable and confident individuals. This is what I experienced when working with young people in the ruMAD program. It's also a common experience in the organisations I've just mentioned.

This chapter builds on the concepts and approaches discussed in previous chapters and begins with a discussion of how teachers can source potential real-world problems and challenges that are meaningful and relevant to their students. A two-phase design-based process is then outlined to show how teachers can create open-ended STEM projects that are authentic and have no single solution or answer. The chapter ends with a lesson-planning template that can be used to ensure that the design process is embedded in the flow of learning throughout a project or unit.

COLLECTING POTENTIAL OPEN-ENDED CHALLENGES

The first barrier that many teachers encounter when designing open-ended challenges is finding worthwhile real-world problems and challenges that students can connect with and become invested in. The best way to approach this dilemma is not to take a just-in-time approach to sourcing open-ended challenges, but instead create a problem bank. Built over time this problem bank represents a list of potentially relevant real-world challenges within the school, the local community, and even nationally and globally.

SCHOOL

School-based challenges can be sourced in a number of ways. Listen to what students, teachers, school leaders and parents complain about! Have them list the things they would like to change around the school. Talk to non-teaching staff such as gardeners, maintenance people, librarians, administration staff and counsellors too as they are often aware of challenges that others may not identify.

School-based challenges are often a great place to start as they are relatively easy to coordinate and organise and can provide great STEM vehicles for the younger year levels or when students are beginning to address open-ended challenges. For example, the students and staff of one primary school were concerned about the amount of waste that was being produced every day and the amount of litter in their school grounds. As a result of following the design process the students created a range of initiatives including setting up worm farms and compost bins to productively use food scraps, introducing a school-wide nude food policy to reduce packaging, recycling ink cartridges and rebuilding computers rather than throwing them away, and creating a canteen menu that minimised litter. Some students even wrote a rap song that was played on local community radio! This particular open-ended STEM challenge had students applying their knowledge and skills from science, maths, economics, civics and citizenship, collecting and communicating data, design thinking, and even art.

COMMUNITY

Students, teachers and parents can collect community-based challenges by observing local issues, scanning the local newspaper and even reaching out to local-government agencies, non-profits, community groups and local businesses. Some businesses and organisations will share problems, others will decline to engage at all, and some might even want to partner with students. Some examples of community-based challenges and problems that schools have tackled include:

- pesticides and fertiliser flowing from farms into the local lake

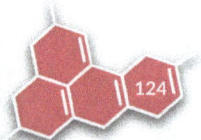

Getting real-world with open-ended STEM projects

- lack of community connection experienced by the elderly in aged-care facilities
- lack of public transport limiting the ability of young people to participate in activities or visit friends
- the local cinema not catering to the interests of young people
- the impact of a major urban-growth plan on the liveability of a local suburb
- the unsustainability of recreation, overuse and the flora planted at a local reserve
- lack of local community facilities for young people (or knowledge of such facilities) in a regional town.

Open-ended community STEM projects can take on a life of their own and lead to highly empowering, rich learning outcomes. As part of the ruMAD program, Whitfield District Primary School in country Victoria created an open-ended STEM project to tackle the polluted, stinky and weed-infested creek that surrounded the school (Bertolini, 2007). The students and teachers had become frustrated that, despite multiple town meetings, nothing had been done about the problem. The project began with students researching what flora and fauna were native to the local area and producing a biodiversity report and posters. They then wrote persuasive letters to a range of environmental groups and the local council, arguing the need for assistance and support. This led to students presenting their biodiversity study findings to Landcare and the local catchment management authority. The project ultimately attracted funding of over $40,000 to rejuvenate the creek (Zyngier, 2009). The teachers supported students to use maths to work out the area and volume of rubbish that needed to be removed, create a budget, order materials, manage the finances and organise working bees. One of the students remarked, 'You have to believe in what you are doing and make a fuss to get things moving. People were surprised that kids could do this stuff' (Zyngier, 2009, p. 266).

NATIONAL AND GLOBAL

National and global challenges often involve issues that affect individuals and communities around the world that students can empathise with. They could be issues involving social justice, sustainable development, climate change, health, ethics, technology access, problems particular groups may experience, and much more. Global open-ended projects can be framed within the context of thinking globally and acting locally.

Reid Moule, a former STEM teacher from Humpybong State School in Queensland, posed a challenge to his Year 5 and 6 students to come up with possible solutions to an issue many elderly people experience. Reid's mother fell and was hurt in an aged-care facility and had not been found for hours. The occurrence of falls increases in the elderly and the injuries sustained not only impact their quality of life but also may indicate other health issues (Eto, 2001). Around 30 per cent of adults over 65 experience at least one fall per year and the medical the cost of falls in Australia is expected to rise to around $1.4 billion by 2051 (Australian and New Zealand Falls Prevention Society, n.d.). In a co-constructed STEM unit, Reid's students learned about electronics, coding, science, ethics and human-centred design thinking to design a sensor package using accelerometers and dermal sensors to detect when an individual falls over so that a notification signal can be sent to alert carers.

National and global STEM challenges can be sourced by staying abreast of current issues in the news, keeping an eye on global affairs and exploring science news. Teachers can also source global open-ended STEM challenges from organisations' lists and collections, including the United Nations Sustainable Development Goals, the Global STEM Challenges collection

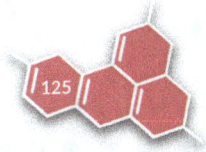

compiled by the Association for Science Education and the list of open challenges maintained by Open IDEO.

PLANNING OPEN-ENDED TRANSDISCIPLINARY STEM PROJECTS

A great way to begin with real-world, open-ended STEM projects is to provide an opportunity for students to discuss and then choose a STEM project topic out of a limited selection of challenges from the problem bank. For younger year levels, teachers might offer two or three school-based challenges for selection. As the students become more experienced and capable, they could choose from between three and five school and community challenges. The national and global STEM challenges should be reserved for student cohorts that are deeply passionate about the topics and are skilled in creating and presenting solutions to school or community challenges. Regardless of the type of challenge offered to the students, the selection process should occur at least a term ahead of the open-ended STEM project being run to give teachers sufficient time to plan the unit.

Once a topic has been selected, teachers should use a two-phase design-based process to flesh out and plan the open-ended STEM project. The intention of the first phase of planning, the empathise phase, is for teachers to use their skill in research to gather a wide range of articles, websites, images and videos. The research ensures that teachers have not only a deeper understanding and breadth of knowledge about the chosen challenge, but also a collection of resources that can be used throughout the STEM project to provoke discussion, possible ideas and potential solutions. The second phase of planning, the define phase, follows a similar planning process to what was outlined in Chapter 5 with teachers using the GRASPS model to create a draft STEM assessment task and sequence of activities and actions for the unit. By the end of the two-phase planning process, teachers will be clear about what aspects of the Australian Curriculum will be addressed, what the learning destination is intended to be and a possible flow of learning activities and experiences that can be designed to support students in creating viable, real-world solutions.

THE EMPATHISE PHASE OF PLANNING

As discussed in Chapter 1, empathising is a process in which information and data are gathered about a topic or challenge with the aim of gaining a deeper appreciation and understanding of the needs, behaviours and dimensions of the issues involved. In design, the process of empathising enables the designer to become clearer about the key issues and needs so that they can focus their ideation–prototyping–testing cycle in a planned way. This is the intention of the three steps of empathise-phase planning: to gather resources and do the preliminary thinking so that teachers have sufficient background and depth of knowledge about the topic to effectively plan an authentic transdisciplinary STEM project.

STEP 1: RESEARCH

Empathise-phase planning begins with teachers researching and identifying relevant and useful websites, news articles, reports, videos and images for their STEM project. Given the breadth of materials likely to be available, the resources chosen should be age appropriate, engaging and from well-respected local, national and global sources. The resources selected should also capture a wide range of perspectives, challenges and potential solutions in the topic area. This will support

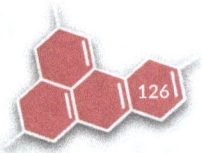

Getting real-world with open-ended STEM projects

teachers to be clearer about the possible directions in which they could guide students during the project. Finally, teachers can list potential contacts from organisations and experts who might be able to assist in the STEM project. These can be from universities, local councils or organisations that are passionate about the particular project topic.

Figure 6.1 is a collection of research resources gathered for 'Paucity of pollinators', a Year 4–6 STEM project that challenged students to create solutions that address the loss of pollinators in the environment. The resources are sequentially numbered for later referencing and contain news articles, reports and videos from organisations as diverse as National Geographic, the Australian Broadcasting Corporation, the Food and Agriculture Organization of the United Nations, the History Channel, the Australian Museum, the Australian Academy of Science and many more. The resources highlight that students should be concerned about not only the loss of bees, which is often showcased in the media, but also the human-induced impact on all pollinators.

Research resources

Useful websites and articles

1. Research report – Rapid assessment of pollinators' status (2008): www.fao.org/3/a-i1046e.pdf
2. Honeybees hog the limelight, yet wild insects are the most important and vulnerable pollinators (April 2018): https://theconversation.com/honeybees-hog-the-limelight-yet-wild-insects-are-the-most-important-and-vulnerable-pollinators-93247
3. Loss of wild pollinators could substantially reduce soybean yields (European Commission, March 2014): http://ec.europa.eu/environment/integration/research/newsalert/pdf/367na1_en.pdf
4. 9 ways you can help bees and other pollinators at home (May 2015): www.nationalgeographic.com/animals/article/150524-bees-pollinators-animals-science-gardens-plants/
5. Bees are dying. What can we do about it? (Jun 2018): www.abc.net.au/news/2018-06-25/bees-are-dying-are-we-next/9904464
6. Getting the buzz on the value of bees: www.science.org.au/curious/everything-else/bees
7. Pollination of crops in Australia and New Zealand (2012): www.agrifutures.com.au/wp-content/uploads/publications/12-059.pdf
8. What's the buzz about bees? (Dec 2017): www.aph.gov.au/About_Parliament/Parliamentary_Departments/Parliamentary_Library/FlagPost/2017/December/Whats_the_buzz_about_bees
9. Pollination (Nov 2018): https://australianmuseum.net.au/learn/animals/insects/pollination/
10. What is it about bees? Three experts on why they're fascinating, why they're dying, what can save them (Sept 2013): https://blog.ted.com/what-is-it-about-bees-three-experts-discuss-why-theyre-fascinating-why-theyre-dying-and-what-can-save-them/
11. Plummeting insect numbers 'threaten collapse of nature' (Feb 2019): www.theguardian.com/environment/2019/feb/10/plummeting-insect-numbers-threaten-collapse-of-nature?

Continued ...

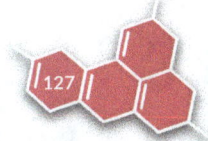

Useful videos
12. A plea for bees (2008): *www.ted.com/talks/dennis_vanengelsdorp_a_plea_for_bees*
13. People, plants and pollinators – Nat Geo Live (Sept 2011): www.youtube.com/watch?v=rmL_XTrPOMw
14. Every city needs healthy honey bees (2012): *www.ted.com/talks/noah_wilson_rich_every_city_needs_healthy_honey_bees*
15. Why bees are disappearing (2013): *www.ted.com/talks/marla_spivak_why_bees_are_disappearing*
16. A world without bees – History (Jun 2014): *www.youtube.com/watch?v=7X1xIIyZw3M*
17. What happens if all the bees die? – AsapSCIENCE (March 2015): *www.youtube.com/watch?v=JilYBVrFiLA*
18. Bee extinction: Why we're saving the wrong bees (May 2021): *www.youtube.com/watch?v=VSYgDssQUtA&ab_channel=DWPlanetA*
19. How to increase food production by using native pollinators (Nov 2015): *www.youtube.com/watch?v=eCLbmOEsrb0*
20. How to attract more bees and pollinators to your garden (Aug 2017) *www.youtube.com/watch?v=6yv7I-Ifxcw* Pollination for kids (Sept 2017): *www.youtube.com/watch?v=CUPzbTuJlgc*
21. Providing a pollination service – a 'how to' video from the Honey Bee & Pollination Program (Sept 2015): *www.youtube.com/watch?v=JEylihp9DX4*

Useful organisations and contacts
22. Wheen Bee Foundation: *https://www.wheenbeefoundation.org.au/about-bees-pollination/*
23. Australian Honey Bee Industry Council: *https://honeybee.org.au/organisation/*
24. Save the Bees: *https://www.beethecure.com.au/*
25. Australian Native Bee Association: *https://australiannativebee.org.au/*
26. Australian Pollinator Week: *https://www.australianpollinatorweek.org.au/*

Figure 6.1: Research resources for Year 4–6 'Paucity of pollinators' STEM project

STEP 2: CREATE A SITUATION DESCRIPTION

The next step is to extract information from the gathered resources to describe the background and key issues inherent in the challenge. This situation description is organised as a logical flow of information and highlights the urgency of developing solutions to the selected challenge. It should explain why it is important for students to act. The information gathered in the situation description will be used later in define-phase planning.

Figure 6.2 is a situation description for 'Paucity of pollinators', building on the research resources gathered in figure 6.1. The information is organised to firstly explain what a pollinator is and how they influence plants, their importance to the production of our food, medicine and clothes (textiles), the widespread decline of pollinators and what may be causing the decline, and then ends with the problem it will cause for all humanity. The numbers in brackets at the end of each statement refer to the numbering of the resources listed in the Figure 6.1.

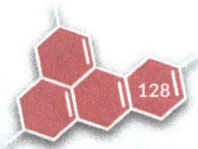

> **Situation description**
> - A pollinator is an animal that causes plants to make fruit or seeds. (2, 6, 7, 9, 17, 27)
>   - Insects, birds and bats pollinate plants. Plants and animals interact in their search for food. Bees and other insects, as well as some birds and bats, transfer pollen from plant to plant. While stopping at a flower for a sip of sweet nectar, the animals or insects get dusted with pollen.
>   - When the animals or insects fly to another flower of the same or similar species, some of that pollen brushes off and the pollinated flowers are then able to produce seeds.
>   - Pollination is important not only for wild plants, but also for crop plants.
> - It is estimated that 65% of all flowering plants and some seed plants (e.g. cycads and pines) require insects for pollination. This percentage is even greater for economically important crops that provide fruits, vegetables, textile-related fibres and medicinal products. (9, 17)
> - Pollinating insects like bees, butterflies and flies have had a rough time of late. Evidence suggests there has been a widespread decline in their abundance and diversity since the 1950s. This matters because such insects are critical both for the reproduction of wild plants and for agricultural food production. (2, 27)
> - The decline of these pollinators is linked with destruction of natural habitats like forests and meadows, the spread of pests such as Varroa mite and diseases like foulbrood, and the increasing use of agrochemicals by farmers. Although there have been well-documented declines in managed honey bees, non-Apis (non-honeybee) pollinators such as bumblebees and solitary bees have also become endangered. (2,8)
> - The loss of bees and other pollinators would have an enormous impact on food production and therefore the viability of resources that humanity relies on. (17)

Figure 6.2: Situation description for Year 4–6 'Paucity of pollinators' STEM project

STEP 3: SPECULATE ON NEEDS, CHALLENGES AND QUESTIONS

The final step of empathise-phase planning involves further thinking and speculation around stakeholder needs, challenges that could be addressed and possible questions to ask students. While this process is used to provoke teacher thinking and planning, it is worthwhile to work through this step with students during the project. The goal of this step is to provoke deeper thinking about the relationships and connections between the issues, needs and questions that could be explored during the project.

The best approach to this final step is to begin by identifying the groups or individuals who may be affected by the issues arising from the identified problem or problems. Who are the primary groups and individuals affected by the issues? How are they affected? Are there flow-on effects to other groups? For example, noted in response to the first prompt in figure 6.3, a lack of pollinators would have a primary impact on growers and farmers, but this impact would flow on to consumers in terms of the food and clothing they use, businesses that use the grown produce to create other goods, and ultimately the government with economic and political impacts. The list is purely speculative, but the intention is to stand in the shoes of each stakeholder and think about their specific needs. What are their particular considerations and wants?

Teachers should then use the understanding gained from the gathered research resources to brainstorm a range of challenges that could be addressed during the STEM project. In effect, this is about identifying the potential causes of the problem or issue. It is important to not only identify some of the direct causes, but also to speculate on what other factors might be causing the situation and the effect of competing needs. In the 'Paucity of pollinators' example, the decline of pollinators might be caused by a wide range of factors such as drought, land clearing, pesticides, introduced species and monoculture farming. Consumer overpopulation and growing desire for fast food are more systemic issues, but they are also likely to highlight the issue of sustainability and cause students to reflect on their own behaviours.

The remaining two fields require teachers to brainstorm possible questions that could focus the direction students will take during the task and speculate about why the students should be personally and emotionally connected to the challenge. The teachers who developed the 'Paucity of pollinators' STEM project struggled at this point because their school was in a metropolitan area and didn't have many connections to farming and agriculture. Once they began exploring the challenges and possible questions to ask, they realised that they should focus on the local challenges and impact to make it relatable and personal to themselves and their students. This made the thinking and planning easier.

What are the needs of the users?
- Need to keep genetic diversity in plants – growers, farmers, government
- need pollinators for the production of food – growers, farmers, consumers, government
- need to eliminate pests and weeds to minimise loss of agricultural products – growers, farmers
- need to have land for the growing demand of meat and raw materials such as coffee, cotton, canola etc. – government, farmers, businesses
- need for fast food – consumers.

What are the challenges that we want to address?
- Loss of forests and brush due to land clearing for meat producing animals (sheep, cows etc.)
- impact of droughts and floods on production of food to meet demands – government, farmers, growers
- growing population and increase in wealth of people in developing countries – government, consumers
- consumers are eating more meat and thus need more land
- use of pesticides to kill pests is also killing pollinators
- introduced species could be killing the pollinators
- issues with monoculture farming
- loss of appropriate indigenous flora
- students could approach council and appropriate organisations to source specific local challenges to pollinators.

Potential questions that could be asked:
- How are plants pollinated?
- Why are bees and other pollinators dying?
- How are we contributing to the loss of pollinators?
- How can we use the area of the school to improve the survival of pollinators?
- What things do we need to consider if we improve the survival of pollinators?
- Why are some people allergic to bees?
- Are the needs of pollinators different in different parts of the world compared to Australia?
- Can we encourage certain pollinators?
- Is our behaviour as humanity destroying the future of the world?
- How can we use our brilliance to create a safe world for pollinators?
- How can we maintain a thriving environment for pollinators whilst meeting humanity's needs?

Why is this important for students?
- They are the future generation/protectors of the environment.
- If pollinators die out, they are the ones who will be most impacted.
- Our demand for particular foods and products is driving the situation. (6)
- Without pollinators, most of our food sources will disappear. (2, 8 ,9, 27)

Figure 6.3: Needs, challenges and questions for Year 4–6 'Paucity of pollinators' STEM project

Igniting STEM Learning

Exercise: Empathise-phase planning

Use the template below and its guiding questions to perform the research and thinking to come to a deeper understanding of the selected open-ended STEM project. The aim is to gather enough age-appropriate resources and do sufficient thinking so that both teachers and students can connect to the urgency of taking action on this open-ended challenge.

Research resources

Useful videos
-
-

Useful organisations and contacts
-
-

Situation description
Use the information gathered during the research stage to describe the background of the challenge.
-
-

What are the needs of the users?
Speculate on who may be the stakeholders (those impacted by the issue) and their possible needs.
-
-

What are the challenges that we want to address?
Speculate on the potential challenges, causes of why the problem or issue exists and the impact of competing needs.
-
-

Potential questions that could be asked:
Brainstorm a range of potential questions that could be asked.
-
-

Why is this important for students?
Why should students care? How is their behaviour causing the situation? How can they become personally and emotionally connected to the situation?
-
-

Reproducible available

THE DEFINE PHASE OF PLANNING

While empathise-phase planning is predominantly a divergent process with the aim of gaining a deeper appreciation of the dimensions of the issues involved, define-phase planning is a convergent process which involves synthesising and defining exactly what the STEM project is going to focus on. This is an essential step for teachers because real-world STEM challenges have multiple possible challenges that can be addressed, and each will lead to very different design and solution paths. The goal during define-phase planning is to specify the driving or essential questions to

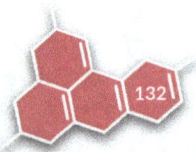

focus on, identify the curriculum outcomes the STEM project should address, and define and plan the culminating STEM assessment. The two steps of define-phase planning support teachers to design a STEM project that meets the curriculum requirements and ensures students apply their knowledge, skills and thinking to an authentic real-world challenge.

STEP 1: ESSENTIAL QUESTIONS AND CURRICULUM OUTCOMES

The brainstorming and speculation about challenges, questions and why students should care carried out in the empathise phase of planning can now be used to design one or more possible essential or driving questions. As discussed in Chapter 4, an essential or driving question frames a STEM project as a problem to be solved. It launches students into a learning journey that is meaningful to them, actionable and provokes deep thought, lively discussion, sustained inquiry and understandings as well as more questions.

The essential question created for the 'Paucity of Pollinators' STEM project has two parts (see figure 6.4). The first sentence captures the problem and one of the major causes of the problem:

Human activities are destroying the population of pollinators globally and this could lead to the loss of most of our food sources.

The second sentence challenges students to design solutions that will result in a thriving environment for pollinators while meeting humanity's needs:

How can we maintain a thriving environment for pollinators while meeting humanity's needs?

This second sentence highlights the underlying tension between the needs of the pollinators and humanity. The essential question for this STEM project is deliberately broad because the teachers wanted to have the freedom to tailor the focus of the question to their year-level curriculum requirements. While one essential question was identified in this case, teachers could brainstorm a range of essential questions before deciding on the one they will focus on during the GRASPS model planning to come.

Having articulated the essential question, the specific transdisciplinary curriculum knowledge, skills and thinking that can be addressed by the STEM project should be identified. This will ensure their planning addresses the curriculum. The teachers who created the 'Paucity of pollinators' STEM project identified possible useful content and skill descriptors from science, geography, economics and business, design and technology, and the general capabilities from Year 4 to 6 (figure 6.4). This made them aware of how they could adapt the project to target specific year-level needs. For example, they could focus the STEM project on the science and geography aspects, involve the cross-curriculum priorities of sustainability or Aboriginal and Torres Strait Islander histories and cultures, or even explore how consumer choices impact the sustainability of the environment. The teachers could have also identified related content and skill descriptors from maths, English and art, which would have enabled them to involve the time and resources of those teachers and specialist areas.

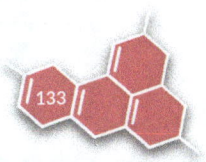

Igniting STEM Learning

Driving/essential questions:
- Human activities are destroying the population of pollinators globally and this could lead to the loss of most of our food sources. How can we maintain a thriving environment for pollinators while meeting humanity's needs?

What curriculum outcomes do we want from students grappling with this topic?

Science
- Year 4
  - explain the roles and interactions of consumers, producers and decomposers within a habitat and how food chains represent feeding relationships (AC9S4U01)
  - consider how people use scientific explanations to meet a need or solve a problem (AC9S4H02)
- Year 5
  - examine how particular structural features and behaviours of living things enable their survival in specific habitats (AC9S5U01)
  - investigate how scientific knowledge is used by individuals and communities to identify problems, consider responses and make decisions (AC9S5H02)
- Year 6
  - investigate the physical conditions of a habitat and analyse how the growth and survival of living things is affected by changing physical conditions (AC9S6U01)
  - investigate how scientific knowledge is used by individuals and communities to identify problems, consider responses and make decisions (AC9S6H02)
- Year 4–6 Science inquiry skills

HASS – geography
- Year 4
  - the importance of environments, including natural vegetation and water sources, to people and animals in Australia and on another continent (AC9HS4K05)
  - sustainable use and management of renewable and non-renewable resources, including the custodial responsibility First Nations Australians have for Country/Place (AC9HS4K06)
- Year 5
  - the influence of people, including First Nations Australians and people in other countries, on the characteristics of a place (AC9HS5K04)
  - the management of Australian environments, including managing severe weather events such as bushfires, floods, droughts or cyclones, and their consequences (AC9HS5K05)

HASS – economics and business
- Year 5
  - types of resources, including natural, human and capital, and how they satisfy needs and wants (AC9HS5K08)
- Year 6
  - influences on consumer choices and strategies that can be used to help make informed personal consumer and financial choices (AC9HS6K08)

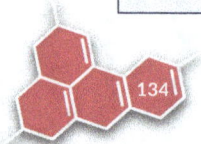

Getting real-world with open-ended STEM projects

> **Design and technology**
> ⚡ Year 3/4
>   • describe the ways of producing food and fibre (AC9TDE4K03)
> ⚡ Year 5/6
>   • Explain how and why food and fibre are produced in managed environments (AC9TDE6K03).
> ⚡ Year 4–6 Design and technology: Processes and production skills
>
> **General capabilities**
> ⚡ Critical and creative thinking (generating)
> ⚡ Personal and social capability (collaboration, communication and decision-making)
> ⚡ Ethical understanding (explore ethical concepts; making and reflecting on ethical decisions)

Figure 6.4: Essential question and student outcomes for the Year 4–6 'Paucity of pollinators' STEM project
Source: Adapted from ACARA (n.d.-d, -f, -g, -i, -m, -q)

Once teachers have formulated the essential question and identified the curriculum to be addressed they should follow the process outlined in Chapter 4 to deconstruct the curriculum into learning intentions and success criteria (from page 73). This will prepare them for the GRASPS model planning in the next step of define-phase planning and provide the necessary aspects for assessing student progress, which will be discussed in Chapter 7.

STEP 2: GRASPS MODEL PLANNING AND DESIGN PROCESS CHECKLIST

As explained in Chapter 5, completing GRASPS model planning and creating a checklist of steps supports teachers to design learning that enables students to cycle through the design, prototype, evaluate and refine stages and demonstrate the knowledge and skill they have acquired. The planning process from this point has been outlined in Chapter 5. By the end of this step, teachers will have a map of the flow of activities across the project aligned with the design process. Teachers can then create a student version of the checklist of steps in partnership with students.

Figure 6.5 (page 136) shows the GRASPS model planning and design process checklist for the 'Paucity of pollinators' STEM project. There are two aspects to note about this planning. First, the empathise phase of planning has made the task of unpacking the logical sequence of understandings shown in the situation section of the GRASPS model much easier. This sequence of understandings has been carried into the planning of learning activities in the design-process template. Secondly, the planning indicates that there will be three smaller milestone deliverables as part of the project: a research report, a persuasive presentation and a designed product that will make a difference to the pollinators' environment. By spacing the deliverables across the length of the unit teachers can provide multiple opportunities for students to go through a drafting, feedback and refinement process to achieve high-quality products.

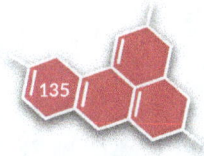

Igniting STEM Learning

Goal and driving question	Question: Human activities are destroying the population of pollinators globally and this could lead to the loss of most of our food sources. How can we maintain a thriving environment for pollinators whilst meeting humanity's needs? Demonstrate your ability to use science and design to communicate and persuade people to take actions to improve the environment for pollinators
Role	Environmental scientists You are a community of concerned environmental scientists and activists who are committed to creating a sustainable future for pollinators, yourselves and your children.
Audience	Peers, the principal, and parents and guardians.
Situation	Logical sequence of understandings: 1. Over 65% of plants on earth require pollination by a variety of species like bees, birds, butterflies and flies to be able to reproduce. 2. Humans rely on many of these plants for food and a sustainable ecology. 3. Humans have a profound impact on the sustainability of pollinators in the environment. 4. We have a responsibility to create a safe world for pollinators to secure the future of the environment and ourselves.
Product/performance	Your goal in this project is to come up with one way to: 1. change people's perception about pollinators 2. encourage pollinators in our school environment 3. create a community action to improve the environment for pollinators.
Standards	Rubrics to be designed for the identified skills and knowledge elements.

Design phase	Approx. time to complete	Checklist steps
Empathise		**1. Over 65% of plants on earth require pollination by a variety of species like bees, birds, butterflies and flies to be able to reproduce.** • Excursion outside where they look at plants and the environment • Taste honey • Activity – Match the plant to the pollinator • Activity – Which of these common plants need pollinators to reproduce? **2. Humans rely on many of these plants for food and a sustainable ecology** • Bring baskets of different fruits and ask where this food comes from • Activity – Which foods require pollination? • Activity – Food web: What would happen if we lost our pollinators? • Speculative brainstorm • Video shows what would happen

Define		3. Humans have a profound impact on the sustainability of pollinators in the environment
		• Research task: How do our actions impact pollinators?
		  ◦ Research as teams
		  ◦ Discussion as class (what are we doing that impacts the pollinators)
		  ◦ Draw mind map showing relationship between our actions and the pollinators
		• Research task: What are humanity's needs that must be met?
		  ◦ Research as teams
		  ◦ Discussion (ethics, what needs must be met)
		  ◦ Create a refined mind map
		• Research task: What are some of the ways we make a difference to the pollinators' environment?
		• Research as teams what can be some of the local, national and global actions that could be taken.
		• Discuss potential examples:
		  ◦ Insect hotels
		  ◦ Pollinator attractors
		  ◦ Flora to plant in school/woodlands to attract more pollinators
		  ◦ Elevated bird baths
		  ◦ Bee hospital
		  ◦ Colours that attract different pollinators
		• Student teams to:
		  ◦ Define what challenge they are going to tackle
		  ◦ Create a persuasive presentation which addresses the challenge, the needs and potential solutions
		  ◦ Identify what they are going to design and build to improve the pollinator's environment either within the school or at home

Ideate–prototype–test		4. We have a responsibility to create a safe world for pollinators to secure the future of the environment and ourselves. • Students to iterate through the design process to plan, prototype and build the chosen design • Time to test and gather evidence of the influence of the design in improving the environment for pollinators?
Deliver		• Update and refine their persuasive presentation • Practice the presentation • Culminating event where students present to peers, parents and the principal

Figure 6.5: GRASPS model planning and design process checklist for the 'Paucity of pollinators' STEM project

Igniting STEM Learning

Exercise: Define-phase planning

Use the following template and guiding questions to narrow down the focus of the open-ended STEM project into a viable STEM unit. The aim is to use the thinking and planning performed in the empathise phase to identify the specific aspects of the Australian Curriculum that the unit will address, potential essential or driving questions, the culminating STEM task and a broad checklist of steps for the unit.

Check the downloadables for further examples of define-phase planning.

Driving or essential questions
What possible driving or essential questions could be asked that are meaningful and actionable?

-
-

What student outcomes do we want from students grappling with this topic?
List the specific curriculum knowledge, skills and thinking that could be addressed in this open-ended challenge. Use the Australian Curriculum and the General Capabilities as a guide.

-
-

Use the GRASP model to define the transdisciplinary STEM assessment task:

Goal — Goal, problem, challenge or obstacle for the task	
Role — Role of the students in the scenario and what they are being asked to do	
Audience — The target audience the students will be presenting to	
Situation — Context and explanation of the situation	
Product/performance — The product or performance that needs to be created and its larger purpose	
Standards — The specific standards for success that must be met and how the work will be judged	

Getting real-world with open-ended STEM projects

Unpack the checklist of steps using the design thinking framework:

Design phase	Approx. time to complete	Checklist steps
Empathise Includes research		1. 2. 3. 4.
Define Includes mind-mapping		5. 6. 7. 8.
Ideate–prototype–test This is the iterative improvement cycle		9. 10. 11. 12. 13.
Deliver Preparing for and delivering presentation		14. 15. 16. 17. 18.

Reproducible available

COMPLETING THE PLANNING

Once the empathise- and define-phase planning are complete, the remaining planning for the open-ended STEM project should be as normal for teachers. They can create a one-page assessment sheet (as discussed in Chapter 5) and plan the learning experiences and instruction. The lesson-planning template that follows (figure 6.6, page 140) supports aligning the design thinking process, learning intentions and success criteria, and learning activities and instruction. Formative assessment structures and feedback strategies will be discussed in Chapter 7.

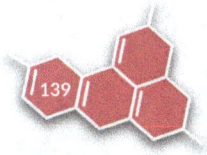

Igniting STEM Learning

Design thinking stages	Learning intention and success criteria	Learning experiences and instruction	Formative assessment / feedback strategy
Empathise Plan motivational learning experiences that immerse students and have them gain a deeper appreciation and understanding of the needs, behaviours and dimensions of the issues that are involved.	We are learning to ... I can <ul><li></li></ul>	Lesson 1: Lesson 2:	
	We are learning to ... I can <ul><li></li></ul>	Lesson 3: Lesson 4: Lesson 5: Specialist lesson:	
Define Plan learning activities that take students through a synthesis process (creatively piecing together the puzzle together to form whole ideas) with the aim of identifying the problem they want to solve. Younger students may need direction. (Update curriculum links based on student identified problems)	We are learning to ... I can <ul><li></li></ul>	Lesson 6: Lesson 7:	
Iterative improvement cycle **Ideate** Students brainstorm and develop creative solutions to solve the problem. They design their solution.	We are learning to ... I can <ul><li></li></ul>	Lesson 8: Lesson 9: Lesson 10: Lesson 11	
Prototype Students bring their designs to life by creating tangible objects/ solutions.	We are learning to ... I can <ul><li></li></ul>	Lesson 12: Lesson 13: Lesson 14: Lesson 15:	
Test Students check and test prototype and evaluate effectiveness.	We are learning to ... I can <ul><li></li></ul>	Lesson 16:	
Communicate Students communicate and/or deliver on the product/ erformance.	We are learning to ... I can <ul><li></li></ul>	Lesson 17:	

Figure 6.6: Sample lesson-planning template
Reproducible available

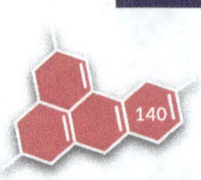

COACHING ON DESIGNING OPEN-ENDED STEM PROJECTS

The purpose of designing open-ended STEM projects is creating authentic, rich STEM learning that requires students to apply the knowledge, skills and thinking they have acquired so far to real-world challenges that have no single answer or solution. The projects should, as much as possible, reflect the learning and processes that occur beyond the bounds of traditional schooling.

The planning process outlined in this chapter takes teachers on the journey that designers, engineers, architects and problem-solvers undertake when they are attempting to solve a challenge. At the start teachers may not have much background knowledge or experience in the chosen open-ended challenge. This is an advantage because 'not knowing' forces teachers to be learners and let go of the expectation that they should know the answers. Many students have come to rely on teachers having the answers rather than working things out for themselves. The space of not knowing is extraordinarily empowering because it frees teachers to be experts in learning and thinking rather than knowledge. The journey that teachers take through the planning process will provide enough certainty and clarity for them to understand where they are going and how they can provide a path for students to reach the desired learning destination successfully.

Effective problem-solvers learn to deal with uncertainty as they work towards a successful outcome. They also learn that the path to desired outcomes is often much longer than first thought or planned for. Real-world challenges demand students deal with the messiness and complexity of making something occur in reality. They will come to learn lessons such as: people don't always respond to your requests in a timely fashion, prototypes don't often work the first time, failure is just a learning experience, and planning does make a difference. For students to authentically grapple with consolidating and transferring their knowledge, skills and thinking, teachers should ensure that significant time is allotted for students to work their way through the ideate–prototype–test cycle. This investment of time will lead to significantly better learning outcomes and final products. Given this, teachers should err on the side of under-planning learning activities and instruction rather than over-planning.

Finally, the process of planning and running open-ended STEM projects is a learning experience for teachers as well as students. The more teachers go through the process, the more skilled they will become and the greater the learning impact will be. The best way to become more effective at planning and leading STEM projects is to set aside time as the project progresses to debrief and capture the lessons that are being learnt. The next chapter explores the thinking that needs to be done to create high-quality STEM assessments.

KEY POINTS

- A never-ending source of open-ended challenges can be created by adding worthwhile and relevant real-world challenges to a problem bank. These challenges can be sourced from within the school, the local community and even nationally or globally.
- Planning open-ended STEM projects begins with gathering resources and doing some initial thinking to gain a deeper appreciation and understanding of the needs, behaviours and dimensions of the issues that are involved. This investment of time and effort supports teachers to become clearer about the possible directions and learning opportunities for the STEM project.

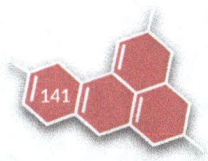

Igniting STEM *Learning*

- Real-world STEM problems have multiple possible challenges that could be addressed, each leading down very different design and solution paths. Define-phase planning enables teachers to create a STEM project that meets the year-level curriculum requirements while focusing the students on manageable challenges and design paths.
- This approach to planning open-ended STEM projects is a process of increasing certainty and clarity for teachers. A lesson-planning template is provided to make aligning the design thinking process, learning intentions and success criteria with learning activities and instruction much easier.
- When planning learning activities and instruction, err on the side of under-planning activities rather than over-planning. The focus is on consolidating and transferring knowledge, skills and thinking to authentic real-life tasks. Consolidation and transfer often takes much longer than we think.

CHAPTER 7
Assessing STEM learning

Learning is about one's relationship with oneself and one's ability to exert the effort, self-control, and critical self-assessment necessary to achieve the best possible results – and about overcoming risk aversion, failure, distractions, and sheer laziness in pursuit of REAL achievement.

(Nilson, 2013, p. xxvii)

BROADENING OUR PERSPECTIVE

Effective assessment of STEM learning is sometimes considered to be a Holy Grail for educators and school systems alike. Everyone knows that great STEM assessment should exist, but no one knows what it looks like or where to find it. As part of my research for this book, I gathered a wide range of STEM learning assessments being used by teachers and schools, as well as those promoted by education systems, to get a sense of the current thinking. What I discovered is that there is currently no consistent agreement about what should be measured in STEM learning – or even how to assess progression. While I did find some examples in which teachers and schools demonstrate a great depth of thinking in the design of their assessment approaches, very few people know what they should be assessing or how to assess it well.

The design of assessment approach reveals an enormous amount about the perspective the teacher, school or education system holds on the purpose of STEM learning. If the designed assessment for STEM learning only addresses what is produced at the end of the learning, then it is ignoring the progression in thinking and skill development that the students make as they take the learning journey. If the assessment only focuses on whether the student has gained the required knowledge or skill in the various disciplines that the STEM unit is designed to cover, then the assessment is not addressing the growth in associated general capabilities. If the assessment is purely to judge the progression of the student for the benefit of the teacher, then it ignores the benefits of students assessing themselves and each other. And if the assessment is designed to meet current reporting requirements, then it is not about learning, but rather it is simply about ticking off those reporting requirements.

This chapter will begin by examining and discussing the strengths and potential challenges of three STEM assessment approaches. Through revisiting the design of the Australian Curriculum, we will define what aspects are worth assessing to achieve the most desirable outcomes from designing and leading STEM learning. We will then explore the thinking that needs to be done to create high-quality STEM assessments and provide a range of possible structures and approaches that can be embedded within a STEM-rich task.

One thing to note is that what follows in this chapter should not be considered a definitive answer. As a result of recent growth in research around developing self-regulated and assessment-capable learners, new evidence is becoming available all the time – meaning there will be new approaches and thinking about what elements are important to assess when developing STEM learners. Rather than being prescriptive, the intent of this chapter is to broaden existing perspectives and thinking about assessment in STEM, and to provide templates and strategies that teachers can use every day.

CURRENT ASSESSMENT APPROACHES

While there is no consistent agreement around assessing STEM learning, the following three approaches and rubrics – one supplied by an education system, another produced for a single curriculum area, and a third built for a transdisciplinary STEM unit – are representative of the majority of STEM assessments currently in use. Each has its strengths and practical issues and provides an insight to general approaches used around Australia.

AN EDUCATION SYSTEM APPROACH

It is pleasing to see that the assessment approaches that are being created and promoted by education systems to their teachers are becoming more nuanced and sophisticated. Many can be used formatively across the length of a STEM unit, and many address more than just the content knowledge. As an example, table 7.1 shows part of the Years 3 and 4 standard elaborations for the Australian Curriculum: Design and technologies as produced by the Queensland Curriculum & Assessment Authority (QCAA; 2019b).

As the QCAA states, its intention with these elaborations is to provide 'teachers with a tool for making consistent, comparable and defensible judgments about how well, on a five-point scale, students have demonstrated what they know, understand and can do' (QCAA, n.d., 'Standards elaborations' section). The QCAA expects teachers to take the standard elaboration progressions and create marking guides for specific tasks, align their reporting and use them in individual assessment of a portfolio of student work.

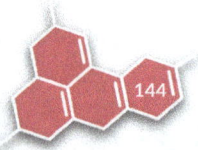

Assessing STEM learning

Table 7.1: Years 3 and 4 Design and technologies – processes and production skills

	A	B	C	D	E
	The student's portfolio of work has the following characteristics.				
Investigating and defining	**comprehensive** explanation of needs or opportunities for each of the prescribed technologies contexts	**detailed** explanation of needs or opportunities for each of the prescribed technologies contexts	explanation of needs or opportunities for each of the prescribed technologies contexts	**description** of needs or opportunities for each of the prescribed technologies contexts	**statement about** needs or opportunities for each of the prescribed technologies contexts
Generating and designing	**considered** development and expansion of design ideas	**informed** development and expansion of design ideas	development and expansion of design ideas	**partial** development and expansion of design ideas	**fragmented** expansion of given design ideas
	thorough and effective communication of design ideas using models and drawings including annotations and symbols	**effective** communication of design ideas using models and drawings including annotations and symbols	communication of design ideas using models and drawings including annotations and symbols	**partial** communication of design ideas using **aspects of** models and **partially labelled** drawings	**fragmented** communication of design ideas using **aspects of** models and drawings
Producing and implementing	**proficient** production of designed solutions: • demonstrating safe work practices • identifying appropriate technologies and techniques	**effective** production of designed solutions: • demonstrating safe work practices • identifying appropriate technologies and techniques	production of designed solutions: • demonstrating safe work practices • identifying appropriate technologies and techniques	**partial** production of designed solutions: • demonstrating safe work practices • identifying technologies and techniques	**guided** production of designed solutions: • demonstrating safe work practices • identifying **aspects of** technologies and techniques
Evaluating	**considered** evaluation of ideas and designed solutions against identified criteria for success, including environmental sustainability considerations	**informed** evaluation of ideas and designed solutions against identified criteria for success, including environmental sustainability considerations	evaluation of ideas and designed solutions against identified criteria for success, including environmental sustainability considerations	**explanation** of ideas and designed solutions against identified criteria for success, including **aspects of** environmental sustainability considerations	**statements about** ideas and designed solutions against identified criteria for success
Collaborating and managing	**considered** planning and **comprehensive** sequencing of major steps in design and production	**informed** planning and **detailed** sequencing of major steps in design and production	planning and sequencing of major steps in design and production	**partial** planning and **partial** sequencing of steps in design and production	**fragmented** planning and **fragmented** steps in design and production

Source: QCAA (2019b)

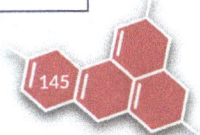

145

POSITIVES

There are several good things about the QCAA approach. First among these positives is that they have indicated assessment should be done on a portfolio of student work. This begins to shift a common teacher practice of assessing only an end product to one of also assessing a student's learning journey. The QCAA also indicates that the standard elaborations should be taken and adapted by teachers for specific tasks. The expectation is that teachers will need to think their way through the design of the assessment they will use for specific STEM learning tasks. Finally, the QCAA has indicated that a progression of skill development exists for each element, as is set out in 'Design and technologies – process and production skills' in the example on page 145.

The investment that the QCAA has made to produce these documents is admirable and a great step forward. However, there are several practical issues with the design of these progressions.

PRACTICAL ISSUE 1: VAGUE 'TEACHER SPEAK'

The first practical issue is with the use of vague terminology and 'teacher speak' to show a progression of skill or capability. While the QCAA does attempt to define each of the terms used, most teachers will still be unclear as to what *comprehensive, thorough, informed, partial, fragmented, effective, proficient* and so on look like in practice. This vague terminology makes it nearly impossible for assessments to be consistent and comparable across schools, unless significant moderation is in place between those schools.

This is a major complaint from teachers attempting to design assessment tasks, and it is especially problematic for teachers new to STEM learning who don't have a design background or in smaller schools that don't have a community to discuss terms and come to a shared understanding of what they mean. Given the normal behaviour of time-poor teachers, they end up having to use the standard elaboration progressions to assess their students.

Secondly, if the progressions are challenging for teachers to understand, they will be virtually unusable by students to self- or peer-assess without an extraordinary amount of scaffolding as to their meaning and a wide range of guiding examples. In other words, if teachers were going to ensure that students independently use the progressions to guide their own learning development, they would need to invest a significant amount of class time into deconstructing the progressions to make them clear enough for students to use them effectively.

PRACTICAL ISSUE 2: POOR PROGRESSION ACROSS YEAR LEVELS

The poor design of skill progression across multiple year levels, which only becomes apparent when you look at the standard elaboration progression documents as a whole set, is another practical issue.

Take the 'Investigating and defining' progression from Prep to Year 6, shown in table 7.2, as an example. In essence, what the standard elaboration documents are saying is that the progression of investigating and defining skills are based solely on student ability to describe and explain needs and opportunities in one or a number of technologies contexts. This is an extraordinarily shallow and narrow conceptualisation of investigating and defining in a STEM context. Investigating should involve identifying the goal of the investigation, coming up with strategies to find out and gather information and data, and even discussing any assumptions that have been made. Defining should then involve synthesising the gathered information to gain insight and describe the given needs or opportunities.

Further, in any well-designed STEM assessment progression, students at any year level should be able to progress their skills beyond those of their own year level. For example, a Year 2 student

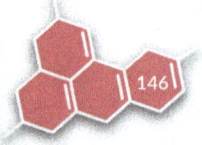

could be demonstrating a skill level commensurate with the statements in Years 3–4 or 5–6. Equally a Year 5 or 6 student might be demonstrating a skill level corresponding to statements in Years Prep–2 or 3–4. As currently defined, there is no clear progression of the skill of 'Investigating and defining' across the year levels. This lack of progression is repeated in all the standard elaboration progressions.

Table 7.2: Standard elaborations for 'Investigating and defining', Prep–Year 6

Year	A	B	C	D	E
Prep–2	clear and informed description of given needs or opportunities	informed description of given needs or opportunities	description of given needs or opportunities	guided description of given needs or opportunities	directed statements about given needs or opportunities
3–4	comprehensive explanation of needs or opportunities for each of the prescribed technologies contexts	detailed explanation of needs or opportunities for each of the prescribed technologies contexts	explanation of needs or opportunities for each of the prescribed technologies contexts	description of needs or opportunities for each of the prescribed technologies contexts	statement about needs or opportunities for each of the prescribed technologies contexts
5–6	identification and explanation of needs or opportunities for each of the prescribed technologies contexts	identification and description of needs or opportunities for each of the prescribed technologies contexts	identification of needs or opportunities for each of the prescribed technologies contexts	identification of aspects of needs or opportunities for each of the prescribed technologies contexts	statements about needs or opportunities for each of the prescribed technologies contexts

Source: QCAA (2019a, 2019b, 2019c)

PRACTICAL ISSUE 3: GRADES VS GROWTH

The final practical issue with education system documents such as the QCAA's standard elaborations is that they have grades associated with each level. Understandably, as a state assessment authority, the QCAA produces documents that teachers can use to summatively assess and produce their reports. However, if the education system is interested in developing an environment in which teachers and students focus on learning growth, then associating knowledge, skill or thinking progression primarily with grades is outdated as a convention.

Grading approaches encourage students to focus on the external motivation of a grade rather than the intrinsic motivation of progressive skill growth. A key outcome of STEM learning is development of students' capacity to self-regulate and become their own teachers. An assessment approach that supports students to collaboratively work together and set goals, apply strategies, seek feedback and gain clarity about their next steps is more consistent with STEM learning than one based on grades (Frey, Hattie & Fisher, 2018).

A SINGLE CURRICULUM AREA APPROACH

The digital technologies assessment rubric shown in table 7.3 (page 148) is representative of the type of rubrics many teachers produce for technology or single discipline units. This rubric has a number of interesting features. First, there is an attempt to use student-friendly language

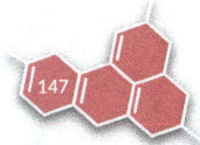

throughout the progression, which means that students can independently self-assess what their current level of skill is and identify the next steps they could take to improve their grade and hopefully deepen their skills. Second, while the rubric does include an A–E grading approach, it is ordered in reverse to what one would normally see. The design of progress from left to right makes it easier for students to read and understand. There is also consistency in the language used at each grade level, from *not attempted* at E, to *with support* at D, then *work independently* at C, and to increasing depth of outcomes and skills at B and A. Overall, the rubric has been designed to be quite specific and age appropriate.

Table 7.3: **Example assessment rubric for a digital technologies project**

Area	E	D	C	B	A
Demonstrate capacity to set up a fruit piano using a Makey Makey kit.	I did not attempt to set up a fruit piano using a Makey Makey kit.	With support, I was able to connect crocodile clips between the fruit and a Makey Makey kit.	I was able to work mostly independently to connect crocodile clips between the fruit and the Makey Makey kit.	I was able to work independently to connect crocodile clips between the fruit and the Makey Makey kit. I was able to problem-solve any issues to make it work.	I was able to work independently to connect crocodile clips between the fruit and the Makey Makey kit, problem-solve any issues to make it work, and support others to have theirs work.
Program the Makey Makey fruit piano.	I did not attempt to code the fruit piano using Scratch.	With support, I was able to follow the coding instructions to program one piece of fruit.	I was able to work independently to follow the coding instructions to program one piece of fruit.	I was able to work independently to follow the coding instructions to program two or more pieces of fruit.	I was able to work independently to follow the coding instructions to program the entire fruit piano and used it to play a simple tune.
Explain the science of the fruit piano.	I did not include an explanation of conductivity.	With support, I was able to explain the difference between something being conductive and something being non-conductive.	I was able to work independently to explain the difference between something being conductive and something being non-conductive.	I was able to explain the difference between something being conductive and non-conductive and draw examples of both.	I was able to explain the difference between something being conductive and non-conductive, draw examples of both, and include references in a bibliography.

Apart from the use of grading, there are two other areas that could be improved. The 'not attempted' column is a common feature of many rubrics. However, if the rubric is to be used formatively to support student learning, there should be no need for a 'not attempted' column. It is simply a convention that has persisted from summative assessment thinking. Over the course

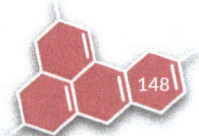

Assessing STEM learning

of a STEM learning unit, every student should be expected and supported to have attempted everything, at least at level D. The second element needing improvement concerns the areas chosen for development. While the rubric addresses setting up the Makey Makey, coding the fruit piano and an element of explaining the science of the fruit piano, it does not appear to be consistent with the requirements of the digital technologies or design and technologies progressions. Depending on the year level, it would be appropriate to include more specific coding statements, such as 'read a program of visual blocks and describe what it might do', 'use if–then statements to create choice', 'design a flow chart to show the sequence of steps for an interactive button' and so on. This would support students to use the language of computational thinking. Similarly, while the rubric does include the words *problem-solve* and *explain*, it misses the opportunity to fully address student growth in elements of science inquiry skills, in particular the 'communicating' skill, and the general capabilities, such as critical thinking and collaboration.

A TRANSDISCIPLINARY APPROACH

Table 7.4 shows an assessment rubric for a Year 6 transdisciplinary learning unit that integrates science, engineering and elements of the design process. The aim of the STEM unit is for students to use their science knowledge of electricity and energy to design a product for a specific purpose.

Table 7.4: Example assessment rubric for a Year 6 transdisciplinary unit

Knowledge and understanding		Processes and production skills		
Technologies and society	Engineering principles and systems	Investigating and defining	Evaluating	Producing and implementing
Describe how design and technologies contribute to meeting present and future need.	Explain how the features of technologies impact on designed solutions for each of the prescribed technologies contexts.	Create designed solutions for the engineering principles and systems context suitable for identified needs and opportunities.	Suggest criteria for success and use these to evaluate their designed solutions using visual representations.	Select and use appropriate technologies and techniques correctly and safely to produce designed solutions.
Describe how electrical designs and technologies contribute to meeting present and future needs, reflecting on the features of designed solutions that ensure safety and wellbeing of users and consider the impact the product has on their lives.	Explain how movement, light or sound can be controlled in a representation of a deconstructed circuit design that shows the features of an electrical system and its impact on designed solutions.	Create electrical designed solutions suitable for identified needs and opportunities, by carefully planning, testing and selecting a range of materials, components, tools and equipment to determine the appropriate technologies needed to perform a specific task.	Suggest criteria for success and use these to evaluate designed solutions in relation to the benefits of the product and its future use and application and the suitability of materials, tools and equipment for specific purposes.	Select and use appropriate technologies and techniques correctly by accurately selecting material and joining techniques to the design intention and work safely, responsibly and cooperatively to produce designed solutions.	A

Continued ...

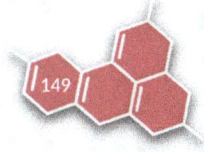

Igniting STEM Learning

Knowledge and understanding			Processes and production skills		
Technologies and society	**Engineering principles and systems**	**Investigating and defining**	**Evaluating**	**Producing and implementing**	
Describe how electrical designs and technologies contribute to meeting present and future needs, reflecting on the features of designed solutions that ensure safety and wellbeing of users.	Explain how movement, light or sound can be controlled through the features of an electrical system and their impact on designed solutions.	Create electrical designed solutions suitable for identified needs and opportunities by testing a range of materials, components, tools and equipment to determine the appropriate technologies needed to make products.	Suggest criteria for success and use these to evaluate designed solutions and the suitability of materials, tools and equipment for specific purposes.	Select and use appropriate technologies and techniques correctly and work safely, responsibly and cooperatively to produce designed solutions.	B
Describe how electrical designs and technologies contribute to meeting present and future needs.	Explain how the features of an electrical system impact on designed solutions.	Create electrical designed solutions suitable for identified needs and opportunities.	Suggest criteria for success and use these to evaluate designed solutions.	Select and use appropriate technologies and techniques correctly and work safely to produce designed solutions.	C
Describe how electrical designs and technologies contribute to meeting present or future needs.	Explain the features of an electrical system.	Create electrical designs.	Suggest criteria for success and evaluate designs.	Select and use technologies and techniques and work safely to produce designs.	D
Describe how an electrical design or technologies contribute to meeting a need.	Explain a feature of an electrical system.	Create designs.	Evaluate designs.	Select and use technologies and techniques.	E

Source: Beckett-Mathews (2020)

A high level of thought is demonstrated in the design of this rubric. It identifies both the knowledge and understanding aspects of the design and technologies curriculum as well as the process and production skills. It attempts to bring some clarity to the progression of knowledge and skill development with clear descriptions and an increase in the complexity of what is required to be delivered by the student as they progress from an E grade up to an A grade. It embeds the science knowledge authentically without the need for a specific column. Finally, each column has a focus description taken directly from the Australian Curriculum. However, the rubric has a certain unwieldiness and complexity to its structure. The higher grade descriptions are much wordier than the lower grades and the verbs used do not change across the progression from grades E to A. This leads to the progression being more about what is produced than about the depth of skill with which students produce it. Without a significant amount of scaffolding and examples, it would also be challenging for students to understand how to improve.

The rubric would be much improved if the Australian Curriculum descriptors were broken down into their elements and if each progression in these were articulate. For example, the descriptor for 'Evaluating' is 'Suggest criteria for success and use these to evaluate their designed solutions using visual representations'. There are two elements to this description that can be unpacked across the progression: (1) developing criteria for success and (2) using the criteria to evaluate a designed solution using visual representations. The progression of skill development would most likely begin with the students needing teacher guidance, then to doing it in collaboration with others, and eventually to doing it independently. The development of the criteria for success might progress from focusing on just the product, to including the processes used, and finally to considering the functionality and sustainability of the designed solution. Evaluating by using the criteria could progress from listing what aspects of the criteria the designed solution meets, to descriptive annotations on images of a designed solution, to showing how well a designed solution meets the criteria for success, to annotations that analyse and discuss the suitability of the processes and the sustainability of the designed solution. If the rubric is decomposed in this way, students will have a lot more clarity about how they can develop their ability.

WHAT SHOULD WE BE ASSESSING IN STEM LEARNING?

As we know, STEM learning brings together multiple curriculum areas to create an authentic learning journey for students. Authentic STEM learning is not bound by the artificial boundaries that are imposed by curriculum documents, but rather nurtures particular mindsets, thinking approaches and capabilities that cross multiple disciplines. Therefore, the first step of designing high-quality STEM assessment is answering this question: 'What knowledge, skills, thinking and mindset do we want the students to develop by participating in STEM learning?' To get a sense of what teachers should be thinking about as they answer this question, we need to revisit the Australian Curriculum.

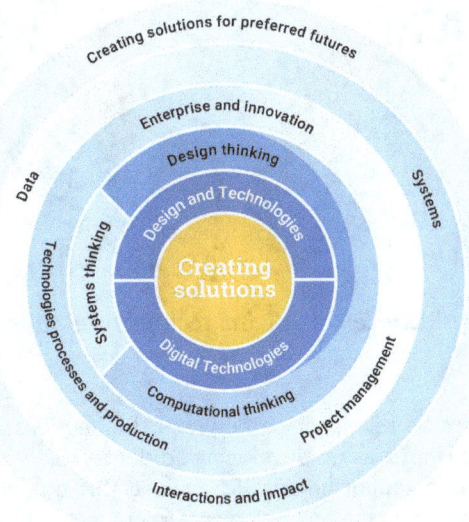

Figure 7.1: Overview of the Australian Curriculum: Technologies core concepts
Source: ACARA (n.d.-s)

Igniting STEM *Learning*

Figure 7.2: Relationships between the design and technologies strands in the Australian Curriculum
Source: ACARA (n.d.-o)

Figure 7.3: Relationships between the digital technologies strands in the Australian Curriculum
Source: ACARA (n.d.-p)

Figures 7.1–3 illustrate the relationships between the key ideas and strands that make up the curriculum. At its core is a focus on developing students' ability to create digital or designed solutions that meet needs or opportunities. To achieve this outcome, a student will need to acquire the knowledge inherent in the technologies curriculum, understand and apply the thinking frameworks and processes, and develop their skills in project management and production. All three aspects are of equal importance. The design of the Australian Curriculum requires teachers to ensure that all three elements are taught and assessed as part of developing STEM learning across a year. Similarly for science, mathematics and every other curriculum area, students will need to acquire discipline-specific knowledge, and understand and apply discipline-specific skills and thinking. Again, the discipline-specific knowledge, skills and thinking need to be taught and assessed if we are to honour the design of the Australian Curriculum.

The trap many teachers fall into is ignoring the fact that discipline knowledge, skills and thinking are all of equal importance and connected to one another. One cannot become a good designer or engineer without understanding the design process and having a design mindset. One cannot be a great mathematician without being fluent in the language of mathematics, and able to use mathematical reasoning and problem-solving strategies. One cannot be a scientist if one is not scientifically literate or does not follow the scientific methodology. Therefore, across a year, teachers will need to ensure that students are developing themselves in the knowledge, skills and thinking specific to the curriculum areas being covered.

Since authentic STEM learning is transdisciplinary, there is one more aspect I recommend teachers also focus on teaching and assessing: targeted elements of the general capabilities. The general capabilities in the Australian Curriculum (see figure 7.4) 'equip young Australians with the knowledge, skills, behaviours and dispositions' (ACARA, n.d.-c, par. 1) that are associated with developing highly capable learners, confident and creative individuals, and active and informed citizens. Each capability has been unpacked into a learning continuum or a learning progression that 'describes the knowledge, skills and behaviours that students can reasonably be expected to develop from Foundation to Year 10' (ACARA, n.d.-c, 'General capability structure' section).

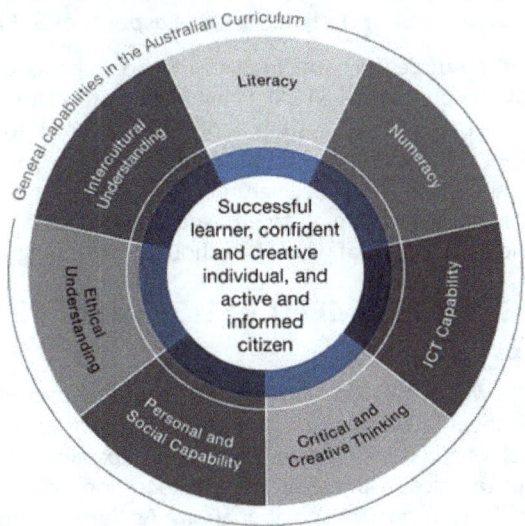

Figure 7.4: General Capabilities in the Australian Curriculum
Source: ACARA (n.d.-h)

The general capabilities documents articulate a wide range of specific skills that are intimately related to the purpose and practice of STEM learning. These include reflective practice, working collaboratively, posing questions, seeking solutions and putting ideas into action, communicating effectively, setting goals and knowing oneself as a learner, and much more. In a well-designed STEM learning program, students should be developing capabilities such as these.

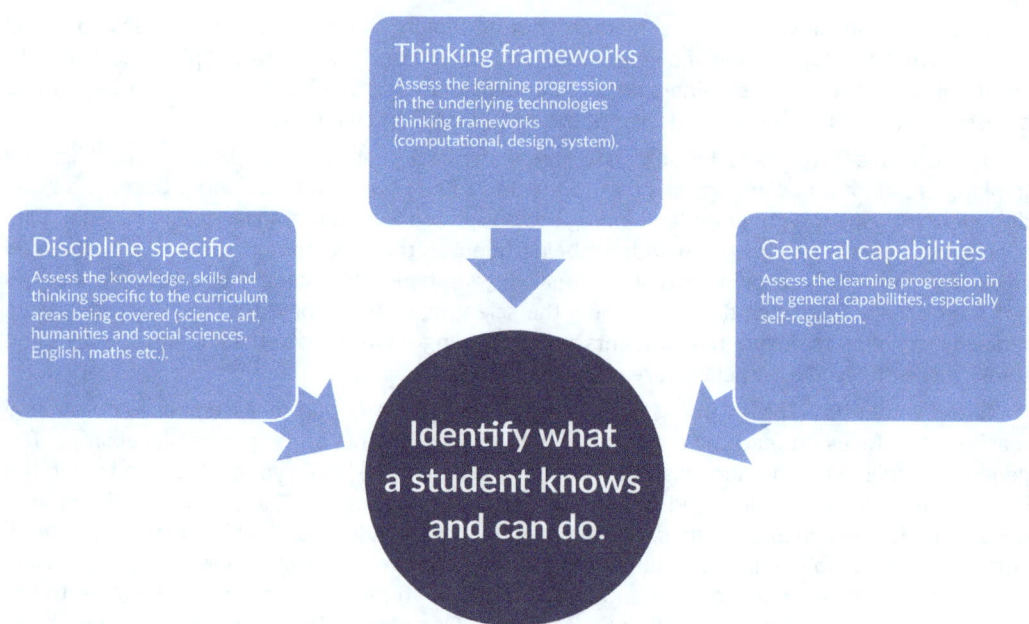

Figure 7.5: Visual representation of three assessable aspects of STEM learning

Figure 7.5 summarises the three key aspects teachers should be assessing to ensure that the learning is delivering upon the purpose of STEM. I have deliberately illustrated the assessment of progression in computational, design and system thinking as separate to the specific knowledge aspects of the technologies curriculum because the former are at the heart of all STEM learning and not specific to the technologies discipline. Naturally, there will be overlap across three aspects (for example, problem-solving is found in all three aspects). The visual representation is useful during planning for reminding teachers of what they should be teaching and assessing.

SHIFTING TEACHER ASSESSMENT BELIEFS AND PRACTICE TO AVOID OVERWHELM

Assessing all three aspects within a STEM learning unit might feel overwhelming. Some teachers are still grappling with effectively assessing student progression in discipline knowledge, let alone in the associated discipline skills and thinking or in the general capabilities and thinking frameworks. Some teachers do attempt to assess aspects such as collaboration, critical thinking, creativity and so on, but they tend do it in an informal, observational way. As the assessment rubrics of tables 7.3 and 7.4 (pages 148 and 149) show, some teachers have attempted to formalise assessing particular skills and processes, but their progressions can be vague or inconsistent. A bottleneck for many teachers is the belief and practice that it is only the teacher who does the assessing. This can lead teachers to focus on summative assessment practices because they are easier to manage. The insight teachers require is the realisation that the process of assessment is an intrinsic part of the process of STEM learning and can be driven by the students.

The process of assessing is fundamentally about evaluating and measuring the progress an individual makes as they work towards a goal, and to provide feedback to allow them to improve their progress towards that goal. In the case of learning, the goal is about acquiring and applying

Assessing STEM learning

the required knowledge, skills and thinking. When students follow the design process to create a solution or achieve a goal they go through the steps of deeply understanding a problem or challenge, defining what they want to achieve, ideating strategies and approaches they could use to achieve their goals, then using the feedback they get from evaluating their trials and tests to refine and progress towards a more effective outcome. Clearly, by students following the design process they will be growing their capacity to self-assess and give, receive and use feedback to improve. Interestingly, the design process also has the benefit of developing students in the five characteristics of assessment-capable visible learners: they know where they are going; they can select from a range of strategies to move their learning forward; they assess and monitor their progress towards desired goals; they identify when they are ready to take the next step; and they know what to do next, even when they don't know what to do (Frey et al., 2018).

In realising that STEM learning naturally requires students to self and peer assess and to use feedback, teachers can achieve multiple goals with two actions. By developing formative assessment structures for the thinking frameworks and the general capabilities, and having the students use these as a habitual part of their learning, they will support students to become assessment-capable learners and thinkers while gathering the information they need to determine the learning progression of each and every student.

STEP 4: DESIGNING THE FORMATIVE ASSESSMENT STRUCTURES

Steps 1, 2, 3 and 5 of the simplified backward-planning process were addressed in Chapters 4–6. We now have enough understanding of the desired outcomes of the planned STEM learning – and the process that students will go through to achieve those outcomes – to begin Step 4, which concerns the design of appropriate assessment structures.

The formulation of the ways to assess STEM learning is much like a design problem. Whatever approaches are created must meet certain design criteria and constraints. Having explored the strengths of and possible improvements that should be made to three current approaches, let's now consider how STEM learning should be assessed.

Assessment should be designed and communicated in way that meets as many of the following criteria as possible:
- written in age-appropriate language that is clear to students, teachers and even parents
- minimises wordiness and complexity as much as possible
- avoids the use of subjective or ambiguous terms, negative language and artificial increases in the numbers of a deliverable to indicate quality or sophistication
- uses terms that are directly observable and measurable without the need to make an inference in order to assess the stage of development
- allows students to know where they are and what their next steps should be
- articulates a minimum expectation to the students
- can be used by students formatively throughout the unit to self- and peer-assess
- encourages students to collect evidence of their progression
- can be used by teachers to summatively assess
- is developmental in design – whether that is through developmental taxonomies or developmental supporting structures
- can be supported by scaffolding and examples to deepen student understanding

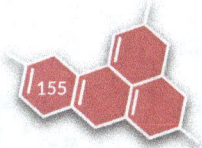

- supports consistent assessment practices across year levels
- presents learning progressions as part of a continuum so that there is a clear and coherent progression of skills and thinking across years of learning
- is consistent with Australian Curriculum language and level standards.

This may be quite a checklist of criteria, but it is consistent with contemporary, evidence-based research performed by the Assessment Research Centre at the University of Melbourne (Griffin, 2017) and the VCAA (2019).

The following structures and approaches have been designed to not only meet these criteria, but also to be embedded by teachers in their normal class routines to assess each of the three STEM learning aspects. A further benefit is that most of the elements to be used as part of these assessment approaches will have arisen during the planning process or from standardised progressions deconstructed from the Australian Curriculum.

ASSESSING DISCIPLINE-SPECIFIC ASPECTS

The first step of the backward-planning process outlined in Chapter 4 involves deconstructing the discipline-specific content descriptors and elaborations into learning intentions and success criteria. This deconstruction process has the benefit of supporting teaching teams to collaboratively articulate a sequence of success criteria that captures what they believe it is important for students to know and be able to do.

Table 7.5 is an extract of the deconstruction for the Years 5/6 earth and space sciences STEM unit first shown in Chapter 4 (table 4.2, page 80). The success criteria created as part of this deconstruction process meet many of the desired design criteria; they are written in age-appropriate language, are directly observable and consistent with the Australian Curriculum, can be used formatively and summatively, use a developmental taxonomy (Bloom's taxonomy in this example), and to a certain extent allow students to know where they are and what their next steps should be. However, if the success criteria are simply listed, a student could say they have achieved the success criteria by demonstrating it once. This would result in a very surface-level approach to learning. A skill is not learned when a student is able to do it once – that requires practice in a variety of situations over time.

Assessing STEM learning

Table 7.5: Extract of the deconstruction for a Years 5/6 earth and space sciences STEM unit

Descriptor and elaborations	Potential misconceptions and roadblocks to learning	Learning intentions and success criteria
Year 6 Science: Inquiry skill – Processing, modelling and analysing Construct and use appropriate representations, including tables, graphs and visual or physical models, to organise and process data and information and describe patterns, trends and relationships (AC9S6I04): • exploring how different representations can be used to show different aspects of relationships, processes and trends • representing circuits using virtual simulations or circuit diagrams and indicating the direction of electricity flow • using line graphs to show changes in growth over time under different physical conditions • developing a physical model of the sun and Earth using objects or role-play to describe their relative positions when a place on Earth is in day or night • organising information in graphic organisers to describe patterns and trends. **Year 4 Digital technologies: Knowledge and understanding** Recognise different types of data and explore how the same data can be represented differently depending on the purpose (AC9TDI4K03): • describing different types of data and how they can be used, for example numbers, letters, symbols and pictures • explaining how the same data can be represented in different ways and why some representations are better than others in certain contexts, for example four vs 4 vs IV vs |||| vs quatre, and that numerals are better for calculation than words • explaining that the same information can be represented differently, for example the term 'stop' can also be represented with an octagon-shaped red sign or a hand icon • identifying rock paintings and other cultural expressions to understand that images are used to encode and represent ethnobotanical knowledge, for example the representation of plant use in the Kimberley cave paintings and ancient engravings including important data on medicinal and food plant classification and their usable parts. *Note: consolidation and transfer of Year 4 data representation content descriptor*	• Students don't realise that data can be categorised. • Students don't know how to use Excel. • Students don't know how to identify patterns or trends.	We are learning to represent and use data appropriately in a range of different ways. **Science** I can: • identify the different categories my data can be organised into • accurately arrange my data in a table with appropriate columns and rows • enter my collected data into an Excel spreadsheet. **Computational thinking** I can: • accurately organise data in Excel • use the organised data to generate a chart/graph • use Excel to order my data in different ways for different purposes. **Computational and design thinking** I can: • discuss the patterns I notice in my data • represent the same data in a range of different ways and justify selecting one particular way over others • create a presentation that explains my investigation and explains why earth has regular changes such as day and night.

Source: Adapted from ACARA (n.d.-m, -r)

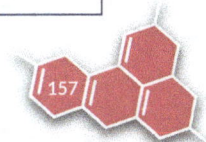

If the success criteria for this particular unit are placed into a CAN DO template as shown in table 7.6, the assessment approach can be built to require students to demonstrate a skill a number of times with increasing depth (a blank reproducible version of the CAN DO template is available for download). This template should be used formatively across multiple lessons and multiple activities during a STEM unit to ensure that each success criteria is addressed multiple times. This will not only support deeper acquisition of a skill by students, but also force teachers to design learning activities in which students are required to demonstrate and transfer the skills across multiple situations. Teachers can also set differing levels of minimum expectations for different students in their class (for example, high-performing students could be required to reach the level of teaching a peer). Finally, the template requires students to collect evidence of their progression, perhaps in a portfolio, teaching them the much-needed skill of gathering evidence to prove an outcome. Teachers simply need to gather filled-in CAN DO templates from students every few lessons plus their portfolios to get sufficient data on student progression and where target teaching may be required. The template can be tailored to different year levels, as shown in table 7.7, and even to address multiple disciplines, as shown in table 7.8.

Table 7.6: CAN DO template for the success criteria shown in table 7.5

I have heard of this	I can do this with help	I can do this on my own	I have taught this to a peer	I CAN list items	Evidence of level
				We are learning to represent and use data appropriately in a range of different ways.	
				I can **identify** the different categories my data can be organised into.	
				I can accurately **arrange** my data in a table with appropriate columns and rows.	
				I can **enter** my collected data into an Excel spreadsheet.	
				I can accurately **organise** data in Excel.	
				I can **use** the organised data to **generate** a chart/graph.	
				I can **use** Excel to order my data in different ways for different purposes.	
				I can **discuss** the patterns I notice in my data.	
				I can **represent** the same data in a range of different ways.	
				I can **justify** selecting one particular way of representing my data over others.	
				I can **create** a presentation that explains my investigation.	
				I can **explain** why Earth has regular changes such as day and night.	

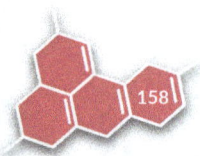

Table 7.7: Sample CAN DO template for a Foundation science unit

I CAN list items	I have heard of this	I can do this with help	I can do this on my own
I can **have** a go and try new things.			
I can **ask** questions about an everyday object or material.			
I can **guess** what will happen in an experiment.			
I can **draw** an accurate picture of my guesses.			
I can **perform** an experiment safely.			
I can **state** what I have observed.			
I can **list** 3 differences and similarities between my guess and my observation.			
I can **identify** patterns in what I have observed.			
I can **use** what I have learnt to **make** better guesses in new experiments of the same type.			
I can **tell** others about my findings.			
I can **use** scientific language.			

Igniting STEM Learning

Table 7.8: Sample CAN DO template for a Year 2 packaging and marketing design unit

	I've heard of this	I can do this with help	I can do this by myself	I can teach this to a peer	Evidence of level
Generating and designing					
I can **sketch and label** a design for my market day product.					
I can **describe** my design idea to my teacher.					
I can **share** what I like and dislike about my design idea.					
I can **list** the materials and tools I need to make the product.					
Producing and implementing					
I can **join** materials in different ways.					
I can **test** my product and packaging and modify the way I make it.					
I can **tell** my teacher how I made it.					
I can **use** tools and equipment safely.					
Evaluating					
I can **explain** why my product sold or didn't sell.					
I can **share** about the environmental impacts of my product.					
I can **identify** ways I could minimise the environmental impacts of my product.					
Collaborating and managing					
I can **list** the main steps I will take to make the product.					
I can **work** productively with a partner.					
Creating persuasive text					
I can **persuade** others to buy my product.					
I can **create** advertising for my product using digital tools.					

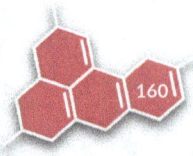

Assessing STEM learning

Frey et al. (2018) point out a range of characteristics displayed by visible learners. Key here is the understanding that visible learners:

- *can talk about how they are learning – the strategies they are using to learn ...*
- *can articulate their next learning steps ...*
- *actively seek feedback (Frey et al., 2018, pp. 1–2).*

With these key characteristics in mind, table 7.9 shows that additional questions can be added to CAN DO templates to embed reflective and strategy-focused discussions in the learning and assessment process. To use these effectively, teachers should begin by explicitly teaching and modelling the reflective process with students through either individual or group conferencing. As students develop their capacity to follow the outlined reflective structure, teachers can create opportunities for students to reflect, discuss and give feedback to one another. By making this a habitual practice, teachers support students to develop desirable self-regulatory attributes such as self-monitoring, self-evaluation, self-assessment and self-teaching (Hattie, 2009).

Table 7.9: Student reflection questions that can be added to the CAN DO templates

Student self-reflection	What I can do:
	What I don't yet know how to do:
Teacher/peer feedback	What you can do:
	What you need to work on:
Strategies to improve	I can improve my skills by using the following strategies:

ASSESSING THE GENERAL CAPABILITIES

In the Australian Curriculum, the general capabilities have been created to capture the 'knowledge, skills, behaviours and dispositions' that will assist students 'to live and work successfully' (ACARA, n.d.-c, par. 1). As we've established, the general capabilities – critical and creative thinking, digital literacy, ethical understanding, intercultural understanding, literacy, numeracy, and personal and social capability – are closely related to the skills that students develop through STEM learning. To help teachers develop scope and sequence documents to assist in planning and assessing student development, ACARA designed learning continuums for each of the capabilities.

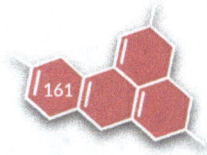

Table 7.10: Examples of deconstructed Foundation to Year 6 personal and social capability, and critical and creative thinking capability statements

Skill	F	1	2	3	4	5	6
Develop questions	I can ask 'why' questions about something I am familiar with.	I can ask questions to find out more information about something I am familiar with.	I can ask 'how' and 'why' questions that are on topic about something I am familiar with.	I can turn 'I wonder' ideas into questions to investigate who, how, what, when and why about something I am unfamiliar with.	I can develop questions to compare and contrast to support my understanding a topic. I can develop questions to make connections.	I can develop questions that challenge points of view. I can develop questions to clarify processes or procedures.	I can develop questions to uncover bias and provoke debate. I can develop questions to interpret processes or procedures.
Identify, process and evaluate information	I can say my opinion about information provided by my teacher. I can group things that are most relevant to a topic.	I can talk about the difference between fact and opinion in information provided by my teacher. I can identify the similarities and differences in information provided by my teacher.	I can identify and explore information from a range of sources provided by my teacher. I can explain the similarities and differences in information provided by my teacher.	I can identify the relevant information and opinions in a range of sources. I can use a graphic organiser to summarise information related to a topic.	I can examine relevant information and opinion from a range of sources. I can put the information related to a topic into my own words.	I can select an appropriate graphic organiser to collect, compare and categorise information and opinions from a range of sources. I can talk about bias.	I can make and explain judgements using evidence on the worth of information and opinions from a range of sources.
Collaboration	I can share my classroom equipment with the class. I can follow the class routine.	I can participate well in group play, tasks and activities.	I can contribute and work cooperatively in group tasks and activities.	I can carry out my role in a group. I can explain how I helped my group.	I can keep track of the things the group have to get done. I can explain how each person in the group contributed to achieving our goals.	I can support group members to contribute ideas to improve the way we work and how we succeed in our goals.	I can encourage others, negotiate roles and manage time/tasks to improve the way we work and succeed in our goals.
Goal setting	I can use one or more strategies to join in with others during class activities.	I can co-create goals with my teacher to help my learning when working by myself or with others.	I can work with others to develop goals to improve my learning.	I can set improvement goals in my learning. I can make plans to achieve the goals.	I can set SMART goals to improve my learning. I can make plans to achieve the goals successfully.	I can select and use strategies to monitor my learning.	I can refine my learning goals and plan for further improvement.

Source: Adapted from ACARA (n.d.-g)

While most primary schools have invested a significant effort in teaching and assessing the literacy, numeracy and digital literacy capabilities, many are still in the process of implementing the teaching and assessment of the remaining general capabilities. Part of this delay is due to many Australian states having an extended reporting timeline for the remaining general capabilities, but it may also be due to schools and researchers still working out the best approaches to teaching and assessing the remaining capabilities (Scoular et al., 2020). Ultimately, the practical obstacle to most schools developing usable scope and sequence documents for the four remaining capabilities is that the statements in the ACARA designed learning continuums are quite broad and open to interpretation.

To assist the teaching and assessing of critical and creative thinking, ethical understanding, intercultural understanding, and personal and social capability, teaching teams could deconstruct the Foundation to Year 6 capability statements into directly observable success criteria (these documents can be downloaded).

Table 7.10 shows some skills related to STEM learning from the deconstructed critical and creative thinking capability and the personal and social capability continuums. In building this resource, the teachers I worked with grappled with how to support students along the continuum without limiting the structures and tools used. This led to the inclusion of broad statements and terms such as *graphic organiser* without specifically identifying which graphic organiser would be used. This approach gives teachers freedom to choose different graphic organisers at different year levels and in different disciplines. What is important is the process – not the tool.

The benefit of having the deconstructed general capability documents is that teachers can pre-assess the existing levels of student capability in specific skills and then use statements pertaining to appropriate levels in a formative assessment rubric. In the Years 3/4 rubric sample shown in table 7.11, the level 2 statements have been placed in the essential column, the level 3 statements in the developing column, the level 4 statements in the capable column, and the level 5 statements in the proficient column. If a teacher has a high-performing class, they can choose a higher sequence of statements; likewise, they can include a lower sequence for students who have a lower starting point. These rubrics can also be tailored to relate to a specific STEM activity, such as the digital technologies project of table 7.3 (page 148), or be used formatively across a whole year to develop student capacity across all learning.

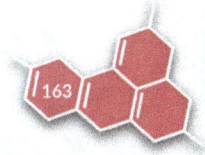

Table 7.11: Sample Year 3/4 progression rubric

Aspect	Essential (below standard)	Developing (at standard, low)	Capable (at standard, high)	Proficient (above standard)	Evidence of level
Develop questions	I can ask 'how' and 'why' questions that are on topic about something I am familiar with.	Plus: I can turn 'I wonder' ideas into questions to investigate who, how, what, when and why about something I am unfamiliar with.	Plus: I can develop questions to compare and contrast to support me understanding a topic. I can develop questions to make connections.	Plus: I can develop questions that challenge points of view. I can develop questions to clarify and interpret processes or procedures.	
Collaboration	I can contribute and work cooperatively in group tasks and activities.	Plus: I can carry out my role in a group. I can explain how I helped my group.	Plus: I can keep track of the things the group have to get done. I can explain how each person in the group contributed to achieving our goals.	Plus: I can support group members to contribute ideas to improve the way we work and how we succeed in our goals.	
Perseverance and adaptability	I can persist when faced with unfamiliar tasks. I can work independently and use strategies when I get stuck.	Plus: I can persist when I feel challenged. I can discuss possible new strategies to solve challenging or unfamiliar tasks.	Plus: I can learn from successes, setbacks and failures. I can apply new strategies to solve challenging or unfamiliar tasks.	Plus: I can discuss coping strategies for managing setbacks when faced with challenging or unfamiliar tasks.	

The personal and social capability elements of these documents attempt to address student self-regulation, which is relevant to STEM learning because, as we've discussed, the development of self-regulated learners is a key outcome. Therefore, it is critical to provide greater distinction and depth to the measurement and assessment of student progression in self-regulation. A research team at the University of Melbourne has performed some wonderful research on self-regulation as part of the Realising the Potential of Australia's High Capacity Students project, defining and calibrating a written description progression of self-regulated learning as it relates to maths, problem-solving and reading comprehension (Harding et al., 2018). The progression describes student behaviour from level A (teacher directed) through to level G (self-regulated learners). While the progression was validated for use only in the three stated areas (mathematics, problem-solving and reading comprehension), it does provide a useful tool for teachers to use in conjunction with the general capabilities progressions.

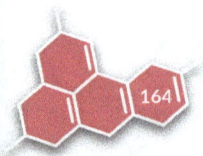

Assessing STEM learning

Table 7.12: Levels A–C of the deconstructed self-regulation progression mapped to Zimmerman and Moylan's (2009) model

Phase	Level A (teacher directed)	Level B (engage in class tasks if interested)	Level C (beginning to monitor approach to learning)
Forethought phase	When given a task by my teacher: • I believe that the task might be too hard. • I want my teacher to tell me I can do it. • I want to have help from my teacher to have a go at the task.	When given a task by my teacher: • I believe that the task might be hard, but could be interesting. • I want my friends to think I am clever. • I ask my teacher how I can have a go at the parts of the task I don't know how to do.	When given a task by my teacher: • I believe that I can learn how to do the task. • I want to have a go at the whole task because I want to learn how to always get the answers right. • I can set goals related to the task with help.
Performance phase	As I work on the task: • I follow the steps the teacher tells me to do for the task. • I have a go at those parts I know I can do or I think aren't too hard. • I sometimes hand in unfinished work or work that is not my best effort. • I can become distracted easily. • I rely on other students to model task-focused behaviour for me. • I am motivated to work on the task because I want a good report or I want to please the teacher.	As I work on the task: • I have a go at parts of the task by myself. • I become distracted when I think the task is too difficult. • I can recognise the learning strategies that work for me when doing difficult tasks. • I focus only on the information provided. • I am motivated to work on the task because I want to get it right.	As I work on the task: • I have a go at the whole task with help from my teacher/peers. • I make an effort to ignore distractions when I am getting distracted. • I am more comfortable doing tasks that I have done before because I know I can do them well. • I hand in my best effort when I respond to a task.
Self-reflection phase	After I complete the task: • I forget what I worked on. • I don't ask for feedback. • If I don't do well on a task I think it is because I am not good at it. • I enjoy learning when I find the task easy.	After I complete the task: • I don't reflect on or check my work. • I don't use any feedback I have been given. • If I don't do well on a task I don't think I can do much about it. • I enjoy learning when I find the task interesting.	After I complete the task: • I check my work with help from my teacher. • I trust my teacher's advice and rely on them to give me feedback. • If I don't do well on a task I think it is because the teacher didn't help me enough. • I want to improve and will put in more effort next time. • I enjoy learning because I want to do well at school.

Source: Adapted from Harding et al. (2018), and Zimmerman and Moylan (2009)
Reproducible available

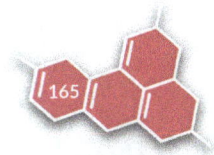

Table 7.12 (page 165) builds on this work, showing levels A–C of the written description progression deconstructed into student friendly language and mapped to Zimmerman and Moylan's (2009) cyclical model of self-regulated learning, which we discussed in Chapter 1 (page 30). This student-friendly progression is valuable because it can be used by both teachers and students to assess the level of student self-regulation. It asks students to reflect and become self-aware about their beliefs, feelings and practices when it comes to learning, and specifically addresses the influence of distractions on performance – something that is not otherwise captured in the general capabilities. By framing the statements within Zimmerman and Moylan's (2009) cyclical model it links self-regulation more closely to the design-process cycle and will support students to first manage and organise their thoughts and then convert them into skills used for learning. Much like the general capabilities progressions, the statements in the self-regulation progression can be put into a rubric form with some tweaking of language and be used by students to self- and peer-assess.

ASSESSING THE TECHNOLOGIES THINKING FRAMEWORKS

The third aspect that should be assessed in STEM learning is student progression in computational, design and systems thinking. Apart from the attempts by organisations such as the QCAA (see table 7.2 on page 147) and some individuals (see table 7.4 on page 149), no one has developed coherent and practical learning progressions for computational, design and systems thinking. The most useful publicly available approach to assessing these three thinking frameworks can be found as part of sequenced teaching resources hosted by the Digital Technologies Hub.

The Digital Technologies Hub contains a sequenced set of units that address the digital technologies curriculum from Foundation to Year 10. Each digital technologies unit has a matrix, based on Biggs and Collis's (1982) SOLO taxonomy, that can be used to assess progression of knowledge and skill development. Table 7.13 shows a matrix for a F–2 hardware and software unit.

Table 7.13: F–2 hardware and software unit matrix

	Learning intention: We are learning about digital systems			
SOLO level	One	Many	Relate	Extend
SOLO verbs	Identify Define	Combine Perform serial skills	Apply Integrate	Create Evaluate
Success criteria	I can **identify** a digital system. I can **point** to the hardware of a computer. I can **name** some software we use in class.	I can **match** the software to its use.	I can **use** some software to write a story, draw a picture or send a message.	I can **choose** and **use** software for a particular purpose. I can **create** a model of a digital system and **explain** the parts and software it uses.
Digital technologies ways of thinking		Computational thinking	Computational thinking	Design thinking

Source: Adapted from Australian Government Department of Education (n.d.-a)

These matrices are extraordinarily useful because they link Biggs and Collis's (1982) SOLO-level success criteria to computational, design and systems thinking, and can be used in conjunction with the CAN DO templates discussed earlier in this chapter to promote depth of practice within a unit. I suspect that the designers of the resources and matrices imagined that in achieving the success

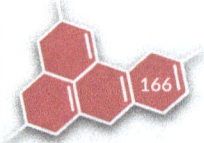

criteria, students will develop their capacity in specific digital technologies ways of thinking. While the matrices do meet many of the recommended design criteria, they are still related to year levels rather than growth in expertise. This means they cannot be used to provide a clear and coherent progression of depth in the thinking frameworks across years of learning.

Table 7.14 (page 168) is an excerpt from a developmental design process rubric that I created to help teachers unpack and assess the design process while also addressing computational and systems thinking. The rubric, which can be downloaded, was developed using all the production and processes content descriptors and elaborations of the F–10 Australian Curriculum: Design and technologies. Though I followed the five-step design thinking model proposed by Stanford's Hasso-Plattner Institute of Design (2020), I also added a collaborating and managing field to the complete rubric, which is not specifically addressed in that model. I took this approach because it is easier to understand and is more consistent with the language and physical processes that design thinkers use as they iterate towards a solution. If schools are going to develop students to follow the design process, then the model should be upwardly consistent with practices found in the global environment.

The leftmost column of the rubric contains three components for each design thinking skill: a definition, key features to be addressed in the progression, and a note about the production and processes, and computational skills that are addressed. These components provide clarity about the meaning of the skill and support teachers and students to recognise what areas they need to develop for each design process skill. The six computational thinking skills (as identified by ACARA: decomposition, pattern recognition, abstraction, algorithms, evaluation, and modelling and simulation) are also linked to the most appropriate design process skills to capitalise on the synergy between the two thinking frameworks.

As discussed in Chapter 1, systems thinking is the process of identifying and examining the interactions between different components (or subsystems) of a system to understand how the components influence each other and the function of the entire system. This is why an attempt has been made to address the required analysis skills for systems thinking in the statements at the capable and proficient levels. The best approach to teaching and assessing system thinking skills is to support students to discuss the interconnected interactions between components of their designed solution.

The rubric is developmental in design and progresses from 'essential' to 'developing', then to 'capable' and finally to 'proficient'. The statements in each column broadly reflect the SOLO taxonomy ranges, plus an increasing depth in skill application. Achieving the 'developing' level requires students to be able to demonstrate they can do what is described in both 'essential' and 'developing' columns. Similarly, to achieve the 'capable' level students must be able to do everything in the 'essential', 'developing' and 'capable' columns. This structure minimises the wordiness of rubrics like those sampled in tables 7.3 and 7.4 (pages 148 and 149). It also creates a clearer and more measurable progression of directly observable behaviour than in the progressions shown in QCAA examples of tables 7.1 and 7.2 (pages 145 and 147).

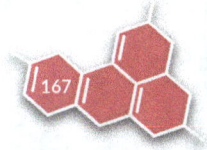

Igniting STEM Learning

Table 7.14: Empathise and define skills excerpted from a developmental design process rubric

Skill	Essential (below level standard; uni-structural)	Developing (at level standard, low; multi-structural)	Capable (at level standard, high; relational)	Proficient (above level standard; extended abstract)	Teacher practices / modelling / graphic organisers — What strategies and approaches will you use to develop your students?
Empathise Process of completing the following to come to a deep understanding of a challenge and who you are designing for. **Elements** <ul><li>identifying goals and sub-goals of the challenge/task</li><li>giving up assumptions</li><li>gathering information and data about needs, opportunities and possible resources</li><li>putting yourself in the shoes of the user.</li></ul> Note: Empathise phase includes skills of decomposition (computational thinking) and the investigating elements of design and technologies strand: Production and Processes.	<ul><li>I can identify the overall goal of the task/challenge.</li><li>I can adopt a 'beginner's mindset'.</li><li>I can ask questions to find out information about the task/challenge.</li><li>I can identify that I made certain assumptions as I gathered information.</li><li>I can identify ways I can gather information.</li></ul>	Plus: <ul><li>I can break down the goal into small sub-goals/-tasks.</li><li>I can ask questions to clarify information and to more deeply understand each sub-goal/-task and the resources that could be used.</li><li>I can describe the assumptions I made as I gathered information.</li><li>I can describe ways I could gather information to understand the sub-goals/-tasks.</li></ul>	Plus: <ul><li>I can use two or three strategies from the strategy document to gather information to understand the sub-goals/-task, the user and the resources that could be used.</li><li>I can justify the assumptions I made as I gathered information and data.</li></ul>	Plus: <ul><li>I can use multiple further strategies from the strategy document to gather information that deepens my understanding of the sub-goals/-tasks, the current and future user(s) and the resources that could be used.</li><li>I can compare and contrast the effectiveness of the strategies I used to gather information and data.</li><li>I can reflect upon how the strategies I used to gather information can be used in other situations/areas.</li></ul>	Create a skill-level appropriate strategy document of approaches that can be used to gather background information. This should include: <ul><li>asking questions</li><li>trialling ideas</li><li>observations</li><li>iterating</li><li>expert knowledge</li><li>collaborating with others</li><li>identifying, gathering and playing with possible resources</li><li>investigating and researching First Nations Australians' designs and resources</li><li>experimenting with traditional and contemporary technologies</li><li>examining tools, techniques, equipment and relationships of properties for complementary materials for product development.</li></ul> Note: Resources includes materials, components, tools and equipment.

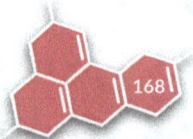

Assessing STEM learning

		Plus:	Plus:	Plus:

Define
Process of synthesising the information that was created during the empathise stage for the purpose of looking for patterns and gaining insight to articulate what to focus on or the problem that will be solved.
 	
Elements
• defining the needs and wants that need to be addressed
• identifying what is important or not
• strategies to recognise patterns and narrow down the design space
• defining specific problems and the causes of problems to be worked on
• identifying possible resources and techniques that could be used
• creating a design brief.
 	
Note: Define phase includes skills of pattern recognition and abstraction (computational thinking) and the defining elements of esign and technologies Strand: Production and Processes.
	• I can identify the wants and needs that the end product/result must address.
	• I can name possible categories that the information and data could be organised into.
	• I can identify what is relevant to a topic and what is not.
	• I can list some of the resources that may be required to create a solution.
		• I can describe the wants and needs that the end product/result must address and rate the importance of each one to the user.
		• I can sort and classify the information and data I have collected into categories.
		• I can identify patterns in the information and data.
		• I can use the patterns I identified to discuss what is important and what is not.
		• I can explore and test the suitability of a range of the resources and techniques that could be used to create a solution.
			• I can explain the possible causes of the wants and needs that the end product/result must address and discuss the opportunity a designed solution will present.
			• I can use a range of ways to represent/ visualise the information and data to help make sense of patterns, relationships and trends (e.g. mind maps, graphs, trends, cause and effect diagrams).
			• I can investigate already existing designs and associated technologies and resources.
			• I can explain how I selected the resources, technologies and techniques that could be used to create a solution that satisfies a design brief.
				• I can make generalisations and insights based on the data I have collected, organised, sorted and analysed.
				• I can create a design brief that reflects the wants and needs to be addressed, identifying:
				  ◦ the goals of design (needs and wants)
				  ◦ target market
				  ◦ constraints
				  ◦ sustainability requirements
				  ◦ resources, technologies and techniques to be used to create a solution
				  ◦ budget and schedule.
				
				Create a skill-level appropriate strategy document of approaches that can be used to narrow down and define the specific problem and needs that the designed solution will address. This should include:
				• considering sustainability
				• exploring tools that could be used
				• exploring suitability and sustainability of potential materials
				• exploring techniques to use to create models and product
				• considering existing products and processes to inform thinking
				• considering environmental and social impacts of manufacturing approach
				• considering accuracy, quality, safety and efficiency of production processes.
				
				Note: Resources includes materials, components, tools and equipment.

Reproducible available

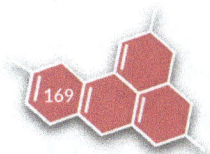

The final column is perhaps the most important for teachers. It was designed so that teachers can capture the strategies, structures and practices they will use to grow student capacity in the specific design process skill. What is listed in this column will change or grow over time as teaching teams select the strategies, structures and approaches that work best for the students within their school learning model. The main strategy currently listed in this column asks teachers to create a skill-appropriate strategy document for each design process skill. The bullet points show a list of possible strategies taken directly from the Australian Curriculum elaborations. Since this design process rubric is applicable F–10, the strategy document and expectations that are created in response to this column will be different depending on the skill level of the students. It is entirely possible for Years 5–6 students to have strategy documents that would be applicable to Years 9–10 students. Equally, it is possible for students not exposed to the design process previously to initially have a strategy document pertaining to a lower skill-level sequence. Ultimately, it is up to the teachers to create a rubric that enhances the skill levels of the students in front of them.

Please note that it is unlikely that this iteration of the sample rubric captures all the necessary elements to sufficiently indicate learner progression from 'essential' to 'proficient'. Rather, the aim here is to create a viable progression of skill that is related to expertise and depth of understanding – not age or year level. This allows the learning of computational, design and systems thinking to be unhooked from the constraints of a curriculum created for year-by-year consumption.

The rubric should not be used as is by primary school teachers. It is too complex and detailed to be enacted straight away in primary schools unless used for lengthy STEM projects with a group of students who have been using the design process for a number of years. The intention is that teachers take the design process rubric and tailor it to be more appropriate to the language and understanding of their learners and the project or design challenge those learners are working on.

Table 7.15 is an example of a simplified version of the design process rubric that could be used across a range of STEM projects in a year. Depending on the students' skill levels and the activity or project, teachers might not use the entire design process rubric. In fact, a better strategy would be teachers focusing on having students acquire and consolidate one or two design process skills at a time, and then introducing the whole design process rubric when they feel confident that the students have a sufficient foundation to self- and peer- assess using the entire rubric.

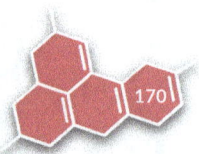

Assessing STEM learning

Table 7.15: Sample simplified design process rubric

Skill	Essential	Developing	Capable	Proficient	Teacher practices / modelling / graphic organisers
Empathise<ul><li>Identifying the goal of the task</li><li>Gathering information and data</li><li>Identifying assumptions</li></ul>	<ul><li>I can identify the overall goal of the task.</li><li>I can identify ways I can gather information.</li></ul>	Plus:<ul><li>I can use a strategy to find out information about the task and the possible resources that could be used.</li></ul>	Plus:<ul><li>I can use different strategies to gather more information and data about the task and the possible resources that could be used.</li><li>I can describe the assumptions I made as I gathered information</li></ul>	Plus:<ul><li>I can compare and contrast the effectiveness of the strategies I used to gather information and data.</li><li>I can justify the assumptions I made as I gathered information and data.</li></ul>	Create an empathise strategy document of approaches. Include:<ul><li>asking questions</li><li>experimenting</li><li>iterating</li><li>expert knowledge</li><li>identifying, gathering and playing with possible resources</li><li>investigate and research First Nations Australians' designs and resources.</li></ul>Note: Resources includes materials, components, tools and equipment.
Define<ul><li>Identifying needs and wants</li><li>Identifying what is important or not</li><li>Looking at existing products and processes</li><li>Exploring resources and techniques</li></ul>	<ul><li>I can identify the wants and needs that the end product must address.</li></ul>	Plus:<ul><li>I can identify the wants and needs that the end product must address.</li></ul>	Plus:<ul><li>I can research already existing designs and associated technologies.</li><li>I can explain what is important and what is not.</li></ul>	Plus:<ul><li>I can use the aspects in the define strategy document to compare and contrast the resources and techniques that could be used to make models and the end product.</li></ul>	Create a define strategy document of approaches. Include:<ul><li>tools and techniques that could be used to create models and products</li><li>considering sustainability</li><li>exploring suitability and sustainability of potential materials</li><li>considering environmental and social impacts of manufacturing approach.</li></ul>Note: Resources includes materials, components, tools and equipment.
Ideate Generating:<ul><li>strategies for generating design ideas.</li></ul>	<ul><li>I can brainstorm the features I would like in my designed solution.</li></ul>	Plus:<ul><li>I can list the features of existing designs to generate new ideas.</li></ul>	Plus:<ul><li>I can compare and contrast the features of existing designs to provide new ideas.</li><li>I can use Safety by Design principles to generate a range of design ideas.</li></ul>	Plus:<ul><li>I can combine or modify ideas to generate a range of innovative design ideas.</li></ul>	Create a skill level appropriate ideation strategy document of approaches that can be used to generate, develop and communicate design ideas. Generating includes:<ul><li>drawing or modelling designs</li><li>using prior knowledge, skills and research</li><li>critical and creative thinking strategies such as brainstorming, sketching, 3D modelling and experimenting.</li></ul>

Continued ...

Igniting STEM Learning

Skill	Essential	Developing	Capable	Proficient	Teacher practices / modelling / graphic organisers
Ideate cont... Developing: strategies to analyse, develop, and improve design ideas		Plus: • I can list the pros and cons of a design idea. • I can talk about the changes made to a design idea.	Plus: • I can seek feedback on the benefits and drawbacks of my design ideas. • I can develop several alternative versions or models of design ideas based on the feedback.	Plus: • I can identify techniques and resources to use for each design idea. • I can use feedback to improve my design ideas or the resources and processes used.	Developing includes: • feedback from users and others • enhancing and improving the sustainability of the design ideas • properties of materials and processes that could be used • considering the selection of materials and joining techniques to suit the purpose of a product.
Communicating: strategies to document and communicate the design ideas	• I can draw/sketch 2D drawings or create a model of the design idea(s). • I can name and label the design idea(s).	Plus: • I can annotate the drawings to clarify the pros and cons of each design idea. • I can describe the results from exploring design ideas.	Plus: • I can annotate the drawings to explain the features and the resources used using the appropriate technical terms.	Plus: • I can annotate the drawings to explain the techniques that could be used to make it.	Communicating includes: • changing perspectives (front vs plan view) • using a range of technologies including digital tools to plan, share and document designs, ideas and processes • including scale, symbols and codes in plans and diagrams; using pictorial maps and aerial views; and using digital mapping applications or infographics to present research and ideas to others. Ensure the students have a design portfolio to track the evolution of their ideas and to learn the process of annotation. *Note: Resources includes materials, components, tools and equipment.*
Prototype/test Making: techniques to create a model or prototype	• I can make a model of the design idea by exploring how available materials could be used or reused in various ways. • I can check that the assembled components work as planned.	Plus: • I can explore ways of joining, connecting and assembling components for the design idea. • I can explain the importance of accuracy when designing and making.	Plus: • I can use the appropriate terminology to describe the making techniques used. • I can use tools and equipment accurately when making.	Plus: • I can practice making techniques to improve my expertise and the quality of the model. • I can describe the environmental impact of the materials, components, tools, equipment and processes I selected and used in the making process.	Create a prototype/test strategy document of approaches. Include: • using discarded materials to design, make and model • cutting and joining • sewing • gluing • safe work practices • experimenting • innovative combinations • considering alternatives.
Safety: strategies to work safely	• I can safely practise a range of making skills using tools and equipment.	Plus: • I can explain the importance of demonstrating safe, responsible and cooperative work practices.	Plus: • I can work safely, responsibly and cooperatively to ensure safe work areas.	Plus: • I can independently develop safe working practices. • I can identify potential risks in the development of a project.	

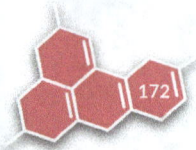

Assessing STEM learning

		Plus:	Plus:	Plus:	
Evaluate Design criteria: developing design criteria to evaluate a designed solution	- I can identify design criteria for a designed solution.	- I can discuss why each design criteria is important.	- I can negotiate design criteria with others.	- I can include design criteria to evaluate the success for processes and planning of a designed solution.	Create an evaluation strategy document of approaches. Include: - personal likes and dislikes - capturing user feedback about what they like and dislike - rating how well the designed solution meets the wants and needs.
Evaluating/ reflecting: evaluating how well the designed solution meets the design criteria	- I can record judgements about what I like and dislike about the designed solution.	- I can describe how well the designed solution meets the original design criteria.	- I can record experiences of the techniques used and challenges of producing the designed solution.	- I can evaluate the choices we made at various stages of a design process.	
Refining/revising: refining/revising the designed solution	- I can suggest how the designed solution could be improved.	- I can seek feedback from others on how we could improve the designed solution.	- I can revise the designed solution to more effectively meet the wants and needs.	- I can modify the production processes used to make a higher quality design solution and improve the costs.	
Planning and collaborating Planning: designing and making a plan	- I / we can create a step by step list of actions or storyboard to take to make the designed solution.	- I / we can collaborate with others to create a plan of the processes and resources to make a designed solution.	- I / we can set milestones of when things are due - I / we can identify and minimise any risks to ensure success.	- I / we can use digital tools to outline and manage the planning and production steps needed to make a designed solution.	Create some simple planning templates for students to use. Develop a conferencing template to use with the students to support them developing their planning, managing and collaboration skills.
Collaborating: collaborative team behaviour	- I can contribute and work cooperatively in a group.	- We can identify roles for each member of a group. - I can model responsible behaviour.	- We can encourage each other and manage our time/ tasks.	- We can give and receive constructive feedback to work effectively as a team.	

Igniting STEM Learning

ASSESSMENT IN PRACTICE

It may take some time for teachers to embed assessing the three STEM learning aspects effectively into their practice. Teachers will need to think through, do the appropriate pre-planning and provide the explicit teaching, pedagogy and activities to support their students to think from and use the new templates and structures effectively.

For example, CAN DO templates such as shown in tables 7.6–8 (pages 158–60) will need constant revisiting in everyday classroom practice through a variety of activities. Students will need to be explicitly taught about and discuss what each success criteria means and looks like, and learn the process of collecting evidence to demonstrate achievement to a particular level. This is the only way students will be able to progress across the levels of the gradual release of responsibility. With the rubrics shown in tables 7.11 and 7.15 (pages 164 and 171), it is important that teachers explicitly teach students the expectations of key aspects. There will be no point using the rubrics if students do not understand the expectations and what is being asked of them. Good practice would be to provide samples of student work of similar tasks to deepen their understanding of what each level looks like. Teachers could even encourage students to assess and provide feedback on the samples.

Table 7.16 is an example of an assessment rubric for a Year 5–6 natural disasters Minecraft unit. The teacher identified the skills he wanted to focus on within the unit and then used the deconstructed general capabilities documents for critical and creative thinking, and personal and social capability to identify the elements of each skill. He then used this to guide his construction of a skill progression from 'essential' to 'proficient' within the rubric format introduced in table 7.11 (page 164). As part of his preparation to introduce the rubric to his students, the teacher highlighted particular words in yellow to remind himself to explicitly teach the meaning of these words. He did this though leading discussions, providing examples of what they could look like and explicitly teaching key skills such as researching.

Table 7.16: Assessment rubric for a Years 5/6 natural disasters Minecraft unit

Skill	Essential	Developing	Capable	Proficient	Observations, evidence, strategies
Questions and possibilities • clarifying questions • identify what my questions are • questions about possible outcomes	• I can create a list of questions that can be used to guide my research.	Plus: • I can ask clarifying questions to gain a better understanding of my topic. • I can identify follow-up questions to further my investigations.	Plus: • I can create questions about future outcomes (what might happen if ...).	Plus: • I can make reasonable predictions for my questions.	• brainstorming questions, wonderings and 'what if's before, during and after planning and creating • recorded in the Google Slide challenge brief

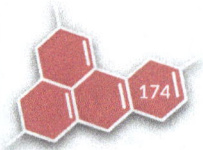

Assessing STEM learning

Research • investigating using digitech • reliable sources • relevance (key words match questions) • summarising information	• I can identify the key words from the questions I have posed. • I can search online using my key words.	**Plus:** • I can list the important information from a research piece. • I can identify the difference between a reliable source and an unreliable source.	**Plus:** • I can organise my information using a graphic organiser. • I can combine information from a variety of sources to create a fluent piece. • I can summarise all my research.	**Plus:** • I can evaluate the author's credibility and expertise. • I can compare and contrast related sources of information.	• evidence of research collected and references in the challenge brief • summarised research • websites sourced • evidence of author's credibility • evidence of cross-referencing of sources • evidence of summaries being in your own words
Collaboration • delegate roles • contribute to my group • reflect on my group's progress/ success/ where to next • provide feedback	• I can identify my role in a group project.	**Plus:** • I can describe my role in a group project. • I make contributions to my group's success.	**Plus:** • I can provide feedback for my peers. • I can reflect on my progress and determine my next steps.	**Plus:** • I can reflect on the group's progress and guide where we will go next. • I find ways to lead my team in different aspects of the project.	• group reflections • creating goals and expectations for future work • created clear roles for individuals • delegate tasks equally • evidence of feedback through comments in slides
Communication • verbal • visual • use of headlines • platform that supports the communication • drafted, planned and well-organised • appropriate	• I can brainstorm different ways to present my project.	**Plus:** • I have a detailed plan for how I communicate my project to others.	**Plus:** • My presentation is creative but also meets the purpose of the topic.	**Plus:** • I have extended my presentation to incorporate extra elements to enhance our work. • I can justify how the extra elements enhance my final presentation.	• evidence of a final product that presents their product • evidence of a brainstorm and plan • reflections and justifications about added elements • evidence that my presentation meets the purpose

Source: Velez and Frattin (2020)

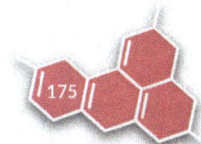

The rubrics shown in this chapter are all designed to be used both formatively and summatively. Throughout a STEM learning unit, students should be using the rubrics to self-evaluate and self-reflect on their current levels of development. At the end of the unit or project, teachers can determine the progress the students made in each skill area and use this as a developmental measure for writing their reports. Alternatively, if they are required by their school's reporting approach, they can assign grades to the achievement levels. Note that the 'capable' column in these rubrics is normally considered to be 'at level', while 'proficient' is typically 'above level'.

Teachers can support students' skill development by creating simple templates (for example, planning sheets) for students to use and ensuring that there are multiple opportunities for conferencing so they can learn to self-reflect and evaluate their progression. The consistent use in STEM learning of templates, such as the conferencing template provided in table 7.17, supports students to acquire and consolidate the language, processes and thinking of STEM.

Table 7.17: STEM conferencing template

Name(s) and date	Topic/project	Design process stage
		☐ Empathise ☐ Define ☐ Ideate ☐ Prototype/test ☐ Evaluate
Prompting questions	**Student comments**	**Teacher notes**
▪ What have I learnt? ▪ What have I achieved? ▪ What is next and how will I get there? ▪ What changes do I need to make? ▪ What resources do I need? ▪ How can I work more effectively? ▪ What are my wonderings/questions?		
Future goal/s (to be negotiated by teacher and student)	**Strategies to improve**	

Reproducible available

KEY POINTS

- There is currently no consistent agreement around assessing STEM learning. Many of the existing assessment approaches suffer from practical issues, such as vague terminology, not showing authentic skill progression across year levels, having a focus on summative assessment, being unwieldy and too wordy, or including extrinsic motivators such as grades.
- The first step of designing high-quality STEM assessment is answering the question 'What knowledge, skills, thinking and mindset do we want the students to develop by participating in STEM learning?'

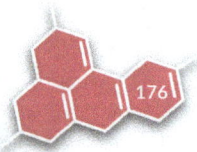

Assessing STEM learning

- The three assessable aspects of STEM learning are:
    1. assessing the knowledge, skill and thinking specific to the curriculum areas being covered (for example, science, art, humanities and social sciences, English, maths and so on)
    2. assessing learning progression in the underlying technologies thinking frameworks (computational, design, system)
    3. assessing learning progression in the general capabilities (especially self-regulation).
- STEM learning requires students to self- and peer-assess, and use feedback.
- A range of structures and templates can be used to embed assessment within the everyday practice of STEM learning, including:
    - CAN DO template for success criteria
    - deconstructed general capability documents
    - a template for a developmental formative rubric
    - use of Biggs and Collis's (1982) SOLO taxonomy
    - design process rubric
    - a STEM conferencing template.
- Teachers should use these structures and templates to design assessments that enhance students' skill levels and follow the criteria set out in 'Assessment in practice' (page 174).
- Regardless of the structures or templates used, teachers need to think through, do the appropriate pre-planning and provide the explicit teaching, pedagogy and activities to support their students to think from and use the new elements effectively.

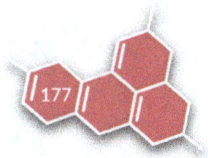

CHAPTER 8

Growing teacher capacity to lead STEM learning

There is no such thing as failure, there's just giving up too soon.

Jonas Salk, quoted in *The Little Book of Medical Quotes*

THE PATH TO LEADING EFFECTIVE STEM LEARNING

Teachers will have many different starting points and individual school circumstances to negotiate as they explore what it takes to lead STEM learning. Some teachers will have been asked to lead STEM learning despite having little to no background in it, while others may have deep expertise in science or maths but little experience in using technology or developing transdisciplinary units. Some teachers will plenty of resources on hand and some will have very little in the way of support. Some will have thriving and engaged students, but others will be struggling to have their students turn up to class. Some teachers will have access to face-to-face professional development and coaching; meanwhile, others will have to glean their wisdom from online sources and conversations via email or video calls. Each teacher's path to being effective at leading STEM learning will be different.

In addition to the challenges and obstacles teachers face throughout their typical practice, it is important to also acknowledge that leading effective STEM learning is challenging in the current educational environment. Schools as institutions are often quite rigid in their structures and approaches, and these traditional structures and approaches can act as subconscious constraints – regardless of the intentions of school leadership. Some of these manifest in STEM learning being given little time in the timetable, unit planners not reflecting a backward-planning process, teachers having negative mindsets about STEM or technology more broadly, learning assessments being predominantly summative or end-product focused, and even the way reporting is done within the school simply not being conducive to STEM learning and assessing.

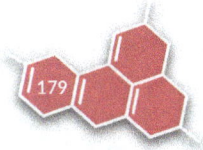

Igniting STEM *Learning*

Developing teacher capacity to be effective in leading STEM learning is not just a professional development issue – it is a whole-school culture and thinking issue. The embedding of an authentic STEM program will transform the way a school operates. While Chapter 9 will address leading transformational change in schools, it is necessary for teachers to understand that one of the obstacles they may face is an educational system that is not aligned to the type of learning and outcomes that STEM is designed to create.

The challenges seem to be enormous! You might be asking yourself: 'Why would a teacher or school ever take it on?' One of the key messages that teachers who have made the journey of enacting an authentic STEM program in their school share is that doing so unleashed their creativity and made them better learners and teachers. The journey of overcoming the obstacles and challenges they encountered nurtured the mindset and skills that made them effective STEM teachers.

Great STEM teachers are creative and passionate activators of thinking and learning. They are problem-solvers and critical thinkers – and they are resourceful. They are clear that they don't know everything and they see themselves and their students as co-learners. They challenge the status quo and nurture students to be change agents. They take risks, fail, learn and strive to be effective with their cohort of students, in their particular school community and with the resources they have to hand. This chapter will feature stories and experiences from a range of Australian teachers to highlight some of their paths and the lessons that they learnt on their journeys towards teaching STEM effectively. We will then discuss six broad areas in which teachers will need to develop their skill and capacity to be effective at creating, planning and running STEM learning.

TEACHERS' STORIES

There is no single path that teachers take as they learn to lead STEM learning. Each teacher has different passions, drivers, strengths, areas of expertise and areas for development. They also exist within schools and communities that have unique challenges and opportunities. As you will discover in the following stories from teachers around Australia, while their paths are different, the passion for empowering and enabling young people to be change makers in the world is present in all of them.

HAVING A GO AND FINDING A WAY

Ann Adams teaches Years 5 and 6 at the Alekarenge School in the Northern Territory. It is considered very remote and services the local First Australians community. Over 95 per cent of students have a language background other than English and many students don't have access to a computer or the internet at home. In 2019 the school received a grant to purchase a range of iPads and technologies devices, with the aim of teaching digital literacy and supporting construction, science, robotics and artificial intelligence learning.

Ann's journey of leading STEM learning began with overcoming a range of resourcing obstacles. Due to the school's remoteness, the technology she ordered took over six months to arrive and it was a further six months before she could get the IT support to connect the technology to the school network. If anything broke down, more months would normally pass just to get it fixed. Ann found that this was an issue for many of the remote schools in the region. The turning point came when Ann and Colin, the school's principal, were able to speak to the right people in positions of authority and, as a result, the regional office was able to get things moving.

While all the resourcing issues were being addressed, Ann began introducing her students to robotics and coding. She created online units of work so the students could have plenty of

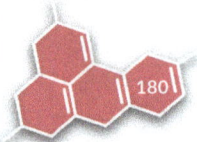

experience with a wide range of platforms. She completed a Master of Education unit on web 2.0 tools and began to understand the relationship between teaching with technology, critical thinking strategies and the use of appropriate pedagogies – including First Australians pedagogies. She is currently encouraging the other teachers embrace technology in the classroom. Her strategy is to empower each teacher to take charge of one technology resource and organise an activity that students and families can get involved in.

Ann and the teachers of Alekarenge School are dealing with challenges most teachers will never face. Initially Ann felt completely out of her depth and believed she didn't know enough. There were times when she felt frustrated and upset, and thought she was a failure because nothing was changing. Yet Ann never gave up, and her self-confidence and her ability to make things happen is growing. She took on the belief that things were going to happen and gradually developed a mindset of 'we can figure it out'. There is still a long way to go, but Ann's expertise in digital technologies and STEM has grown exponentially. What has made the difference to her is the support of her principal and her passion for making a difference in her students' lives.

EMPOWERING STUDENT SELF-REGULATION

Anna Danson teaches Years 1 and 2 and is the STEM teacher at Our Lady of the Assumption Cheltenham Primary School in Victoria. Anna began her career as an art teacher before completing a master's degree in IT in support of her interest in using technology to engage students in their learning.

Anna and her colleagues have taken on the mission of developing students to be independent learners who use their creative thinking and problem-solving skills to build on what they already know. In maths, rather than teaching the content first, teachers give a question and answer on their SMART Boards and invite students to identify the process for getting to that answer. Similarly, in English, teachers share a piece of unedited student writing and invite students to collaborate and edit the work together. The students identify spelling errors and where the author can improve each paragraph, authentically teaching one another at their level. What Anna and her colleagues have found is that students get excited about trying to figure things out and love connecting and relating their learning to their experiences.

Prior to taking on this flipped approach in her lessons, Anna found that she and her students always focused on the end products. There was no empathising about a problem and no purpose behind what they designed or built. This led to students becoming quite passive and reliant on teacher instruction. Anna applied the design process to her program and now has students explore and identify problems that they feel a connection to, breaking down and explaining the design process of empathising and why things are invented for a purpose. While students in the older classes struggled with this approach initially, the benefits over time have far outweighed the challenges. Anna has found that students are much more self-directed, their learning is more purposeful and they are much more in control of their learning.

The school is now enacting the flipped approach in the broader curriculum with the older students. Teachers of older students have found that it takes a bit longer at the beginning of a topic for students to create a learning path and to develop the skill of expressing themselves and explaining their thinking and approaches. Anna feels this is because these students are used to having their teachers model the processes rather than having the opportunity themselves to think their way through and navigate their own learning. While some teachers are trying the approach and finding it valuable, others have yet to buy in.

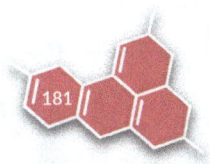

CO-LEARNING WITH STUDENTS

Josh Velez is a Years 5 and 6 teacher and English learning specialist at Malvern Valley Primary School in Victoria. He is also an Apple- and Google-certified teacher. While technology is a big part of his practice, Josh didn't begin exploring STEM until he realised how it linked with his passion for drones. He realised that the ability to build, use and program drones not only made him excited – it made the kids excited too. This personal interest plus his disposition to give things a go kick-started his interest in STEM teaching and learning.

Josh is happy to admit he was clueless when he began. Despite having a strong background in instructional models and framing lessons in normal units, Josh was unclear how to begin with STEM learning. Given Josh's nature, he jumped in anyway. Josh spent his first year learning on the fly with his students. There were times he literally went into lessons and said, 'Well, this is what we're going to try to do. I really have no idea how we're going to do it, so let's just try and do it together.' He discovered that it was okay if things went wrong because that was actually part of the design process. Better yet, he noticed that students found their voice and agency when they saw him learning through trial and error. Josh realised that he didn't need to be an expert in STEM to lead great STEM learning, but it made a difference if he understood what learning he was trying to achieve.

In Josh's three years of exploring how to enact STEM learning, he has learnt to let go of having a rigid instructional structure and instead allow the back and forth of the design process phases to progress as he learns alongside his students. Sometimes he cycles through the design process within one lesson as he and the students figure out why something isn't working, and sometimes they have to go backwards because they realise they haven't empathised enough or defined the problem they are trying to solve. One thing that has become clear is that students need to develop the capacity to know where they are in their knowledge or skill, reflect on their expectations, and think through and plan the next steps to get to their goals.

Josh highlighted that what helped him was having good mentors, decent resources and school leaders who provided him the time to do the planning and necessary professional development. He acknowledges that STEM does take time, and that teachers need to grapple with the thinking and processes and understand how they all fit together in STEM learning. Ultimately he feels that teachers need to discover the excitement of learning with their students, and unleash kids' creativity and imagination on how they can make a positive contribution to the future.

PERSISTENCE PAYS OFF

Before he retired, Reid Moule was the head of curriculum for digital technologies at Humpybong State School, north of Brisbane. Reid came to teaching later in his life, having worked a variety of jobs after leaving school when he was thirteen. Following night school and then studies in journalism, anthropology and psychology, Reid finally found his place with an education degree and moved into the classroom.

Reid's interest in teaching technology was sparked by what was happening in other countries. He could see that Australian schools would soon go down a similar path to the UK, where a digital technologies curriculum had been implemented. In 2014 Reid and a friend started an after-school club at the local library to teach kids about Raspberry Pi, Arduino, coding and electronics.

With no experience with electronics or coding, it is not surprising Reid found it extremely challenging to start with. He found much of the code that he took from the internet to support his teaching was full of errors. Like many people learning something new, he thought it was his lack

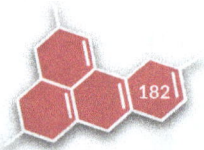

of experience that was the problem, not that the code was wrong. Reid shared that he spent many nights banging his head on the kitchen bench out of sheer frustration. But he persisted because he could see how technology and coding authentically linked maths and science to applications that kids were excited about.

After the success of the after-school club, Reid convinced his school principal to allow him to run a class each week with a group of gifted and talented students. The students loved the sessions so much that the following year Reid was given two days each week to teach the digital technologies curriculum to Foundation and Year 6 students, teaching his normal classes the other three days. The following year, Reid was teaching the technologies curriculum five days a week, cycling through every class in every year level. By the time he retired, Reid was supporting and coaching teachers to integrate technology in innovative ways through their normal lessons and units.

Reid found the digital and design technologies curriculum intrinsically motivational for students and therefore easier to teach than other subjects. To do it effectively, he realised, he had to find the right analogies, decompose the problem, define the parameters (formative and summative assessment) and the curriculum links. The more experienced Reid became, the more he saw the enormous opportunities that this type of learning represented for education. His understanding of the curriculum deepened, the connections between different subjects and how they fit together became clearer, and he developed a more nuanced understanding of how concepts and content were connected and built upon across year levels. His thinking expanded from a focus on simply understanding coding and devices to a more global understanding of the spiral nature of the curriculum.

DEVELOPMENTAL STAGES OF EFFECTIVENESS

Teachers will go through a number of stages as they develop their capacity to effectively lead STEM learning. Each story shared here conveys snapshots of the emotions and challenges that four teachers experienced as they developed themselves. The stages of competence, developed in the 1970s by Noel Burch, articulates what individuals go through when learning a new skill (Gordon & Burch, 1974). I have found that awareness of these stages of development (illustrated in figure 8.1, page 183) makes a profound difference for teachers as they journey towards being effective STEM teachers.

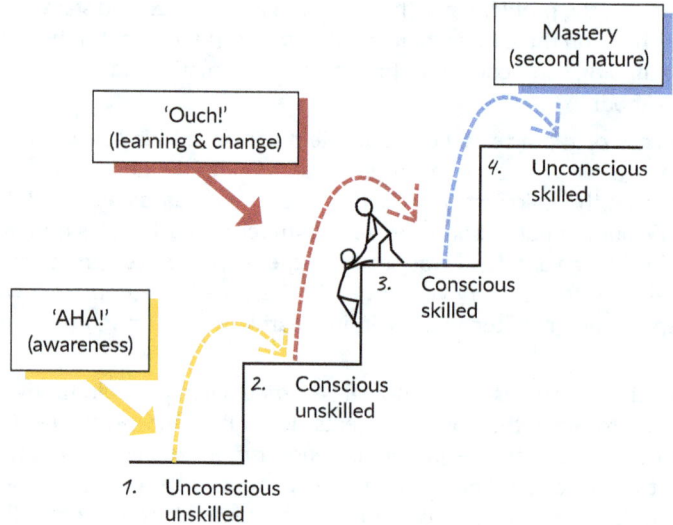

Figure 8.1: The stages of conscious skill
Source: Adapted from Gordon and Burch (1974) and Richens (2017)

STAGE 1: UNCONSCIOUS UNSKILLED

When we learn something that is completely new to us we are often completely unaware of how little we know. Learning to create and plan for authentic STEM learning will be that way for many teachers. We don't know what we don't know, but we think we should know what we are doing! This stage is particularly challenging for teachers who have ingrained practices and beliefs about how learning should look that have been reinforced over many years of practice. In this stage it is common for teachers to feel self-conscious and awkward as they enact STEM approaches in their classes. When the activity or planned learning doesn't work, teachers can become frustrated and deny the importance and value of STEM learning.

The aim in this first stage is for teachers new to STEM learning to become aware of how much they don't know and the benefits to student learning of changing that. For the people coaching these teachers it is important to be sensitive and give plenty of positive feedback to keep motivation high. They may need to keep the case for urgency present (see Chapter 9, page 199) and explain how these skills align with their goals.

STAGE 2: CONSCIOUS UNSKILLED

As teachers begin to recognise what they don't know and the value of learning the new planning and pedagogical approaches, they may become demoralised and lose confidence. This stage of learning can be uncomfortable and teachers can feel overwhelmed by what they need to learn to be effective. When coaching teachers in this stage I suggest providing plenty of encouragement and support, as well as introducing the concept of beginner's mind to support the necessary shift in thinking. Beginner's mind is a concept in which learners, at any stage of expertise, have an attitude of being open and putting aside preconceptions when studying a subject, just as a beginner in that subject would (Suzuki, 2011). Having teachers begin to relearn this mindset will not only make a difference to their teaching and growing their confidence it also sets them up to lead the design process effectively as it is a pre-condition for being able to empathise well. Teachers should keep a diary or use a thinking tool like the Helen Sanderson Associates' (2015) now-ubiquitous 4 + 1 Questions thinking tool (see figure 8.2) to record and reflect on what strategies and approaches worked, what didn't and what can be done next time. The aim is to build self-confidence, which will take teachers to Stage 3.

Figure 8.2: 4 + 1 Questions thinking tool
Source: Adapted from Helen Sanderson Associates (2015)

STAGE 3: CONSCIOUS SKILLED

A teacher reaches Stage 3 when they consciously think their way through planning and leading STEM learning. For example, consciously using the steps and language of the thinking frameworks (such as the design process) to guide planning and classroom pedagogy. It isn't yet automatic or second nature. The imperative in this stage is to practise, practise, practise and learn from mistakes and successes. As teachers try various strategies, and reflect on and refine their approaches and thinking they will gradually internalise the methodology, language and thinking of STEM learning.

STAGE 4: UNCONSCIOUS SKILLED

Finally, in Stage 4 teachers have had so much practice with planning, delivering and assessing STEM learning that these tasks can be performed quickly and easily without much thought. The danger in this stage is that teachers may regress if they become complacent about the skills and thinking they have developed. A great way to keep thinking and practice fresh at this stage is to teach and coach others.

BECOMING EFFECTIVE LEADERS OF STEM LEARNING

There are six broad areas in which teachers need to build their capacity to move from unconsciously unskilled to unconsciously skilled: mindset, capacity to influence, backward-planning habits, formative assessment practices, pedagogical practices and action research.

1. DEVELOP A MINDSET THAT WILL OVERCOME CHALLENGES AND OBSTACLES

Much like we did for students in Chapter 2, teachers need to create a mindset motto that empowers them to not be stopped by challenges or obstacles. There are many ways this mindset is described by STEM teachers: from beginner's mindset, as we encountered earlier, to 'have a go', 'risk-taking', 'I can figure it out' and so on. A big barrier that many teachers face is the perception that they need to know and understand science or technology or engineering or maths and how to use and teach them well before they start. This perception stymies learning, creativity and innovative problem-solving – and is the opposite of what is needed to create effective STEM learning. As one expert STEM teacher expressed, 'There is a real fear of failure and many teachers seem to believe they can't teach STEM as they don't have all the answers.'

One of the major shifts that teachers experience in their journey to leading effective STEM learning is the shift in mindset from 'sage on the stage' to being an activator and seeing failures and mistakes as learning experiences for everyone. Teachers can learn alongside their students. This might sound risky, but many STEM teachers have found this to be the best approach to leading STEM learning. This approach allows teachers to authentically model the appropriate thinking and problem-solving process, while empowering their students to drive their own learning. It also allows teachers to focus on something they are really good at: learning. While it does help if teachers know the 'how' of technology and be a highly trained scientist or mathematician, what matters more is instilling a love of learning, being curious and figuring things out as a community of learners.

2. DEVELOP THE CAPACITY TO INFLUENCE AND ENGAGE OTHERS

In every STEM teacher's journey is a story about how they shared and convinced someone in a position of influence to support expanding STEM learning beyond what they were doing. The ability to communicate clearly and convincingly is an extraordinarily valuable skill. Effective STEM teachers engage and convince students who don't believe they can, that they actually can. They engage students in the possibility that they are more capable and extraordinary than they think they are. They interact with parents and influence them by sharing the importance of STEM thinking and learning. They share stories about the learning growth of students with other teachers and influence their thoughts about STEM. They share the progress students are making with school leaders, and influence their decisions about embedding STEM learning in the school timetable. They even sometimes influence industry and companies to partner with schools for new STEM initiatives. And some, like Ann Adams (see page 180), take on educational systems to remove barriers.

Effective STEM teachers have developed the ability to make their cases for action and tell engaging stories that influence the heads, hearts and hands of listeners. This will be unpacked further in Chapter 9 as part of a discussion about how to cause change.

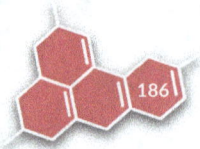

3. DEVELOP BACKWARD-PLANNING HABITS

Forward planning is a common habit that teachers need to overcome when developing their capacity to lead STEM learning effectively. Many teachers plan learning from beginning to end. In other words, they look at the curriculum content knowledge that needs to be addressed and then they sequence the learning to ensure that the curriculum content knowledge is covered. This approach is like building a house piece by piece without having a clear vision and goal of what the house should look and feel like. Even worse, it doesn't address that each student is actually building their own personal house of learning and understanding. Each student begins with different levels of knowledge, skill and thinking and will build their learning at different rates.

STEM learning is based on the habit of planning backwards with a learning destination (knowledge, skills, thinking and even mindset) in mind. The backward-design approach frees teachers from following the curriculum as a checklist and instead allows a more creative and authentic approach to the creation of learning. The process supports teachers to have a deep understanding of what the curriculum is asking, but then shifts the focus to the progressive development of knowledge, skill, thinking and mindset framed within an authentic journey. Backward-planning also helps teaching teams to be much more collaborative and share their expertise and knowledge. Teaching teams need to come to a deep common understanding of the curriculum and authentically identify what students need to know and be able to do by the end of their learning journey. They can then, upfront, create STEM projects or authentic STEM tasks sufficiently complex for students to undergo a series of trial-and-error episodes. Through these they learn to self-regulate, problem-solve, use design thinking and become skilled lifelong learners. The learning that occurs as a result of these backward-planning practices is far richer and has students test their ideas against reality to determine their worth.

It should be no surprise that learning to backward plan effectively, which was unpacked in detail in Chapters 4–6, does take a significant amount of time to begin with. Of all the areas to become skilled in as a teacher, backward planning takes the greatest investment of time and the most rigour. However, the more teachers practise this skill, the easier and quicker it becomes.

4. DEVELOP APPROPRIATE FORMATIVE ASSESSMENT PRACTICES

Consistent with the common forward-planning approach is a focus on summative assessment in STEM learning. When attempting to enact STEM learning, many teachers seem to be only assessing the end product or result. As Anna Danson shared, this fixation on the end product and summative assessment often leads to teachers and students losing sight of the learning journey. Summative assessment, while an important part of assessing the ability of a learner to deliver a quality product or outcome, is a small part of measuring learning growth.

Teachers need to develop their capacity to create formative assessment structures and approaches that not only allow them to measure learning progression but also supports learners to develop their own capacity to self- and peer-assess. Effective STEM learning requires a systemic drafting–reflection–evaluation–refinement approach, meaning that assessment approaches must reflect the design process. This won't just empower students to become self-regulated drivers of their own learning; it will allow teachers to provide more point-of-need teaching and support. Learning to create and effectively use formative assessment approaches and structures, such as those outlined in Chapter 7, is an investment that teachers of STEM learning will need to make on their journey to being effective.

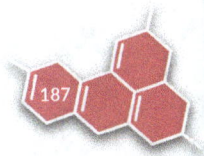

5. DEVELOP EFFECTIVE PEDAGOGICAL PRACTICES

Many teachers will find themselves on a pedagogical journey as they weave the design, computational and systems thinking frameworks into their day-to-day learning – and all while leading learning that empowers and enables students to drive their own learning. As part of this process, teachers will need to let go of any preconceived notions about their role as teachers, their students' role as learners and what learning should look like.

Skilled STEM practitioners relate to students as co-learners, co-teachers and co-designers of learning. Over time, these teachers develop templates, graphic organisers and pedagogical practices that nurture the growth of this environment and culture. They deliberately train learners in the skills of being self-regulated through individual and group conferencing, setting goals, building portfolios, drafting processes, using critique groups, establishing thinking routines and much more. They consistently use language that underpins the thinking frameworks (*deconstruct, algorithm, empathise, ideate, interconnected, hypothesis, evidence, evaluate, strategy* and so on), as discussed in Chapter 1. They become masterful learners and activators, always reflecting and adjusting or adapting their pedagogical techniques to the circumstances and the students in front of them.

6. BRING RIGOUR TO ONE'S OWN LEARNING THROUGH ACTION RESEARCH

The final area that teachers need to develop their capacity in is bringing rigour to their own learning growth. It is surprising how many teachers do not have consistent practices in which they strategically plan, reflect on and gather evidence of their growth. This often has more to do with the culture of the school and how it supports teachers to grow their capacity than teachers as individuals. Many schools are beginning to integrate data-informed inquiry cycles or reflection as part of individualised professional growth plans, but these can still be quite narrow or not very rigorous.

While we will address rigour in whole-school curriculum and pedagogical change in the next chapter, teachers do need to take personal responsibility for developing habits of planning, trialling and evaluating mini action-research projects as part of their personal learning growth. Great STEM teachers apply the design process to their own learning. They gather information and data so they can come to a deep understanding of what they are not yet skilled in. They identify what they are going to focus on and then iterate through the ideate–test–evaluate cycle in learning sprints to grow their capabilities. This approach not only improves their ability as leaders of STEM learning, it deepens their understanding and application of the thinking frameworks.

Exercise: Action research 1

For each of the broad areas of development identified in this chapter, identify your current stage of conscious competence: unconscious unskilled, conscious unskilled, conscious skilled, unconscious skilled (Gordon & Burch, 1974). With this in hand, write a list of actions you could take to move up a developmental stage in each area.

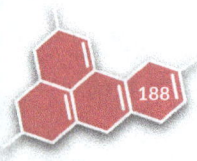

DESIGNING A PERSONAL MINI ACTION-RESEARCH PROJECT

Personal mini action-research projects are not intended to be multifaceted and as complex as many long-term whole-school projects or university research projects can be. They are designed for teachers to focus on one area where they desire to improve their practice. Teachers should be able to sprint quickly through the desired learning within a term or two – trialling ideas, gathering evidence of what works and what doesn't, and refining their practice.

In the coming pages we will work through the five steps of designing a personal mini action-research project. This planning process is supported by the template shown on page 192 (check the downloads for a reproducible version), the relevant elements of which will be featured alongside each of the five steps. Used in conjunction with Helen Sanderson Associates' (2015) 4 + 1 Questions thinking tool, shown in figure 8.2 (page 185), this simple design-thinking structure will support teachers to create their own learning sprints and improve the rigour of their practice.

Step 1: Identify the challenges

Begin by identifying the broad area in which you would like to improve your capacity. Using the first column of the template elements shown in table 8.1, write down the challenges you are experiencing in this area. For example, you may want to research the general area of developing student agency and helping students see themselves as co-teachers in your STEM classes. In this case, some challenges might include:

1. Students are passive learners.
2. Most students wait for teacher prompting before beginning a task.
3. Students don't yet understand how to use the design process.
4. Students give up easily when they get stuck.

Be authentic about what you are seeing in the classroom. List as much observable evidence (qualitative and quantitative) as you can. This can be considered the empathise phase of the action-research process.

Table 8.1: Template element supporting Steps 1 and 2 of designing a personal mini action-research project

Challenges this action-research project is trying to address	Research question What improvement is evident in *[learning area where I desire improvement]* when I implement *[the strategies that I am researching the effect of]*?

Step 2: Articulate the research question

Writing a good research question can take an enormous amount of time. University researchers can take months to develop high-quality, rigorous questions. Teachers don't have that amount of time, so the following format (replicated in the second column of table 8.1) is a simple way to create them:

> *What improvement is evident in [learning area where I desire improvement] when I implement [the strategies that I am researching the effect of]?*

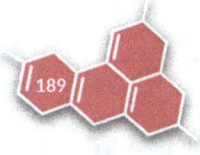

Here are some examples of research questions following this structure:
- What improvement is evident in student voice and agency when I co-design formative assessment rubrics with the students?
- What improvement is evident in student agency when I create and value a trial-and-error learning environment?
- What improvement is evident in student agency when I explicitly teach metacognitive strategies to students?
- What improvement is evident in student mindset when I consistently use James Nottingham's (2017) learning pit metaphor in my classes?
- What improvement is evident in learning growth when students are trained to give, receive and use focused feedback as part of the STEM learning process?
- What improvement is evident in critical and creative thinking when students consistently use the design process in all learning?

The benefit of this format is that it includes what will be measured and the broad strategies that will be used. This makes the next step, where desired outcomes are defined, a lot easier.

Step 3: Define the outcomes, evidence, strategies and resources

There are two sets of outcomes to define in this step (with the support of the template elements shown in table 8.2): those for the students and those for the teacher (table 8.2). Both are equally important as there should be learning growth in both groups during the period of the mini action-research project.

Table 8.2: Template supporting Step 3 of a personal mini action-research project

Outcomes			
Outcomes — What is your vision of success? What do you expect to see as a result? How will you know you have succeeded?			
Outcomes	What evidence do I need to be gathering to measure progress towards this outcome? How will I gather it?	Strategies and possible actions to accomplish this outcome (what, who, by when)	What resources will I need to take these actions? Include $$, PD, research & human resources.
Student outcomes: 1. 2. 3.			
My outcomes: 1. 2. 3.			

When completing this step, imagine what the results could be at the end of the research project. In other words, after going through the mini action-research project for four learning sprints over twenty weeks, what outcomes should be observable in student and teacher practice and behaviour? For example, the student outcomes expected from the research question 'What improvement is evident in student agency when I create and value a trial-and-error learning environment?' could be:

- *Students demonstrate a greater willingness to collaborate and help one another.*
- *Students improve their capacity for self-regulation.*
- *Students demonstrate a measurable improvement in their engagement with STEM.*

Meanwhile, teacher outcomes from the same question could be:

- *I have grown my capacity to trust the students.*
- *I have grown my capacity to encourage and empower student self-confidence.*
- *I am using the computational and design thinking vocabulary consistently with the students.*

Once the outcomes have been defined, teachers then go through the process of ideating what evidence they might gather to measure progress, what strategies and actions can be taken, and what resources will be needed to achieve each outcome. In many cases they will need to be inventive about how they measure progression. For example, teachers could gather evidence using pre- and post-surveys of students, video observation using technology such as Swivl, external observations, audio evidence, personal reflections captured throughout the project, rubrics, anecdotal stories, student work, formative feedback such as exit cards, student feedback and learning reflections, and so on. Be creative and try out different qualitative and quantitative ways of measuring progress.

Step 4: Plan the logistics

As part of Step 3 teachers will have ideated a number of strategies and actions that they could take during the research project. Step 4 provides an opportunity to map out these strategies, actions and ways of gathering of evidence across the learning cycles (scaffolded by the template elements shown in table 8.3). As part of this process, teachers will need to consider the time they have available in their teaching calendar during each five-week cycle. They may not have the time or opportunity to implement all the strategies and actions they ideated. While Step 3 is about creative ideation, Step 4 is about creating a prototype plan of attack to be implemented and trialled. This plan is most likely to change as teachers come to a deeper understanding of what strategies and actions are more useful and valuable in the classroom.

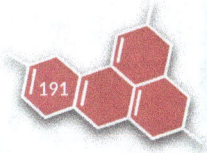

Table 8.3: Template supporting Step 4 of a personal mini action-research project

	Actions What are the actions required in each cycle to successfully accomplish the goal? (Include milestones.)			
Outcomes	**First 5-week cycle**	**Second 5-week cycle**	**Third 5-week cycle**	**Fourth 5-week cycle**
Student outcomes: 1. 2. 3.				
My outcomes: 1. 2. 3.				

Step 5: Consider challenges and solutions

The last step, which pairs with the template elements shown in table 8.4, provides an opportunity for a teacher to think about the potential challenges or obstacles that may arise during the period of the mini-action research project. This is an important step as it challenges the teacher to acknowledge any barriers that could arise and articulate ways they could overcome and get around those obstacles and challenges. This is a solution-oriented approach and is specifically included to develop the 'I can figure it out' mindset.

Table 8.4: Template supporting Step 5 of a personal mini action-research project

Challenges/obstacles to achieving the outcomes	Potential solutions

Exercise: Action research 2

Having identified potential for improvement in Exercise: Action research 1, use the following template to design a mini action-research project for one area that you want to grow your capacity in.

Challenges this action-research project is trying to address	Research question What improvement is evident in *[learning area where I desire improvement]* when I implement *[the strategies that I am researching the effect of]*?

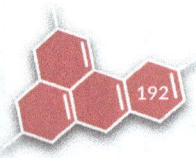

Growing teacher capacity to lead STEM learning

Outcomes What is your vision of success? What do you expect to see as a result? How will you know you have succeeded?			
Outcomes	What evidence do I need to be gathering to measure progress towards this outcome? How will I gather it?	Strategies and possible actions to accomplish this outcome (what, who, by when)	What resources will I need to take these actions? Include $$, PD, research & human resources.
Student outcomes: 1. 2. 3.			
My outcomes: 1. 2. 3.			

Actions What are the actions required in each cycle to successfully accomplish the goal? (Include milestones.)				
Outcomes	First 5-week cycle	Second 5-week cycle	Third 5-week cycle	Fourth 5-week cycle
Student outcomes: 1. 2. 3.				
My outcomes: 1. 2. 3.				

Challenges/obstacles to achieving the outcomes	Potential solutions

Reproducible available

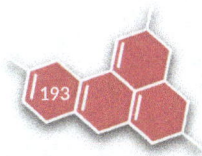

193

LEARN BY DOING

The best short-term action a teacher at the very beginning of leading STEM learning can take is to begin. Take a risk! Go through trial and error along with students and see what happens. Little by little, teachers will see the path forward and identify what they need to grow their skills and capabilities. As teachers try, reflect, evaluate and refine their pedagogy, lessons and units, they should be ready to be surprised by how clever and amazing their students are.

KEY POINTS

- There is no one pathway that teachers take as they learn to lead STEM learning. Each teacher has different passions, drivers, strengths, areas of expertise and areas for development.
- Teachers also face different obstacles and challenges along the way. This can include traditional structures and approaches within schools and school systems that may act as barriers to embedding an authentic STEM program.
- Great STEM teachers use the obstacles and challenges on their journey to improve. They take risks, fail, learn and strive to be effective with their cohort of students, in their particular school community and with the resources they have to hand.
- Teachers will go through four stages of development as they grow their capacity to lead STEM learning effectively: unconscious unskilled, conscious unskilled, conscious skilled and unconscious skilled.
- There are six broad areas in which teachers must develop their capacity to be effective: mindset, capacity to influence, backward-planning habits, formative assessment practices, pedagogical practices and action research.
- The best course of action is to just get started.

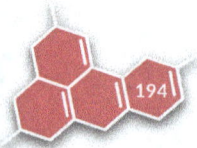

CHAPTER 9

Leading the STEM curriculum and pedagogical change

> Many great projects go through a stage early on where they don't seem very impressive, even to their creators. You have to push through this stage to reach the great work that lies beyond. But many people don't. Most people don't even reach the stage of making something they're embarrassed by, let alone continue past it. They're too frightened even to start.
>
> Paul Graham, 'Early work'

LEADING ORGANISATIONAL CHANGE

There is no one-size-fits-all solution to causing the organisational change required to embed a sustainable and authentic STEM program. Great STEM programs that deliver great outcomes are the result of a series of good decisions that accumulate over a very long period of time. If a school's goal is to develop young people to be collaborative, adaptable thinkers and learners with a STEM mindset, this will only be built by thoughtful and strategic alignment of the school's systems, processes and policies. School leaders will have to explore questions such as, does the timetable need to change? What resources will be required? What time release will teachers need to take their learning journeys and build their capacities? How can the school support teachers to grow and develop their professional practice and thinking? What systems will be needed to ensure continual improvement? What will assessment look like? What will reports look like? What documentation will be needed? How will new staff be inducted into the STEM learning approach? How will parents be inducted and supported into the STEM learning approach so they are more effective in empowering and enabling their children? Are there any misalignments that could stop us achieving our goals?

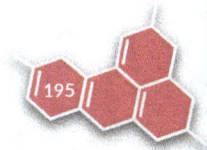

Like any organisation, schools can be subject to change initiatives that are poorly thought through, rolled out too fast or put in place without sufficient preparation. These types of change often lead to teachers expressing change fatigue and resisting subsequent change, regardless of how valuable or transformative it could be (Dilkes et al., 2014). Sometimes the issue is that the skills and commitment to ensure that change can be sustained over time is missing. Sometimes it is because the decisions, planning and implementation have excluded the input and voices of teachers, students and, to a lesser extent, parents. Sometimes it is due to a lack of clear communication and ownership of the change agenda. Whether change is mandated externally or internally, school leaders need to develop their capacity to effectively lead curriculum and pedagogical change within their school. The sustainability of major change initiatives in schools takes concerted and long-term strategic thinking, planning and acting.

This chapter will explore the concept of socially constructed organisational change and consider how it applies to embedding an authentic STEM program. John Kotter's (1995) eight-step change management model will be used to identify key steps that school leaders can take as they lead and enable required organisational change. As we unpack each of the steps, we will draw lessons from the experiences of a range of teachers and school leaders on their journeys to embedding a STEM program in their school.

SOCIALLY CONSTRUCTED ORGANISATIONAL CHANGE

Schools are relational learning organisations; the educational process is relational and experiential, the individuals involved are relational beings, and the systems, processes and policies of a school are built on a culture of collaboration, relationships and learning (Giles, 2018). As in any relationship, the nurturing of trust and psychological safety within a school is central to achieving sustainable change. Leading the curriculum and pedagogical change to embed an authentic STEM program effectively is a social process that involves students, teachers, staff and parents trusting and owning the processes (Breakspear, 2017).

The problem is that in many schools change has traditionally been something initiated and managed from the top. Generally, curriculum or pedagogical change is motivated by one of three situations: the educational system has mandated change, a school review has suggested change, or a new leader has arrived and wants specific changes to be made. To make change happen 'efficiently', the traditional approach has been for school leaders identify what needs to happen, create a roll-out plan and then enforce it through hierarchical systems and processes (Dilkes et al., 2014). This approach to organisational change often leads to teachers resisting change and expressing change fatigue.

Socially constructed organisational change recognises the importance of building trust, and empowering and enabling the school community to own and drive change. This approach involves school leadership setting up the agency and platform for committed stakeholders to initiate change, recruit a coalition of early adopters, suggest solutions and launch experiments. An effective socially constructed change platform encourages individuals to tackle significant organisational challenges that they would normally consider beyond their remit, explore and come to a shared understanding of the root causes of the challenges and barriers, brainstorm a wide range of potential solutions before converging on an approach, generate a portfolio of experiments that can be used to determine what will work in their local setting, and take personal responsibility for initiating the change they want to see (Hamel & Zanini, 2014).

Socially constructed organisational change overcomes factors such as interpersonal fear, beliefs about failure and risk, groupthink, and the normal human behaviours that hold teams and

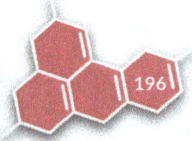

communities back from continuous improvement (Edmondson, 2018). It is sustainable because it provides the active building of relational trust, ownership of the change processes, and freedom to take risks and learn new approaches that systems and social processes require. As leadership is progressively distributed throughout the community, it leads naturally to a significant positive influence on school culture, improved conditions for teaching and learning, teacher autonomy and sustained improvement in pupil behaviour, engagement and outcomes (Leithwood et al., 2020).

THE EIGHT-STEP CHANGE MODEL

Kotter's (1995) eight-step change model, which incidentally mirrors the design process, was founded on this concept of socially constructed organisational change. The model is built on what Kotter terms a 'dual operating system' (Kotter, 2012). The first operating system is the traditional leadership hierarchy found within most organisations, including schools. This is a valuable operating system since it is designed to provide clarity and certainty for the long term as well as manage the normal operations of a school. However, in periods of rapid change, Kotter (2012) finds that normal hierarchical processes tend to be risk-averse and resistant to change with leadership concentrated in the few at the top. To allow for nimbleness and adaptation in periods of rapid change, Kotter recommends that a second operating system be established that nurtures and distributes leadership to trial and embed change. The second operating system is a strategy network – a group of focused, committed and passionate people who drive the change process through problem-solving, creativity and collaboration. This group is populated by people who have a genuine desire to contribute to positive change and be change agents. The idea is that the two operating systems work in concert with one another. If we apply this to managing change in schools, the job of school leadership here is to provide the resources, management and accountability support so that the strategy network can focus on researching, developing and prototyping strategies, processes and thinking that align with their school's vision and goals.

Astute readers might notice that professional learning communities (PLCs) in schools are an attempt at creating this sort of strategy network operating system within schools. The problem with the way that many PLCs are formed is that they aren't populated by teachers and stakeholders who specifically desire to be change agents and risk-takers. They are generally made up of a mix of teachers: some who are eager to drive change, some who resist change and others somewhere in between. Well-formulated and well-managed strategy networks and PLCs tend to involve nimble working parties of early adopting teachers and stakeholders who sprint through cycles of inquiry in action-research projects. They develop a strong sense of community responsibility for their school and for student learning, they identify shared norms and values, and they have collective accountability to achieve a big-picture vision for all stakeholders (Servage, 2008).

Kotter (1995) came up with his model after examining change across hundreds of businesses and organisations. He found that leaders who successfully led sustainable transformation in their organisations did eight things right – and in the right order. As illustrated in table 9.1, which adapts the eight-step change model for the school context, Kotter's (1995) model involves three phases of action:
1. creating a climate for change
2. engaging and enabling the organisation
3. implementing and sustaining change.

Change ripples through a school, beginning with the nimble strategy networks, and then flows through that school as those strategy networks lead change for remaining teachers and key stakeholders.

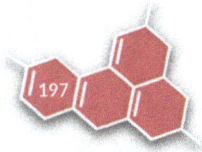

Table 9.1: An adaptation for schools of Kotter's (1995) eight-step change model

Phase	Step	Description	Notes
Creating a climate for change	1. Create a sense of urgency.	<ul><li>Examine the current reality of the school against desired outcomes.</li><li>Identify and highlight challenges and major opportunities.</li></ul>	Create the foundational pre-conditions for change.
	2. Form a powerful guiding coalition.	<ul><li>Assemble a small group of early adopters and leaders to lead the change effort.</li><li>Support the group to build trust and work together as a team.</li></ul>	
	3. Create a vision for change.	<ul><li>Create a vision to clarify and direct the change effort.</li><li>Develop strategies for achieving that vision.</li></ul>	
Engaging and enabling the organisation	4. Communicate the change vision.	<ul><li>Develop guiding coalition's knowledge, skills and thinking via an action-research project.</li><li>Communicate coherently and consistently the vision and results of action-research project to the staff.</li></ul>	First ripple of change. Cycles of inquiry and action-research project involves only the guiding coalition.
	5. Empower others to act on the vision.	Through the action-research project:<ul><li>Identify and remove obstacles to change.</li><li>Change systems and structures that are not aligned to the vision.</li><li>Encourage risk-tasking and research-based ideas, activities and practices.</li></ul>	
	6. Plan for and create short-term wins.	<ul><li>Plan cycle of inquiry learning sprints.</li><li>Gather evidence of successes and failures.</li><li>Refine the strategies, processes and structures to lead to the greatest success.</li></ul>	
Implementing and sustaining change	7. Consolidate improvements and produce more change.	<ul><li>Use increased credibility to change systems, structures and processes that don't fit the vision.</li><li>Potentially hire and promote those who implement the vision.</li></ul>	Following ripples of change. Guiding coalition leads the following ripples of developing and empowering change agents at the school.
	8. Anchor the new approaches.	<ul><li>Articulate the connections between the new behaviours and practices and learning success.</li><li>Develop the means to ensure leadership development and succession.</li></ul>	

Source: Adapted from Kotter (1995)

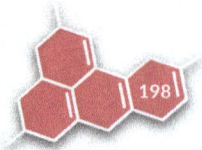

CREATING A CLIMATE FOR CHANGE

Teachers are not afraid of change. Every day they adapt and learn and nurture the growth of the students in front of them. If they do resist change, that resistance has been shown to arise from a range of fears: the fear of wasting their time and energy on a change that won't benefit students, the fear of losing autonomy, the fear of experiencing incompetence when trying something new, the fear of uncertainty and not being in control, and the fear of having more work to do (Ferguson et al., 2010). These normal human fears occur for many of us in times of change. Strategically, the first phase of leading the change necessary to embed an authentic STEM program involves creating an empathetic climate for change. That climate must highlight the need for change, while also finding a way for that change to occur without triggering resistance or change fatigue.

STEP 1: CREATE A SENSE OF URGENCY

It takes courage to take the risk to change existing habits and practices. What makes a difference and empowers people to take that risk is seeing that their current habits and practices are not delivering on their vision for the learners in their care. It is rare to find teachers who are not passionate and committed to making a difference for young people. However, unless there is an embedded continuous improvement process where teachers can reflect, review and refine their thinking and practices, they can fall into the trap of thinking good enough is close enough. This idea of 'good enough' kills the desire and agency for change that delivers outstanding outcomes.

The first step of creating urgency is the most challenging because it is about highlighting the need for change and obtaining the cooperation of many individuals. Creating urgency can be confronting for people as it requires driving people out of their comfort zones and having honest discussions about the impact of the status quo. These types of conversations become much easier and less confronting when a school and its key stakeholders are aligned around a clear vision and mission, and have data-informed review and reflection processes in place.

One way of starting the process is constructing a case for action to persuade people of the urgency. A case for action has three elements: what the current reality is for learners, what will happen if nothing is done and what is possible if action is taken.

1. The current reality

A conversation about the current reality is designed to address both the head (with quantitative data) and the heart (with qualitative data). Both are equally important, as we need to appeal not only to logic, but also to the genuine desire to make a difference to the learning and lives of students. Quantitative data could include student, teacher and parent surveys and macro data such as NAPLAN or whole-cohort, in-school testing. The aim is to demonstrate the impact of current practices and approaches on students' progression. Qualitative data could include work samples, observations and student–teacher conversations. These personal stories and experiences provide a humanising background to the quantitative data.

When looking to share the current reality for STEM learning, qualitative data can be easier to come by than quantitative data. Stories about students who struggle with normal classroom approaches, the disengagement of particular students, as well as the noticeable passivity and focus on grades that students demonstrate as they are enculturated into schooling can create a powerful narrative. Quantitative data typically collected by schools is often insufficient to show the need for urgency. Schools and leaders might need to invent new measurement tools and surveys to explore growth (or lack thereof) in the general capabilities, self-regulation and student agency. Use of the rubrics outlined in Chapter 7 would go some way to providing this type of data.

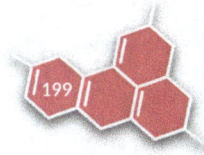

2. What will happen if nothing is done

A great way to articulate this element of the conversation is highlighting the disparity between what the data shows and the vision and mission of the school. Explore the likely outcomes if this situation is not addressed; generally it will be more of the same results. It could also be useful to demonstrate trends in quantitative and qualitative data over time. What difference have the past strategies and approaches made to students' learning growth? Focus particularly on those areas that STEM and the thinking frameworks could make a difference to.

3. What is possible

The intent of this conversation is, again, to address both the head and the heart. Discuss the body of evidence from research and reputable sources. Share stories and samples from any trials or experiences you have had. Share what has happened in other schools and the difference it has made. Be authentic in the picture you paint – the potential benefits and the potential challenges. What difference could it make to teachers? What difference will it make to students? What are some of the other benefits? It is important to link any potential action to the school's strategic plan to align it with the current focus. End the conversation with a recommendation about the next step.

The following sample case for action (figure 9.1) was developed with a teacher who was interested in laying the foundation for a STEM program. Given the school's strategic plan had a focus on causing twelve months of learning growth per year of schooling, the teacher felt the best strategy was to make a case for action for developing student agency. Over time, this would upskill teachers in the necessary thinking and practices so that a STEM program would be easier to integrate in the future. This case for action was presented to the school leadership team, who approved the request for the formation of a professional learning team.

> **What is the current reality?**
> - The school's student attitude to school survey shows poorer levels of differentiated learning challenge, student effort, effective classroom behaviour, student motivation, self-regulation and goal-setting compared to similar schools.
> - A teacher-feedback session about the strategies that worked during the remote learning period highlighted that the majority of strategies developed students to own and drive their own learning.
> - Teachers are not currently aware of the research that highlights the practices that develop student agency.
> - In-class student feedback statements indicate that teachers are using the school instructional model, but it is all teacher directed – the learning in classrooms is seen by some students as boring and repetitive.
> - Recent NAPLAN data indicates that the students are showing less growth compared to students in similar schools. This is also true among upper-quartile students.
>
> **What will happen if nothing is done?**
> - The trend in both the NAPLAN data and the student attitude to school surveys show very little improvement over the past three years despite a range of initiatives.

Leading the STEM curriculum and pedagogical change

> - Students will continue to become disengaged and their learning will not progress across testing years.
> - It is likely that teachers will fall back into their old habits after the period of remote learning and continue to not work towards causing twelve months of learning progress per year in each student, not give homework, not teach to student point of need, and not develop student organisation and planning skills.
> - We will miss providing the challenge the kids want from us.
> - The school will not deliver on its vision or mission.
>
> **What is possible if action is taken?**
> - Student effort and engagement will increase, and their organisational and planning skills will improve.
> - There will be more engagement from staff because they will feel supported and understand the moral imperative. It will increase staff morale.
> - Students will become better learners.
> - Teachers will become more masterful in their thinking and practice.
> - We will be building a research- and evidence-based approach to learning throughout the school.
> - Less time will be wasted doing things that we don't need to do (e.g. if the students are engaged and empowered, behaviour improves).
> - We will achieve better learning growth across the years.
>
> **Request:**
> Recruit a professional learning team to run an action-research project that examines and trials explicit teacher practices that build student metacognition, agency and self-regulation (organisational, wellbeing and planning).

Figure 9.1: Sample case for action

For long-term, sustainable change, school leadership needs to first acknowledge the urgency for change because they have the positional authority to logistically support the required next steps. Without the support of school leadership, it is unlikely there will be much progress. A case for action could be presented to school leaders by members of the school leadership team, the school board, teachers, middle leaders and even parents. At this level, the next-step request should be to form a small working party or professional learning team to run an action-research project that will dive deeper and trial what strategies and approaches could work in the school. Once approval for this small working party has been granted, the next action is to present the case for action to the community of teachers and other stakeholders. This not only heightens the sense of urgency within the community, but also provides an opportunity to extend an invitation for community members to be part of leading the action-research project (the guiding coalition).

STEP 2: FORM A POWERFUL GUIDING COALITION

While the entire school community will become aware of the urgency for a change, not everyone may be ready to change. Stakeholders can be held back by not only their fears, but also by different levels of learning readiness in the area of change. For example, if the change involves bringing technology or design thinking into a classroom, many teachers could feel they don't yet have enough skill or knowledge to be part of driving that change. Equally, there may be individuals who approach new ideas with caution or need evidence that the initiative will work before dipping their toes in the water. Generally, the people who accept the invitation to be part of the action-research working party (the guiding coalition) tend to be early adopters in the area of interest who are ready and willing to take the learning risks involved.

Guiding coalitions that are successful in the early stages of action-research projects tend to be made up of between five and eight volunteers who have bought into the urgency to take action (Kotter, 1995). The team should be kept small because is it logistically easier for a small team to meet and sprint through cycles of inquiry than it is for a large team. However, careful consideration must be given to the composition of the guiding coalition. It is critical that at least one person in the guiding coalition is a member of the senior-leadership team. The positional authority they bring can smooth out many of the logistical and communication challenges that occur when change is being initiated and they can also report back to school leadership. The remaining members should be seen and respected by the community for their credibility, expertise or leadership. This does not mean that graduate teachers or new middle leaders should be excluded. The action-research process is a perfect vehicle for nurturing and growing confidence and leadership in the members of a guiding coalition.

The job of a guiding coalition is to use the cycle of inquiry inherent in an action-research project to systemically find out what works and what doesn't within their school environment. They create a vision for change and an agreement for working together; they articulate the specific challenges the action-research project will address; they define the desired outcomes of the project and the evidence they will collect to measure the impact of their strategies and actions; and they create a plan of attack. As the guiding coalition cycles through the inquiry stages, members will come to a deep understanding of what strategies, structures and processes lead to the best outcomes for their students and the school as a whole. Along the way, they will develop the knowledge, skills and thinking, and the evidence to communicate the benefits and possibilities to their colleagues. The guiding coalition will end up leading the next ripples of change during the implementing and sustaining phase (Phase 3).

Taroona Primary School in Tasmania took on a whole-school approach to implementing the digital technologies curriculum in 2016 (Purdie, 2019). They devised an action-research project based on an eighteen-month coaching model in which a team of teachers studied together to become Digital Technology coaches before co-planning and co-teaching over three terms with partner teachers in their school. They put out a call for anyone interested in being on the guiding coalition, with clear expectations that individuals would need to engage in online and in-house professional learning over a period of two terms. Their guiding coalition was made up of five early adopter teachers, plus four members of their leadership team. The coalition met and established a 'culture of learning' in the team by formulating a 'working together agreement' (Purdie, 2019). They agreed to the following actions:

- *being kind to ourselves and each other as learners*
- *being willing to take risks as learners and leaders*

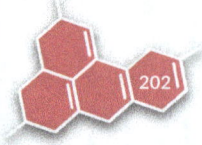

Leading the STEM curriculum and pedagogical change

- *developing 21st century habits of mind*
- *valuing the diversity of learning styles and 'point of readiness' across the school. (Purdie, 2019, 'Creating a guiding coalition' section)*

This set the foundation for trust among the diverse team of people in the coalition and allowed for non-threatening and personalised co-planning and co-teaching.

STEP 3: CREATE A VISION FOR CHANGE

Once a guiding coalition has been formed, one of their first actions is to develop a change vision – a realistic, convincing and attractive depiction of the future – that is relatively easy to communicate and will appeal to the community. Developing this vision is one of the key elements of socially constructed change. Teachers don't teach because they get great holidays or because they love spending their time planning lessons at nights, looking at data walls or dealing with student behaviour. Most become and stay teachers, despite the challenges, because of a passion to make a difference to the lives and futures of the students in front of them. The vision for change should speak to that passion and commitment. Unsurprisingly, Kotter (1995) found in his research that many unsuccessful transformations either had no vision or a vision that was too complicated or blurry to be useful.

Creating a vision requires a guiding coalition to clarify the purpose and direction that they believe the school needs to move in to address the challenges highlighted in the case for action. This vision can then be used to frame the research question for the action-research project, as well as the strategies and outcomes. I recommend that schools create both a vision and a mission during this step. A vision articulates the 'what' or the resulting outcome of the change initiative. The mission articulates the 'how' of achieving that vision. The format I use when I am coaching schools is:

Vision: We are deeply passionate about …

Mission: We want to be known for …

A simplified variation on Jim Collins's (2001) Hedgehog Concept, this format makes it easier for individuals, small teams and schools to articulate their vision and mission clearly and concisely.

When creating the vision statement ('We are deeply passionate about …') teams will need to think about and discuss the visible and concrete outcomes for students, teachers, staff and the community at the end of their project. The vision statement is not a detailed unpacking of these outcomes, but rather captures their essence. Some examples include:

- We are deeply passionate about people being empowered to manage and monitor their learning.
- We are deeply passionate about people striving to be more than what they believe they can be.
- We are deeply passionate about people maximising their potential and striving to be

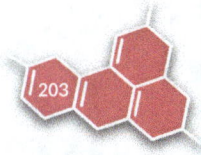

highly literate and successful participants in a twenty-first century context.
- We are deeply passionate about people being active design thinkers and problem-solvers who make a difference to the world.
- We are deeply passionate about empowering and enabling all people to connect, learn and flourish.

One thing you may notice in these vision statements is the choice to refer to people rather students. I am very particular about this because often schools develop visions that only focus on their students. By making statements inclusive of everyone, they are automatically also applicable to teachers, parents, non-teaching staff and school leaders. Teachers need to be empowered, maximise their potential and be active design thinkers too! I have found that this small change means teachers and school leaders begin to think about strategies, processes and structures that can be implemented to support staff and parents as well as students to achieve their vision.

The mission statement ('We want to be known for …') captures how a team is going to achieve their vision. What strategies or approaches will the team have focused on to realise their vision? This statement also doesn't need too much detail, but rather indicates what the team will focus on. For example, the guiding coalition that had the vision 'We are deeply passionate about people being empowered to manage and monitor their learning' articulated this mission statement: 'We want to be known for creating a learning environment that nurtures metacognition, self-regulation, collaboration and agency.' Their thinking was that their vision would be achieved by creating a learning environment where metacognitive and self-regulation skills were explicitly taught, and that their curriculum planning and pedagogy would encourage agency and collaboration.

Other examples include:
- We want to be known for challenging and encouraging people while still being positive and approachable every step of the way.
- We want to be known for being an innovative, highly motivated and collaborative team, inspiring people to apply these valuable skills in all aspects of their lives.
- We want to be known for providing a safe and supportive learning environment that caters for all individual learning styles, models healthy lifestyle habits and allows people a variety of opportunities to succeed and become team players.
- We want to be known for creating innovative learning that challenges thinking, is meaningful and encourages leadership.
- We want to be known for providing learning and pedagogy that nurtures problem-solvers, thinkers and leaders.

Once vision and mission statements have been designed and agreed upon by the guiding coalition, the challenges and the research question to be addressed through the action-research project should become easier to articulate. Table 9.2 is a variation to be used by guiding coalitions on the mini-action research project planning template outlined in Chapter 8 (figure 8.1, page 184).

Leading the STEM curriculum and pedagogical change

Table 9.2: Guiding coalition action-research project planning template

Action-research project planning template	
Name:	**Role:**
Guiding coalition members	
Name:	Role:
Name:	Role:
Name:	Role:
Name:	Role:
Name:	Role:
Vision and mission for the project	
Vision: We are deeply passionate about … Mission: We want to be known for …	

Challenges this action-research project is trying to address	Research question What improvement is evident in *[learning area where I desire improvement]* when I implement *[the strategies that I am researching the effect of]*?

Outcomes			
What is your vision of success? What do you expect to see as a result? How will you know you have succeeded?			
Outcomes	**What evidence do I need to be gathering to measure progress towards this outcome? How will I gather it?**	**Strategies and possible actions to accomplish this outcome (what, who, by when)**	**What resources will I need to take these actions?** Include $$, PD, research & human resources.
Student outcomes: 1. 2. 3.			
Teacher outcomes: 1. 2. 3.			

Continued …

Igniting STEM Learning

Actions What are the actions required in each cycle to successfully accomplish the goal? (Include milestones.)					
Outcomes	**First 5-week cycle**	**Second 5-week cycle**	**Third 5-week cycle**	**Fourth 5-week cycle**
Student outcomes: 1. 2. 3.				
Teacher outcomes: 1. 2. 3.				

Challenges/obstacles to achieving the outcomes	Potential solutions

Reproducible available

The phase of creating a climate for change is complete when the action-research project has been formulated.

ENGAGING AND ENABLING THE ORGANISATION

In the second phase, guiding coalitions sprint through cycles of inquiry in their action-research projects. The intention is for teams to grow their knowledge, skills and thinking in the strategies being applied so they can determine what works and what doesn't work in their school environment.

Guiding coalitions will perform research to identify specific research-based strategies and approaches to use. They will try and reflect on different approaches and share what they are learning. They will take risks, ask for student feedback, gather evidence of impact and refine their approaches and thinking based on the evidence and their reflection. They might even begin to identify the systems, practices and mindsets that are barriers to rolling out change through the school.

This phase can last from six months to a year and is in essence a time of learning and working out what needs to be in place to achieve the desired outcomes.

STEP 4: COMMUNICATE THE CHANGE VISION

While the guiding coalition is running their action-research project, it is important to lay the foundations for engaging the entire school community in the upcoming change. A key strategy for this is constantly and consistently sharing the change vision and what is being learnt. Kotter (1995) discovered that transformation is impossible without a lot of credible communication that captures the hearts and minds of the community. Applied to a school context, it's fair to say that only with communication can levels of engagement and empowerment within school communities improve.

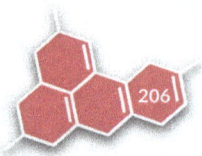

Once the action-research project has been formulated, this communication begins with the guiding coalition formally sharing the vision, mission, research question and outcomes with their community. Engage teachers by inviting them to provide feedback and ideas, and even explore what seeing the vision fulfilled in their classes would look like. Share the project with students, parents and other staff members. The goal here is to begin the process of attracting the interest and commitment of the school community to the change vision. I have led these first communication sessions with teachers in a number of schools and it is surprising how often teachers have approached me afterward to share their interest in what the guiding coalition was doing and how it related to their thinking and practice.

Constant and consistent communication should continue as the guiding coalition sprints through cycles of inquiry and the members meet to reflect, learn and refine their approaches. I recommend that time be set aside in these team meetings for members to share their stories of success and failure as they go. Not only does this storytelling keep the value and the passion for the project alive for the team, but this type of anecdotal information is also perfect to capture and share with the community. The constant sharing – in both formal and informal settings such as the staff room or conversation – gradually creates a culture of authenticity and trust in the process the team is going through as well as ownership of the change.

STEP 5: EMPOWER OTHERS TO ACT ON THE VISION

To a certain extent, the guiding coalition's constant formal and informal sharing will empower others to act. Other staff members, students and even parents become inspired by the vision and mission and will want to help to make it happen. This is something that the guiding coalition and school leadership need to harness, because the more that people actively engage with their vision and mission, the better the outcome. This step is about empowering people by removing obstacles to trying new ideas and providing leadership.

Sometimes the obstacle to transforming a school is a person or group of people who act negatively or pay lip service to the process. This is particularly troublesome if they have positional authority. These individuals can undermine and even block transformation efforts. This is a challenging situation, and they may be talented individuals and worthwhile contributors in other ways. However, it is critical that negativity or lip service be addressed by someone in authority in a way that is fair and consistent with the new vision. For example, a coach I mentored noticed a huge difference in progression between two groups of teachers who were enacting the same strategies in their classes. When she began observing their team meetings, she realised that the group leader did not believe in the intended change and preferred the old ways of doing things. The coach hit upon the idea of having this group leader come along to a professional learning session to learn how to implement a new measurement tool required by their action-research project and then partner the coach in teaching everyone else about how to use it. This shifted the mindset of the group leader as they had all their questions answered by the expert and experienced being empowered to use their expertise to make a difference to others. Empowering negative people to become positive change agents can make a huge difference to the uptake of change.

At other times, the obstacle is that there is no pathway for individuals to try the new ideas being shared with them. Though inspired by the possibilities of the vision and the action-research project, they may not know how to take action on it or doubt themselves and their abilities. I recommend each member of the guiding coalition to begin informally mentoring someone outside the coalition team after a term of enacting their action-research project. This has the benefits of empowering others, developing the coaching capacity of guiding coalition members and growing the confidence of those who doubt themselves. I also recommend exploring how the guiding

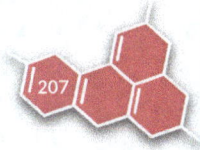

coalition and school leadership could support students and parents to be involved. It could simply mean providing opportunities for students and parents to be involved in giving feedback, or it could result in extending invitations to be involved in the decision-making. Whatever actions are taken, they will build agreement and ownership for the subsequent ripples of change that will occur in the third phase.

Sometimes the obstacle lies in the traditional systems and processes of the school. This is an issue with STEM learning in particular. STEM learning does require a significant amount of time and planning investment because it not only brings together a number of disciplines, but also requires students to develop the capacity to lead their own learning. Schools often bring in STEM via after-school programs, lunchtime activities or specialist subjects that get limited time in a busy schedule. If an authentic STEM program is going to be embedded within a school, that school's guiding coalition will need to examine how structures such as the timetable, assessment approaches and reporting will be adapted to fully realise the benefits of the program. This exploration of alignment or non-alignment of school systems, structures and processes to the vision will ultimately support the community believing in and supporting the proposed vision and change.

STEP 6: PLAN FOR AND CREATE SHORT-TERM WINS

The final step of this phase revolves around proving the validity and credibility of the action-research project quickly. Long-term transformation of practices, structures and thinking is built on a foundation of short-term wins. Without short-term wins being shared and celebrated, the level of urgency for change can drop. It is very easy for people who are not fully enrolled in or who resist the change vision to lose patience and discount the potential benefits of the change. This is particularly true in schools where the community believes they are already doing a good enough job. What I have generally found in schools where this 'good enough' belief is widespread is that teachers and the schools themselves measure their performance using the results of standardised testing (such as NAPLAN and the range of knowledge-based testing) almost exclusively. They do not consider or measure what we discussed in Chapters 7 and 8: growth in students' and teachers' thinking, their mindsets and the skills inherent in the Australian Curriculum general capabilities. Part of the journey of establishing the benefit and value of the change vision and the change project is building the credibility of learning aspects that were not previously measured.

As such, guiding coalitions should plan for and focus on delivering short-term wins in the first six months of their action-research project. This could require weekly team meetings, between which team members are rigorously practicing new strategies and testing new ways of capturing student growth in aspects of learning that are not traditionally measured. In addition to student work submissions, this could also involve student and parent feedback, learning journals, videos of lessons, audio of student discussions, student self- and peer-assessment using rubrics, and much more. Guiding coalitions should be encouraged to find a range of quantitative and qualitative ways to capture growth in the desired outcomes. They should then share these wins with each other and the community as part of building the credibility and value of the change.

This weekly process of planning, acting, reflecting and refining – all normal parts of the cycle of inquiry in action-research projects – will lead to the guiding coalition building an extraordinary depth of knowledge about what strategies, processes and structures lead to the greatest success.

IMPLEMENTING AND SUSTAINING CHANGE

The transformational change needed to embed a great STEM program will require many years and a high level of relentlessness. It will not happen just because a school is ready to move on to the next thing. Until the thinking, strategies and systemic changes sink deeply into the culture, new

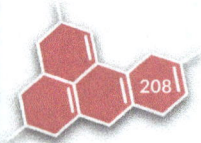

Leading the STEM curriculum and pedagogical change

approaches will be fragile and subject to regression (Kotter, 1995). All teachers, leaders and parents will have already existing thoughts and beliefs about education based on their personal upbringing and education. The relentlessness of implementation is required to overcome these many decades of unexamined and ingrained ways of thinking and operating.

For the best outcomes, the STEM learning program and the ways of thinking and planning will have to become part of the day-to-day way of working of a school. They must become automatic and habitual to survive school leaders and teachers coming and going, changing student and parent cohorts, and the influence of various educational system initiatives. Many great STEM programs have dissipated and disappeared when key individuals have left the school. The two steps in the third phase focus on the skilful and relentless implementation of plans, monitoring of quality results and provision of appropriate supports and incentives.

STEP 7: CONSOLIDATE IMPROVEMENTS AND PRODUCE MORE CHANGE

Once a guiding coalition is clear about the planning, pedagogical strategies, practices and structures that successfully lead to the desired learning outcomes, it is time to begin the next ripple of change. The second ripple of change begins with the guiding coalition presenting their findings to the entire community and inviting the next group of early adopters to be professionally developed to embed the STEM learning approach in their practice. At this point, the guiding coalition will formally mentor and coach the next group of volunteer change agents. They will follow the same rigorous cycles of inquiry the guiding coalition went through in their action-research project (including Steps 4–6), but the approach will this time be informed by all the lessons they learned through the process. This mentoring and coaching will provide a new depth of understanding to the guiding coalition about what works and what doesn't, and how to effectively communicate and develop others in the thinking, planning and pedagogy. The expanding team should continue to share stories of their successes and failures to build the sense of trust, credibility and reliability within the community.

It is important to continue building momentum and to repeat this cycle until all staff members and stakeholders have gone through the change process. In later ripples of change, the expanding group of change agents will start to interact with and attempt to empower and enable those who are change resistors or even refusers. These individuals represent both a challenge and an opportunity. The challenge is shifting the beliefs, mindset and practices of these individuals. The opportunity is that finding constructive ways to communicate and empower these individuals to own the change will lead to a greater level of authenticity, trust and understanding in the community. It will be a clear demonstration of acting consistently with the vision and mission of the change. This doesn't mean that the conversations won't be difficult or confronting. In fact, it is the willingness and courage of school leaders and coalition members to initiate these difficult but constructive conversations that make a difference for everyone. Other strategies that can support and incentivise engagement with the change include implementing accountability structures for all teachers, making the change process part of the teacher professional learning plans and even hiring expert STEM teachers to build momentum in an existing STEM change program. Whatever strategies are used, the aim is to keep building short-term wins and never let up – otherwise traditional thinking and operating will creep back in.

Quite early on in Malvern Valley Primary's journey of implementing design thinking and STEM learning, their approach had been to schedule several hours of 'academy project' time for Year 3–6 students every Friday afternoon from Week 5 of Term 1 to the end of Term 4. Each academy project focuses on a different discipline and is essentially a three-term design challenge. Students can choose from areas as diverse as engineering, coding, entrepreneurship, sport, sustainability, robotics and science. Early in Term 1 each academy project teacher makes a pitch to the students

about their project area and the students then choose which project they want to be involved in for the coming year. One condition is that they cannot be involved with a project that they have already participated in before. From Term 2 the students form multi-age groups within their area and go through the design process in multiple ways to deliver a project.

To consolidate the desired improvement across the school, school leadership worked with the guiding coalition to create a planning template bringing together design thinking, Kath Murdoch's (2015) inquiry process, learning intentions and success criteria into the one document. In the first year, the teachers planned their projects using an early variation of the template and were coached as they enacted their plan. In the following year, whole-school planning was supported by professional learning on how to plan using the template and all teaching teams were expected to use the template to plan. The academy project teachers informally mentored teachers in their teaching teams while they continued to run their projects and receive coaching. In the third year, two teachers who were experienced in STEM and leading change initiatives took up middle-leadership positions. Their roles were to support teachers in embedding design thinking and other strategic initiatives into day-to-day thinking and planning. As part of expanding the rigour of the development of student reflection and learning with academy projects, a design process rubric (see table 7.15, page 171) plus a critical and creative thinking rubric (similar to table 7.11, page 164) were made mandatory for all projects. The aim is to roll these out to the whole staff by the middle of the third year.

STEP 8: ANCHOR THE NEW APPROACHES

As staff and other stakeholders journey through their own cycles of inquiry, guiding coalitions and school leaders must confront the systems and structures that are not consistent with their vision and mission. The aim is to strategically think through how the school can anchor the new thinking and approaches for the long term. Questions to ask include:

- What current system processes, policies and roles are aligned or not aligned with the vision, mission and approaches?
- What new system processes, policies and roles will be needed?
- What are the non-negotiable ideas and priorities?
- What habitual practices do staff members need to develop?
- What further professional learning do the staff members and non-staff stakeholders require to fully embrace the change process?
- How will we support staff members and non-staff stakeholders that resist the change?
- How will we support incoming staff members and non-staff stakeholders?

Some of these questions will have been answered naturally during earlier steps of the change process. However, it is in this step, as the broader school community is engaged in the inquiry cycle, that strategic changes can be instituted.

There are two other factors that help to entrench the STEM learning change vision, mission and approaches so that they become 'the way we do things around here'. The first is consciously and relentlessly showing people how the new approaches, behaviours and thinking are delivering the desired outcomes. When staff members and non-staff stakeholders are left to make their own connections, they can easily misunderstand or misconstrue why the desired outcomes are being achieved. For example, having a good or poor cohort of students is often used as justification for an approach working or not working. Supporting people to make the right connections requires appropriate data and good communication. This means building useful data walls and providing

time and opportunities for staff members to reflect on and discuss why performance is improving. It could also mean staff members and school leaders routinely visiting classrooms, discussing the work and even making the improvement in student work visible to everyone. For non-staff stakeholders, the school communicating via newsletters, on social media platforms and even directly to parents and guardians on how the approaches and vision are making a difference will grow belief and credibility.

The second factor is making sure that people in leadership roles really do represent and personify the vision and mission of STEM learning. Without having a clear succession process that, as Jim Collins (2001) explains, puts 'the right people on the bus, the right people in the right seats, and the wrong people off the bus' (p. 41), transformation rarely lasts. This is not about putting people who don't resist the change in roles or positions. This is about putting people who are champions of the vision and mission in those roles and positions. For example, one school principal shared with me that they achieved very little of the change they were brought in to cause until the former assistant principal retired and he was able to employ two new assistant principals who were passionate about the vision and mission the guiding coalition had created. Poor succession planning and induction processes can undermine years of hard work.

School leadership at Oakleigh State School realised that to create a sustainable approach to STEM learning they had to shift teacher mindsets. To do this they would need to create clearly defined structures and processes that empowered teachers to take full collaborative control of classroom and professional learning without having to rely on a hierarchical leadership structure telling them what to do. Their work with Steve Borthwick from Organic Learning led to the idea of 'transparent and collective accountability'. This was built on the notion of creating explicit expectations, structures and processes that left teachers and teams nowhere to hide. Norms were established that valued integrity, taking initiative, strong internal accountability, working collaboratively and showing agency. Taking risks, making mistakes and failing were acceptable. However, if individuals continually made poor choices, lacked commitment or hid behind a closed mindset, it would quickly become apparent to everyone. Similarly, if teams didn't gel, didn't work collaboratively or lacked cohesion, it was obvious to other teams.

The 'nowhere to hide' approach was embedded through three strategies: hexagonal curriculum mapping, pitch and critique, and professional learning goals. Hexagonal curriculum mapping is a visual planning process for developing transdisciplinary learning units and is done on a shared learning wall. The pitch and critique protocol is a collective accountability strategy in which teachers and teaching teams cycle through pitching plans, receiving feedback, working on their plans and refining their plans as they iterate towards a desired outcome. Setting professional learning goals involves teachers and school leaders identifying learning goals, which are made visible in the staff learning space, and then working together as groups or in coaching relationships to continually learn, fail, take risks and grow across the year. The three strategies propel teachers and leaders into a transparent culture that demands greater internal accountability and personal leadership.

THREE KEY LESSONS

There are three fundamental lessons that I believe all school leaders and teachers need to learn as they lead the curriculum, pedagogical and structural changes needed to embed an authentic STEM program in their schools. First, don't be frightened to start and make mistakes. All transformational changes in any society began with mistakes, failures and reinvention. Second, the change journey will take years. Change can be messy and takes time because there are so many competing demands, drivers and constraints to think about. Be strategic, respect the process and build the

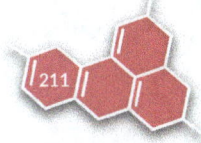

processes and approaches that you find work into the way your school operates. Finally, change is driven by people. When school leaders and school systems honour and respect the time, effort and expertise of the staff that drive the change, trust is nurtured and people are willing give more to achieve the desired change.

KEY POINTS

- Great programs that deliver great outcomes are the result of a series of good decisions that accumulate over a very long period of time.
- The effective embedding of an authentic STEM program will be a socially constructed change process that involves the students, teachers, staff, and parents and guardians trusting and owning the processes.
- Kotter's (1995) eight-step change model is broken down into three phases of action: creating a climate for change, engaging and enabling the organisation, and implementing and sustaining change.
- The change process to embed a STEM program begins by establishing a case for action that compels staff and non-staff stakeholders to urgently take action to break from the status quo.
- A small guiding coalition of early adopters and people with positional authority must articulate a clear and attractive STEM learning vision and mission, and then formulate an action-research project.
- Guiding coalitions should constantly and consistently communicate the successes, failures and lessons being learned through their action-research project while empowering others to act. Short-term wins should be planned for and widely celebrated to quickly prove the validity and credibility of the action-research project.
- Set up successfully, long-term, sustainable change ripples through the school, transforming beliefs, mindsets, systems, processes and practices. For the best outcomes, the STEM learning program and ways of thinking and planning will have to become part of the day-to-day. This will involve the guiding coalition and school leaders aligning school systems, processes and roles to be consistent with the STEM learning vision and mission.

Epilogue

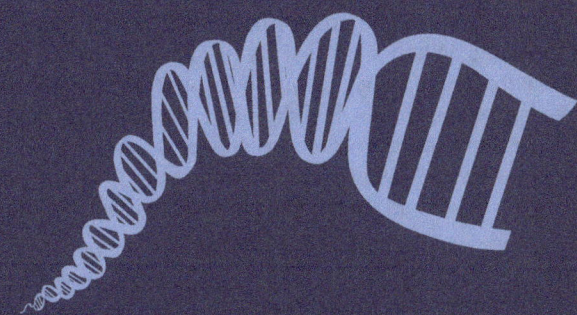

Superlative performance is really a confluence of dozens of small skills or activities, each one learned or stumbled upon, which have been carefully drilled into habit and then are fitted together in a synthesized whole. There is nothing extraordinary or superhuman in any one of those actions; only the fact that they are done consistently and correctly, and all together, produce excellence.

(Chambliss, 1989, p. 76)

When teachers and school leaders read this book they may find quite a lot that is familiar and already understood, as well as ideas and approaches that are new to them. The intention of this book was not to reinvent the whole field of enacting STEM in a school. Rather, it was to take the approaches that I have learned, stumbled upon or reimagined as I worked with schools over the past two decades and to synthesise them into a cohesive and thoughtful whole. Each chapter captures important ideas and processes that will support schools to develop a culture of superlative performance among both students and teachers.

Chapter 1 addressed the habit of schools to implement new initiatives without examining the underlying contexts, structures and practices that already exist. Schools often skip this exploration and then wonder why the enactment of a new initiative is so glacial. This chapter challenged teachers and school leaders to look deeper into what they do and don't know about learning, about the purpose of schooling and about STEM so they can begin to design a more effective learning environment. Creating transformational change in a school begins with revisiting the thinking that has created the existing system. To then achieve the desired change requires the alignment of a range of systems, structures and processes. The approaches discussed in this chapter can be used regardless of the initiative being implemented.

Chapters 2 and 3 arose from seeing how primary schools continue to operate in silos across year levels. When a school invests time in creating progressive whole-school mindset, capability and curriculum maps and partner these with learning ladders, they help students progressively internalise the knowledge, skills and thinking to become independent, self-regulated learners. This is a systems approach that requires a significant amount of pre-planning, yet enables teachers to be creative and inventive in the classroom. Once these maps are developed, schools will find that they are able to adapt quickly to new initiatives with far less disruption and frustration.

Chapters 4–6 took the idea of backward planning, linked it to Hattie and Donoghue's (2016) conceptual model of learning and explained how this could be used to set out the progressive development of learning activities and units across a year. This practice supports teachers to design learning that has students build the required curriculum knowledge and skills before applying it to real-world situations. This is another systems approach, as many teachers are still in the habit of forward planning learning rather than identifying the intended learning destination and then backward planning to achieve it. Students will not only find the learning more meaningful and authentic, but also come to drive their own learning – all while enabling teachers to provide point-of-need teaching. The thinking, templates and processes outlined in these chapters can be used to plan single curriculum units as well as transdisciplinary units.

Assessment of STEM – and most learning in schools – has a history of being considered summatively only. This is problematic because it teaches students to value the end result, whether it is a product or a grade, rather than the learning journey. Formative assessment, in which students learn to self- and peer-assess using clear, student-friendly assessment structures, has the benefit of building student confidence while also developing them to become self-aware, self-managing and self-regulated learners. Chapter 7 showcased how teachers can create and embed student-centred formative assessment structures using the thinking and planning of earlier chapters. The result is a classroom learning environment where students are intrinsically motivated because they understand where they are, where they are going and how they can get there.

Chapters 8 and 9 round out the journey teachers and schools will take as they participate in and lead the process of embedding a STEM program. Effective personal and organisational change takes time. It requires an investment in people as well as consistent and committed action over a long period of time. Too often teachers and school leaders jump from one initiative to the next without going through the process of making sure that they have internalised and systemised new habits. These two chapters are about creating rigorous and sustainable change within the school.

While this book was written with a focus on developing a sustainable and authentic primary school STEM program, in many ways it was not about STEM at all. I am deeply passionate about learners – whether they are novices or experienced, young or old – coming to know themselves as curious, creative and capable problem-solvers and thinkers. I am committed to building an education system that develops people to be the all-important difference in an increasingly complex and challenge-filled world. This is what led me to start my journey in education and sustains me still today. I love seeing students and teachers realise they are far more capable and creative than they believed they were. I am thrilled when a school I have coached starts producing the results they have always wanted to achieve. In my experience, schools are filled with similarly passionate individuals. They want to create learning that makes a difference to the lives of the young people in their care. My hope is that the thinking and approaches outlined in this book will provide the provocation that schools need to get started themselves.

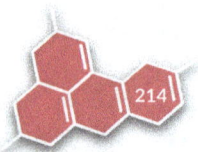

Epilogue

Naturally, every teacher, leader and school community will undertake a different journey to that goal. It is likely that at times this journey will be challenging and confronting, while at other times it will be easy and joyful. Take the time to stop and complete the activities in this book. Some can be completed in a few minutes or hours, while it will take many months to complete others to the desired extent. As with anything worthwhile, it is the journey that leads to the greatest benefits for the community. Students will grow in confidence as learners. They will develop the knowledge, skills, thinking and mindset to become the remarkable and adaptable agents of change we'd all love them to be. Teachers will grow their mastery as leaders of learning and reignite the passion that brought them to the profession. School leaders will know that they have created an environment that harnesses and empowers the human spirit.

The first step is always the hardest, but as one wise educator wrote:

> ... be your name Buxbaum or Bixby or Bray
> or Mordecai Ali Van Allen O'Shea,
> you're off to Great Places!
> Today is your day!
> Your mountain is waiting.
> So ... get on your way!
>
> Dr Seuss, Oh, the places you'll go!

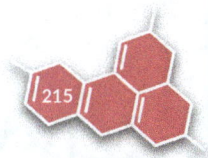

References

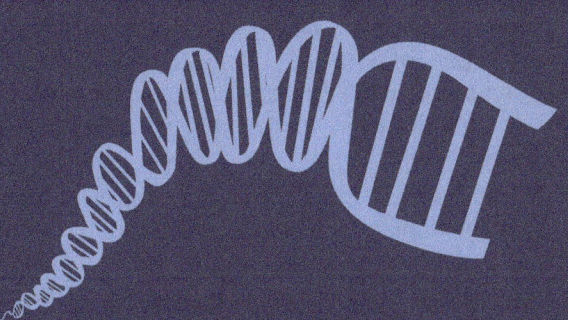

Abramm, F. (2008, May 6). When the lights go on. *The Guardian.* www.theguardian.com/education/2008/may/06/schools.uk

Ames, C., & Archer, J. (1988). Achievement goals in the classroom: Students' learning strategies and motivation processes. *Journal of Educational Psychology, 80*(3), 260–267.

Anderson, L. W., Krathwohl, D. R., & Bloom, B. S. (2001). *A Taxonomy for Learning, Teaching, and Assessing: A Revision of Bloom's Taxonomy of Educational Objectives.* Longman.

Australian and New Zealand Falls Prevention Society. (n.d.). Info about falls. *Australian and New Zealand Falls Prevention Society.* www.anzfallsprevention.org/info/

Australian Curriculum, Assessment and Reporting Authority (ACARA). (n.d.-a). *Computational Thinking.* https://www.australiancurriculum.edu.au/media/4613/dtif_computational_thinking_poster.pdf

Australian Curriculum, Assessment and Reporting Authority (ACARA). (n.d.-b). *F–12 Curriculum Overview.* https://v9.australiancurriculum.edu.au/f-10-curriculum/f-10-curriculum-overview

Australian Curriculum, Assessment and Reporting Authority (ACARA). (n.d.-c). *General Capabilities.* https://v9.australiancurriculum.edu.au/f-10-curriculum/f-10-curriculum-overview/general-capabilities

Australian Curriculum, Assessment and Reporting Authority (ACARA). (n.d.-d). *General Capabilities: Critical and Creative Thinking Version 9.0 – comparative information.* https://v9.australiancurriculum.edu.au/content/dam/en/curriculum/ac-version-9/downloads/general-capabilities/general-capabilities-critical-and-creative-thinking-comparative-v9.docx

Australian Curriculum, Assessment and Reporting Authority (ACARA). (n.d.-e). *General Capabilities Downloads.* https://v9.australiancurriculum.edu.au/downloads/general-capabilities

Australian Curriculum, Assessment and Reporting Authority (ACARA). (n.d.-f). *General Capabilities: Ethical Understanding Version 9.0 – Comparative Information*. https://v9.australiancurriculum.edu.au/content/dam/en/curriculum/ac-version-9/downloads/general-capabilities/general-capabilities-ethical-understanding-comparative-v9.docx

Australian Curriculum, Assessment and Reporting Authority (ACARA). (n.d.-g). *General Capabilities: Personal and Social Capability Version 9.0 – Comparative Information*. https://v9.australiancurriculum.edu.au/content/dam/en/curriculum/ac-version-9/downloads/general-capabilities/general-capabilities-personal-and-social-capability-comparative-v9.docx

Australian Curriculum, Assessment and Reporting Authority (ACARA). (n.d.-h). *General Capabilities (Version 8.4)*. https://australiancurriculum.edu.au/f-10-curriculum/general-capabilities/

Australian Curriculum, Assessment and Reporting Authority (ACARA). (n.d.-i). *Humanities and Social Sciences: HASS F–6 Version 9.0 – Curriculum Content F–6*. https://v9.australiancurriculum.edu.au/content/dam/en/curriculum/ac-version-9/downloads/humanities-and-social-sciences/hass-f-6/humanities-and-social-sciences-hass-f-6-curriculum-content-v9.docx

Australian Curriculum, Assessment and Reporting Authority (ACARA). (n.d.-j). *Learning Area Downloads*. https://v9.australiancurriculum.edu.au/downloads/learning-areas

Australian Curriculum, Assessment and Reporting Authority (ACARA). (n.d.-k). *Mathematics: F–10 Version 9.0 – Curriculum Content F–6*. https://v9.australiancurriculum.edu.au/content/dam/en/curriculum/ac-version-9/downloads/mathematics/mathematics-curriculum-content-f-6-v9.docx

Australian Curriculum, Assessment and Reporting Authority (ACARA). (n.d.-l). *Mathematics: Understanding This Learning Area*. https://v9.australiancurriculum.edu.au/teacher-resources/understand-this-learning-area/mathematics

Australian Curriculum, Assessment and Reporting Authority (ACARA). (n.d.-m). *Science: F–10 Version 9.0 – Curriculum Content F–6*. https://v9.australiancurriculum.edu.au/content/dam/en/curriculum/ac-version-9/downloads/science/science-curriculum-content-f-6-v9.docx

Australian Curriculum, Assessment and Reporting Authority (ACARA). (n.d.-n). *Science: F–10 Version 9.0 – Scope and Sequence*. https://v9.australiancurriculum.edu.au/content/dam/en/curriculum/ac-version-9/downloads/science/science-scope-and-sequence-f-10-v9.docx

Australian Curriculum, Assessment and Reporting Authority (ACARA). (n.d.-o). *Structure*. www.australiancurriculum.edu.au/f-10-curriculum/technologies/design-and-technologies/structure/

Australian Curriculum, Assessment and Reporting Authority (ACARA). (n.d.-p). *Structure*. www.australiancurriculum.edu.au/f-10-curriculum/technologies/digital-technologies/structure/

Australian Curriculum, Assessment and Reporting Authority (ACARA). (n.d.-q). *Technologies: Design and Technologies F–10 Version 9.0 – Curriculum Content F–6*. https://v9.australiancurriculum.edu.au/content/dam/en/curriculum/ac-version-9/downloads/technologies/design-and-technologies/technologies-design-and-technologies-curriculum-content-f-6-v9.docx

Australian Curriculum, Assessment and Reporting Authority (ACARA). (n.d.-r). *Technologies: Digital Technologies F–10 Version 9.0 – Curriculum Content F–6*. https://v9.australiancurriculum.edu.au/content/dam/en/curriculum/ac-version-9/downloads/technologies/digital-technologies/technologies-digital-technologies-curriculum-content-f-6-v9.docx

References

Australian Curriculum, Assessment and Reporting Authority (ACARA). (n.d.-s). *Technologies: Understanding This Learning Area*. https://v9.australiancurriculum.edu.au/teacher-resources/understand-this-learning-area/technologies

Australian Government Department of Education. (n.d.-a). Scope and Sequence (F–10): Learning Programs to Support Implementation. *Digital Technologies Hub*. www.digitaltechnologieshub.edu.au/teachers/scope-and-sequence/f-2/digital-systems

Australian Government Department of Education. (n.d.-b). Student Challenges and Activities. *Digital Technologies Hub*. https://www.digitaltechnologieshub.edu.au/for-families/student-resources/student-challenges-and-activities/

Axford, N., Berry, V., Lloyd, J., Moore, D., Rogers, M., Hurst, A., Blockley, K., Durkin, H., & Minton, J. (2019). *How Can Schools Support Parents' Engagement in Their Children's Learning? Evidence From Research and Practice*. Education Endowment Foundation.

Beckett-Mathews, A. (2020). *Year 6 Design and Technologies – Electrical Innovations* [Unpublished rubric].

Berry, A. E. (2015, September). Exploring classrooms that support the growth of top-quartile students. Masters Thesis. Australia: Melbourne Graduate School of Education.

Bertolini, A. (2007). Transforming the way kids learn sustainability: ruMAD? *Eingana: The Journal of the Victorian Association for Environmental Education, 29*(3), 9–11.

Biggs, J. B., & Collis, K. F. (1982). *Evaluating the Quality of Learning: The SOLO Taxonomy (Structure of the Observed Learning Outcome)*. Academic Press.

Boyes, K., & Watts, G. (2009). *Developing Habits of Mind in Elementary Schools: An ASCD Action Tool*. ASCD.

Breakspear, S. (2017). Embracing agile leadership for learning: How leaders can create impact despite growing complexity. *Australian Educational Leader, 39*(3), 68–71.

Carpenter, S. L. (2007). A comparison of the relationships of students' self-efficacy, goal orientation, and achievement across grade levels: A meta-analysis. [thesis]

Chambliss, D. F. (1989). The mundanity of excellence. *Sociological Theory, 7*(1), 70–86.

Collins, J. (2001). *Good to Great: Why Some Companies Make the Leap and Others Don't*. HarperCollins.

Cotton, K. (1988). *Classroom Questioning. School Improvement Research Series 5*. Northwest Regional Educational Laboratory.

Dam, R. F., & Siang, T. Y. (2021, February). What is empathy and why is it so important in design thinking? *Interaction Design Foundation*. www.interaction-design.org/literature/article/design-thinking-getting-started-with-empathy

de Bono, E. (n.d.). *Six Thinking Hats*. The de Bono Group. www.debonogroup.com/services/core-programs/six-thinking-hats/

Department of Education and Training. (2017). *High Impact Teaching Strategies: Excellence in Teaching and Learning*. Department of Education and Training.

Dilkes, J., Cunningham, C., & Jan, G. (2014). The new Australian Curriculum, teachers and change fatigue. *Australian Journal Of Teacher Education, 39*(11), 45–64. http://dx.doi.org/10.14221/ajte.2014v39n11.4

Duhigg, C. (2014). *The Power of Habit: Why We Do What We Do in Life and Business*. Random House.

Dweck, C. S. (2008). *Mindset: The New Psychology of Success*. Ballantine Books.

Edmondson, A. C. (2018). *The Fearless Organization: Creating Psychological Safety in the Workplace for Learning, Innovation, and Growth*. Wiley.

Eto, F. (2001). Causes of falls in the elderly. *Japan Medical Association Journal*, 44(7), 299–305.

Evidence for Learning. (n.d.). Feedback. *Evidence for Learning*. https://evidenceforlearning.org.au/the-toolkits/the-teaching-and-learning-toolkit/all-approaches/feedback/

Ferguson, R. F., Hackman, S., Hanna, R., & Ballantine, A. (2010, June 1). How high schools become exemplary. AGI conference report. Harvard University.

FranklinCovey Co. (n.d.). What is Leader in Me? *Leader in Me*. www.leaderinme.org/what-is-leader-in-me/

Frey, N., Hattie, J., & Fisher, D. (2018). *Developing Assessment-Capable Visible Learners, Grades K–12: Maximizing Skill, Will, and Thrill*. Corwin.

Giles, D. L. (2018). *Relational Leadership in Education: A Phenomenon of Inquiry and Practice*. Routledge.

Gordon, T., & Burch, N. (1974). *TET: Teacher Effectiveness Training*. Crown Publishing Group.

Graham, P. (2020). Early work. *Paul Graham*. http://paulgraham.com/early.html

Green, J. (2012, November). The nerd's guide to everything online. [Video]. *TED*. www.ted.com/talks/john_green_the_nerd_s_guide_to_learning_everything_online

Griffin, P. (2012). The influence of teaching strategies on student achievement in higher order skills. [Paper presentation]. What does research tell us about effective strategies? ACER. https://research.acer.edu.au/research_conference/RC2012/27august/19

Griffin, P. (Ed.) (2017). *Assessment for Teaching* (2nd ed.) Cambridge University Press.

Hamel, G., & Zanini, M. (2014, October 1). Build a change platform, not a change program. *McKinsey & Company*. www.mckinsey.com/business-functions/organization/our-insights/build-a-change-platform-not-a-change-program

Hansen, E. J. (2011). *Idea-Based Learning: A Course Design Process to Promote Conceptual Understanding*. Stylus Publishing.

Harding, S., Nibali, N., English, N., Griffin, P., Graham, L., Alom, B. M., and Zhang, Z. (2018). *Self-Regulated Learning in the Classroom: Realising the Potential for Australia's High Capacity Students*. Assessment Research Centre, Melbourne Graduate School of Education.

Harvard Graduate School of Education. (n.d.). Project Zero's Thinking Routine Toolbox. *Project Zero*. www.pz.harvard.edu/thinking-routines

Hasso-Plattner Institute of Design. (2020). *An Introduction to Design Thinking: Process Guide*. http://web.stanford.edu/~mshanks/MichaelShanks/files/509554.pdf

Hattie, J. (2009). *Visible Learning: A Synthesis of Over 800 Meta-Analyses Relating to Achievement*. Routledge.

Hattie, J. (2015). *What Works Best in Education: The Politics of Collaborative Expertise*. Pearson.

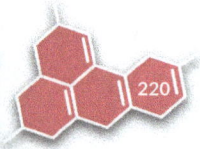

References

Hattie, J. (2017). The science of how we learn. *Visible Learning Plus*. www.visiblelearningplus.com/sites/default/files/VL%20Summit%20John%20Hattie%20Keynote%5B1%5D_0.pdf

Hattie, J. A. C., & Donoghue, G. M. (2016). Learning strategies: A synthesis and conceptual model. *npj Science of Learning, 1*, 16013.

Hattie, J., & Timperley, H. (2007). The power of feedback. *Review of Educational Research, 77*(1), 81–112. https://doi.org/10.3102/003465430298487

Heick, T. (2019, March 3). What to think about backward design? *TeachThought*. www.teachthought.com/pedagogy/backward-design-criticism-ubd/

Helen Sanderson Associates. (2015). *4 + 1 Questions*. www.helensandersonassociates.co.uk/wp-content/uploads/2015/02/fourplusone.pdf

International Baccalaureate Organization. (2014). *MYP: From Principles into Practice*. International Baccalaureate Organization (UK) Ltd.

Kennedy, T. (2018). Effectiveness of applying conceptual change approaches in challenging mathematics tasks for low-performing students. In J. Hunter, P. Perger, & L. Darragh (Eds.). *Making Waves, Opening Spaces: Proceedings of the 41st Annual Conference of the Mathematics Education Research Group of Australasia* (pp. 447–454). MERGA.

Kotter, J. P. (1995, May–June). Leading Change: Why transformation efforts fail. *Harvard Business Review*, 59–67.

Kotter, J. P. (2012, November). Accelerate! *Harvard Business Review*, 45–58.

Lehmann, C., & Chase, Z. (2015). *Building School 2.0: How to Create the Schools We Need*. Jossey-Bass.

Leithwood, K., Harris, A., & Hopkins, D. (2020). Seven strong claims about successful school leadership revisited. *School Leadership & Management, 40*(1), 5–22.

Lemov, D. (2014). *Teach Like a Champion 2.0: 62 Techniques That Put Students on the Path to College*. Jossey-Bass.

Lucas, B. (2018). International perspectives on how education offers solutions to tackle skills mismatches and shortages: Speech to 5th International Conference on Employer Engagement & Training. ResearchGate.

Marton, F. (2006). Sameness and difference in transfer. *The Journal of the Learning Sciences, 15*(4), 499–535. https://doi.org/10.1207/s15327809jls1504_3

McTighe, J., & Seif, E. (2003). *A Summary of Underlying Theory and Research Base for Understanding by Design*. MAC: McTighe & Associates Consulting. https://jaymctighe.com/wp-content/uploads/2011/04/UbD-Research-Base.pdf

McTighe, J., & Wiggins, G. (2013). *Essential Questions: Opening Doors to Student Understanding*. ASCD.

Melbourne Archdiocese Catholic Schools. (n.d.). STEM MAD showcase. *Melbourne Archdiocese Catholic Schools*. https://sites.google.com/vic.catholic.edu.au/stemmad/home

Murdoch, K. (2015). *The Power of Inquiry: Teaching and Learning With Curiosity, Creativity, and Purpose in the Contemporary Classroom*. Seastar Education.

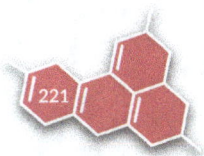

Nilson, L. B. (2013). *Creating Self-Regulated Learners: Strategies to Strengthen Students' Self-Awareness and Learning Skills*. Stylus Publishing, LLC.

Nottingham, J. (2017). *The learning challenge: How to guide your students through the learning pit to achieve deeper understanding*. SAGE.

OECD. (n.d.). *OECD Future of Education and Skills 2030 project*. OECD. www.oecd.org/education/2030-project/about/

OECD. (2019). *Conceptual Learning Framework: Student Agency for 2030*. OECD. www.oecd.org/education/2030-project/teaching-and-learning/learning/student-agency/Student_Agency_for_2030_concept_note.pdf

Ostroff, W. L. (2012). *Understanding How Young Children Learn: Bringing the Science of Child Development to the Classroom*. ASCD.

Pollard, S. (2020). *Code Academy Program Design Task* [Unpublished task].

Purdie, H. (2019, November 1). All aboard: A whole school approach to implementing the DT Curriculum at Taroona PS TAS. *CSER Digital Technologies Education*. https://csermoocs.adelaide.edu.au/news/list/2019/11/01/all-aboard-a-whole-school-approach-to-implementing-the-dt-curriculum-at

Queensland Curriculum & Assessment Authority (QCAA). (n.d.). *P-10 Design and Technologies Assessment Resources*. www.qcaa.qld.edu.au/p-10/aciq/learning-areas/technologies/design-and-technologies/assessment

Queensland Curriculum & Assessment Authority (QCAA). (2019a). *Prep to Year 2 Standard Elaborations – Australian Curriculum: Design and Technologies*. www.qcaa.qld.edu.au/downloads/p_10/ac_tech_design_p2_se.docx

Queensland Curriculum & Assessment Authority (QCAA). (2019b). *Years 3 and 4 Standard Elaborations – Australian Curriculum: Design and Technologies*. www.qcaa.qld.edu.au/downloads/p_10/ac_tech_design_yr3-4_se.docx

Queensland Curriculum & Assessment Authority (QCAA). (2019c). *Years 5 and 6 Standard Elaborations – Australian Curriculum: Design and Technologies*. www.qcaa.qld.edu.au/downloads/p_10/ac_tech_design_yr5-6_se.docx

Richens, M. (2017, January 12). Conscious competence ladder – developing new skills. *UKCPD College Members*. https://ukcpd.net/collegemembers/conscious-competence-ladder-developing-new-skills/

Rider-Bertrand, J. H. (2017). Development of integrative STEM curriculum: A multiple case study of multi-disciplinary teams in two Pennsylvania high schools. [Dissertation] Delaware Valley University.

Robinson, K. (2006, February). Do schools kill creativity? [Video]. *TED*. www.ted.com/talks/sir_ken_robinson_do_schools_kill_creativity

Schraw, G., & Dennison, R. S. (1994). Assessing metacognitive awareness. *Contemporary Educational Psychology, 19*(4), 460–475.

Schwartz, D. L., & Bransford, J. D. (1998). A time for telling. *Cognition and Instruction, 16*(4), 475–522.

References

Scoular, C., Ramalingam, D., Duckworth, D., & Heard, J. (2020). *Assessment of General Capabilities: Skills for the 21st-Century Learner – Final Report*. Australian Council for Educational Research.

Servage, L. (2008). Critical and transformative practices in professional learning communities. *Teacher Education Quarterly, 35*(1), 63–77.

Spencer, J., & Juliani, A. J. (2016). *Launch: Using Design Thinking to Boost Creativity and Bring Out the Maker in Every Student*. Dave Burgess Consulting, Inc.

Suzuki, S. (2011). *Zen Mind, Beginner's Mind*. Shambhala.

Tomlinson, C. A. (2008). The goals of differentiation. *Educational Leadership, 66*(3), 26–30.

Tomlinson, C. A., & Eidson, C. C. (2003). *Differentiation in Practice: A Resource Guide for Differentiating Curriculum Grades K–5*. ASCD.

Tyler, R. W. (1949). *Basic Principles of Curriculum and Instruction*. University of Chicago Press.

Velez, J., & Frattin, L. (2020). *Assessment Rubric for a Year 5-6 Natural Disasters Minecraft Unit* [Unpublished rubric].

Victorian Curriculum and Assessment Authority (VCAA). (2008). *Graphic Organiser – POOCH*. Victorian Curriculum and Assessment Authority. https://view.officeapps.live.com/op/view.aspx?src=http%3A%2F%2Fsccweb.scea.wa.edu.au%2FC3_IT%2FITC3SCC20013%2FICAU3019B_Migrate_to_New_Technology%2FMigrate_IMAGES%2Fpooch_template.doc

Victorian Curriculum and Assessment Authority (VCAA). (2019). *Guide to Formative Assessment Rubrics*. Victorian Curriculum and Assessment Authority.

Waack, S. (2018). Hattie ranking: 252 influences and effect sizes related to student achievement. *Visible Learning*. https://visible-learning.org/hattie-ranking-influences-effect-sizes-learning-achievement/

Walker, K. (2011). *Play Matters: Investigative Learning for Preschool to Grade 2* (2nd ed.). ACER Press.

Walker, K., & Bass, S. (2011). *Engagement Matters: Personalised Learning for Grades 3 to 6*. ACER Press.

Weins, J. W. (1983). Metacognition and the adolescent passive learner. *Journal of Learning Disabilities, 16*, 144–149.

Wiggins, G. P., & McTighe, J. (1998). *Understanding by Design*. ASCD.

Wiggins, G. P., & McTighe, J. (2005). *Understanding by Design* (2nd ed.). ASCD.

Wiggins, G., & McTighe, J. (2011). *The Understanding by Design Guide to Creating High-Quality Units*. ASCD.

Wiliam, D. (2017). *Embedded Formative Assessment*. Solution Tree.

Wujec, T. (2010, February). Build a tower, build a team. [Video]. *TED*. www.ted.com/talks/tom_wujec_build_a_tower_build_a_team?language=en

Yeager, D. S., & Dweck, C. S. (2020). What can be learned from growth mindset controversies? *American Psychologist, 75*(9), 1269–1284. https://doi.org/10.1037/amp0000794

Yero, J. L. (2010). *Teaching in mind: How teacher thinking shapes education*. BookLocker.com, Inc.

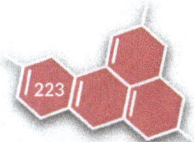

Zimmerman, B. J., & Moylan, A. R. (2009). Self-regulation: Where metacognition and motivation intersect. In D. J. Hacker, J. Dunlosky, & A. C. Graesser, *Handbook of Metacognition in Education* (pp. 299–315). Routledge.

Zyngier, D. (2009). Education, democracy and social Justice: The Australian experience – doing thick democracy in the classroom. [Conference paper] Learning Democracy by Doing: Alternative Practices in Citizenship Education and Participatory Democracy (pp. 259–263). Ontario.

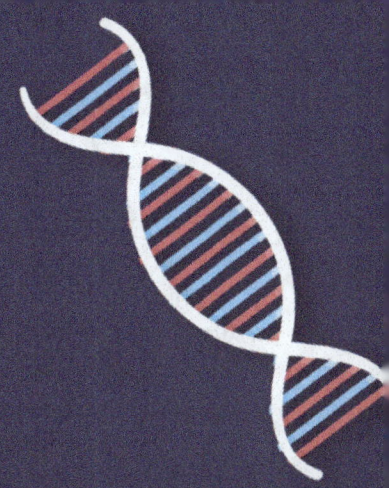

Index

#

100-cup tower challenge, the 104

A

abstraction 17, 23, 77, 94
acceptable evidence 75
acquiring stage of learning, the 87
acquisition strategies 100
action research 188–94, 204–6
Adams, Ann 180–1
agency 53, 76, 196–7
agreements 46, 61, 62
Alekarenge School 180
algorithms 18
anchoring new approaches 210–11
anti-social behaviours 41, 42
assessment
    bounded transdisciplinary STEM assessment tasks 111–14
    current approaches to 144–51
    design of 75, 143–4, 155–6
    diagnostic assessment 100
    discipline-specific content 156–61
    education system approach to 144–9
    formative assessment 75, 148–9, 155–6, 158–61, 163–4, 187
    grades versus growth 147
    of progression 146, 147–8, 155–6
    of STEM learning 143–76
    summative assessment 87, 147, 154, 187
    teacher assessment beliefs 154–5
Australian Curriculum
    interconnectedness of 66
    knowledge, skills, thinking and mindset in 151–4
    requirements of 52
    self-regulation skills in 31
    structure of 70
Australian Curriculum, Assessment and Reporting Authority (ACARA) 161–3
Australian Curriculum: Design and Technologies
    intrinsic motivation in 183
    QCAA approach to 144–7

rubrics 150–1, 167
thinking frameworks in 12
Australian Curriculum: Digital
	Technologies 12, 147–9
Australian Curriculum: General
	Capabilities 39, 40, 45, 153–4,
	161–6
Australian Curriculum: Technologies 4,
	12–28, 57, 152

B

backward planning 73–86, 94–5, 116–22,
	156–61, 187
Bloom's taxonomy 75
Borthwick, Steve 211
bounded STEM activities 97–122

C

CAN DO templates 158–61, 166, 174
'Can you really play?' task, the 106–7
capabilities 40
capabilities planning 39–48
capability statements 161–3
capable learners 28
capacity to influence 186
change, need for 199–201
change agents 207
change fatigue 196
change makers 123–4
change management in schools 195–212
change vision 203–6
checklists 76, 116–22
climate for change 199
coaching
	on backward planning processes 94–5
	on designing open-ended STEM
		projects 141
	on the mapping process 70–1
coding 180–1, 182–3
co-learning 182, 186, 188
collaboration 8, 187
collaborative learning 61–2
Collins, Jim 203
communication (in change management)
	206–7
community-based open-ended challenges
	124–5
competencies 40
computational thinking 13–20, 77, 94,
	166
conceptual model of learning, the 98–101
conceptual questions 91–2
conferencing 161
conscious competence 183–5
conscious skilled stage, the 185
conscious unskilled stage, the 184–5
consolidating stage of learning, the 87
constraints on STEM programs 3–4
content descriptors 66, 68, 156
critical and creative thinking 45
culminating rich tasks 75, 92–4, 111–16
curriculum deconstruction 75, 76–86
curriculum descriptors 79
curriculum design 73–86, 94–5
curriculum maps 51–71
curriculum outcomes 133–5
curriculum progression planning
	frameworks 101–11

D

Danson, Anna 181
data 199
debatable questions 91–2
de Bono, Edward 13
decomposition 15, 77, 94

Index

deconstructing the curriculum 75, 76–86, 156–61
deep-learning phase, the 100, 101
define-phase planning 133–9
defining 23, 146
design briefs 32–4
design process, the 89, 117–19
design thinking 21–6, 166, 167–73, *see also* graphic organisers
development, stages of 56–7
diagnostic assessment 100
digital literacy 180–1
Digital Technologies Hub, the 79, 111, 166
discipline-specific knowledge 152–3
disruptive behaviours 41, 42
distractions 166
drones 182
dual operating systems 197

E

education system approach to STEM assessment 144–9
eight-step change model, the 197–8
elaboration progressions *see* progression
empathise-phase planning 126–32
empathising 8–12, 22, 181
empowerment 207–8
engaging and enabling organisations 206
environment sustainability design tasks 110
essential questions 133–5
ethical understanding 45
evaluation 20
evidence 75, 88
experiments 88
external motivation 147

F

fabulous fabrics task, the 105, 107
factual questions 91–2
feedback 77, 155
formative assessment
    CAN DO templates 158–61
    design of 75, 155–6
    development of practices for 187
    rubrics for 148–9, 163–4
formative feedback cycle, the 104

G

general capabilities 153–4, 161–6, 174–6, *see also* mindset and capabilities planning
global open-ended challenges 125–6
goals 76–7
grade descriptions 150–1
grades versus growth 147
graphic organisers 46–7, 163
GRASPS model, the 111–14, 135–9
guiding coalitions 202–3

H

habits 28–30, 45, 46
Hattie, John 13
Hedgehog Concept, the 203
highly capable learners 40, 42, 877, *see also* self-regulation skills
Humpybong State School 182–3

I

ideate–prototype–test cycle, the 141
ideation 24
Indigenous pedagogies 181
influence 186

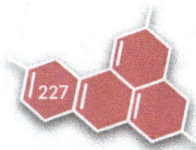

inquiry-based learning 100
inquiry skills 13, 88
instruction, planning of 76
intercultural understanding 45
International Baccalaureate, the 91–2
interrelatedness of ideas and concepts 94
intrinsic motivation 87, 147
investigating 146

K

key understandings 75, 87–90
Kotter, John 197–8

L

language
    in formative assessment 155
    in rubrics 147–8, 150–1
    for success criteria 78–9
    'teacher speak' 146
leadership 186–94, 196–7
learner mindsets 40–3
learning, phases of 99–101
learning continuums 161–3
learning destinations 75, 76–95
learning experiences, planning of 76
learning habits 28–30
learning intentions 77
learning ladders 54, 55, 56–60
learning priorities 74
learning progression *see* progression
learning readiness 202
logical sequence of key understandings 75, 87–90

M

Malvern Valley Primary School 182, 209–10
marble run challenge, the 102

marshmallow structure challenge, the 103
mastery goal orientation 87
mathematical reasoning 13
mentoring (in change management) 207–8
metacognition 100
mindset 28, 31–2, 40–3, 186, 207
mindset and capabilities planning 39–48, 54, 55
Minecraft 174–6
mini action-research projects 189–94
mission statements 200, 203–6
modelling 19
motivation to learn 31–2, 87, 147
Moule, Reid 182–3

N

national open-ended challenges 125–6
needs 152, 181
negativity 207
norms 46, 61, 62

O

Oakleigh State School 211
observations 88
open-ended STEM projects 123–41
opportunities 152
optical illusions 29
organisational change 195–212
Our Lady of the Assumption Cheltenham Primary School 181
outcomes (in organisational change) 210–11
overwhelm 154
ownership (in organisational change) 208

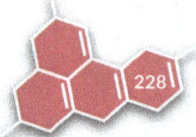

Index

P

paddock-to-plate task, the 105, 119–20
parents 4, 42
passive learners 53
pattern recognition 16, 77, 94
pedagogical practices 188
peer assessment 187
personal and social capabilities 45
planning
    backward planning 73–86, 94–5
    checklists and templates 116–22
    completion of 139–40
    curriculum maps 51–71
    curriculum progression planning frameworks 101–11
    the define phase of 133–9
    the empathise phase of 126–32
    GRASPS model planning 135–9
    mindset and capabilities planning 39–48
    of mini action-research projects 189–94
    of open-ended transdisciplinary STEM projects 126–41
portfolios 146, 158
pre-existing knowledge, skills and thinking 7–12, 79
pre-planning 48
problem-based learning 100
professional development 179–94, 207
professional learning communities 197
progression, *see also* skill development
    across year levels 146–7
    assessment of 146, 147–8, 155–6
    evidence of 158
    and grade descriptions 150–1
    lack of 147
prototyping 25, 38

purposeful learning 87

Q

qualitative data 199
quantitative data 199
Queensland Curriculum & Assessment Authority (QCAA) 144–7
questions
essential questions 133–5
questions to drive learning 90–2

R

Realising the Potential of Australia's Highly Capable Students project 164
real-world challenges 52, 123–41
reflective process, the 161
release of responsibility 53, 174
reports 176
research
action research 188–94
action-research projects 204–6
for empathise-phase planning 126–8
mini action-research projects 189–94
research skills 47
resourcing 180
robotics 107–9, 180–1
routines 61, 62
rubrics 147–51, 163–4, 167–73, 174–6
ruMAD program, the 125

S

schemas 29
school-based open-ended challenges 124
school culture 29
schools, *see also* individual schools
    need for change in 199–201

organisational change within 195–212
structures and approaches of 179, 208
scientific inquiry skills 88
scientific method, the 88, 89
scientific theories 88
scope and sequence learning plans 79, 161–3
self-assessment 187
self-driven learning 42, 147, 181, 187, 208
self-efficacy 87
self-evaluation 176
self-motivation 31–2
self-reflection 176
self-regulation skills 31, 100, 147, 161, 164–6
sequencing 117
short-term wins 208
simulation 19
situation descriptions 128–9
skill development 150–1, *see also* progression
socially constructed organisational change 196–8
software and learning ladders 57–9
SOLO taxonomy, the 79
speculation (in empathise-phase planning) 129–31
stakeholders 129–30
standard elaboration progressions 144, 146
Stanford school model, the 21
STEM programs
constraints on 3–4
developmental stages of effectiveness of 183–5

effective assessment of 143–76
existing perceptions and knowledge about 7–12
implementation of 7–12
laying the groundwork for 37–9
organisational change to embed 195–212
purpose of 12–28, 32–4
strategy networks 197
student agency 76
student capacity 170
student-driven assessment 154–5
student-driven learning 4, 52–4, 62, 77, 90–2, 98–101, 117
students
as change makers 123–4
mindset of 28, 40–3
pre-existing knowledge, skills and thinking of 7–12, 79
self-evaluation by 176
success 76–7
success criteria 77, 163, 174
succession 211
summative assessment 87, 147, 154, 187
systems thinking 166, 167–73

T

Taroona Primary School 202
tasks
100-cup tower challenge, the 104
environment sustainability design tasks 110
fabulous fabrics task, the 105, 107
the marble run challenge 102
the marshmallow structure challenge 103
open-ended STEM projects 123–41
the paddock-to-plate task 105

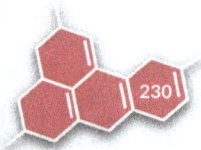

Index

robotics assessment tasks 107–9
taxonomies 79
teacher-driven learning 98–9
teachers
    accountability structures for 209
    assessment beliefs of 154–5
    capacity of to lead STEM learning 179–94
    co-learning by 182, 186, 188
    collaboration by 8, 187
    developing leadership skills of 186–94
    habits and practices of 29–30
    as learners 141
    pre-existing knowledge, skills and thinking of 7–12
    release of responsibility by 53
    stories from 180–3
teacher speak 146
technologies thinking frameworks 166–73
technology, effective use of 57–9
templates 158–61, 176, 189, 190, 192–3
terminology 146
thinking frameworks 13–30, 152
thinking tools 185
thoughtful questions 90–2
transdisciplinary learning units 52, 55, 56, 60–4, 68, 149–51
transfer stage of learning, the 87, 100
transformational change 195–212
trust 196–7

U

unconscious skilled stage, the 185
unconscious unskilled stage, the 184
unit plans 56
urgency 199–201

V

Velez, Josh 182
visible learners 161
vision for change 203–6
vision statements 200, 203–6

W

Whitfield District Primary School 125
whole-school maps 54–5, 62–4, 65–71
whole-school systems of learning 48

Y

year-level maps 55, 65–71

www.ingramcontent.com/pod-product-compliance
Lightning Source LLC
Chambersburg PA
CBHW081719100526
44591CB00016B/2430